IMAGES
of America

MOUNT TABOR

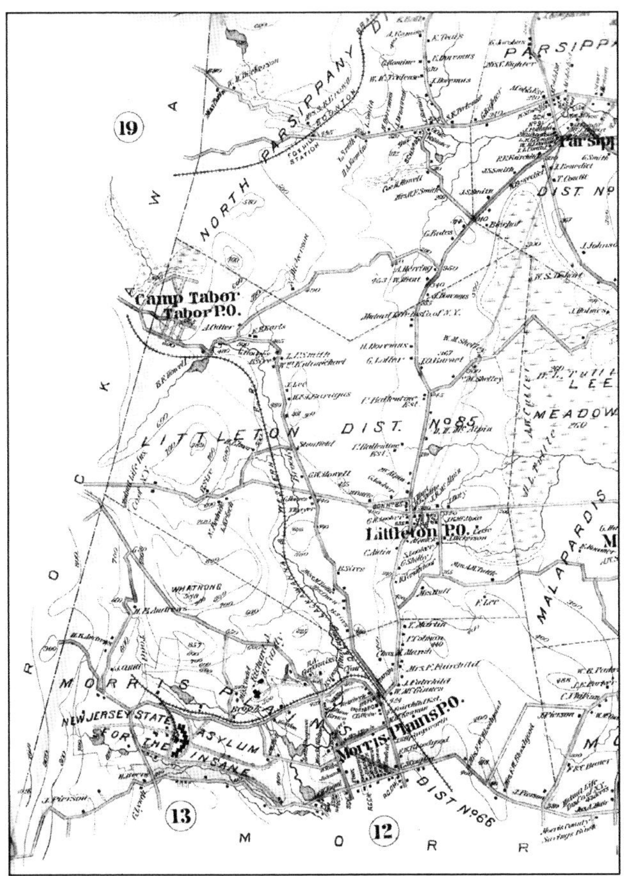

Camp Tabor is shown here as a detail in the 1887 Robinson's map of Hanover Township. Mount Tabor was part of Hanover Township until 1928. The town was described in a brochure as "a beautiful summer resort in the line of the Delaware Lackawanna & Western Railroad, thirty-seven miles from New York, and six miles west from Morristown; under the charge of the Newark Conference of the Methodist Episcopal Church. A large and beautiful chestnut grove; seven hundred nine feet above sea level; streets lined with neat cottages, and well lighted and drained; air pure and invigorating; water in abundance, pure and clear as crystal, from inexhaustible springs, and conducted to cottages through iron pipes, affording hot and cold water, baths, etc. To those desiring a summer home in the midst of religious influences, a refined Christian society and a place of rest, Mount Tabor affords desirable advantages. The grounds are managed by a Board of Trustees, four being elected each year by the lot owners. Lots from 16 x 25 to 50 x 100 feet according to location, and leased to purchasers for ninety-nine years." (Beth Shaw.)

On the cover: The Coit family is shown in front of its cottage tent around 1890. Ella (Nafie) Coit, sitting in the chair on the right, is the mother of Henry Leber Coit, shown sitting on the railing; Catherine Miriam Coit is sitting on the top step, and Carrie Ella (Coit) Meleney is sitting on the left. Carrie Meleney's three sons are pictured: Robert Coit Meleney is standing on the left, his brother Henry Edmund is in the carriage, and Frank Lamont is held in Carrie's lap. Note the Adirondack stick-style fence. The one-room cottage at the rear of the tent takes advantage of the best of both accommodations, a common sight in the transition from early tents to cottages. Henry Leber Coit was an innovative pediatrician in Newark who donated his collection of 500 books to start the Mount Tabor Free Public Library. He also was proprietor of the camp's pharmacy. (Camp Meeting Association.)

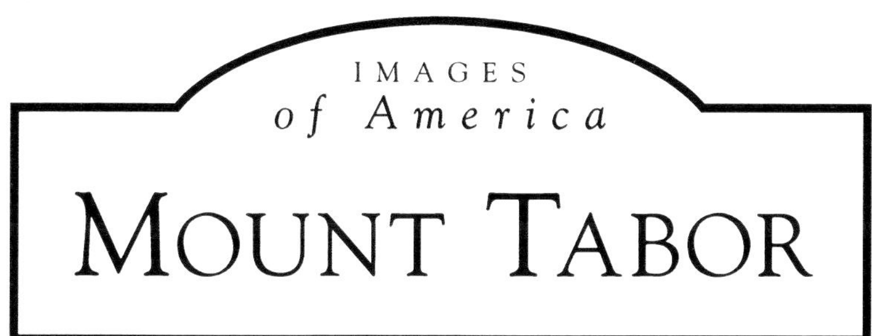

Mount Tabor Historical Society

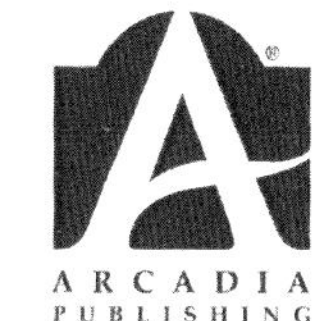

CONTENTS

ACKNOWLEDGMENTS

The Mount Tabor Historical Society was founded in 1990 with a small collection of photographs, postcards, and memorabilia and has grown considerably through the generosity of families and friends of Mount Tabor. Today the society continues to catalog and safeguard an ever-growing collection. This book is a natural progression of those efforts. The families and friends of Mount Tabor answered our call, once again, and we are forever grateful.

A group of novices undertook to author a pictorial history of Mount Tabor. Together we mined our resources, unearthed new information, checked and rechecked facts, wrote and rewrote text, and continually supported and encouraged one another. As always, within a large group, a small group of people merit special acknowledgement.

Beth Shaw, president of the Mount Tabor Historical Society, tirelessly devoted herself to organizing a mountain of information and plunging into every aspect of this book. Her efforts were truly of "biblical" proportion. Michelle LaConto Munn masterminded the project and skillfully scanned, edited, and coordinated the images gracing the pages of this book. She kept us focused. David Jones, our computer guru, safeguarded our output. We were blessed with dedicated authors. Andy Pillsbury diligently researched and wove information into wonderful text. Carol Pillsbury kept us honest by refusing to sacrifice fact for poetry. Lori Brown brought the images to life with heart, humor, and a touch of whimsy.

Photograph credits are individually acknowledged after each caption with our gratitude.

We offer our heartfelt appreciation to all the people who volunteered their time and talents to this effort. We sincerely apologize for any oversights. Our appreciation cannot be overstated. We wish to thank Ruth Lynch Blazure, Jewel Burns, Camp Meeting Association, Robert D'Alessandro, Lori Falco, Bud Knudsen, Bobbi Longstreet, Jeff May, Marc Miller, Morristown Library, Morristown Methodist Church Archives, Mount Tabor Country Club, Mount Tabor Fire Department, Mount Tabor School, Tom Nestor, Renee Nisivoccia, Blanche Ohlsen, Betsy Pauli, Print Communications Group and Michael D'Alessandro, Pat Rolston, and Ann Britten Wilson.

We thank those historians who chronicled the details of Mount Tabor life. Without their dedication and efforts, our rich heritage would have been lost.

INTRODUCTION

In 1866, American Methodism celebrated 100 years on the North American continent. In the century since Philip Embury had begun his ministry in New York City, Methodism had grown from a prayer group of five people to a congregation approaching two million. At the National Centenary Conference in Washington, D.C., the church leadership was heady with the knowledge that Methodism had become the most popular religion of the emerging American middle class. The great Methodist preachers, Philip Embury, George Whitefield, Capt. Thomas Webb, Francis Asbury, and especially John Wesley, were more than just an integral part of the founding of America, they were folk heroes. The leaders of the church were concerned about the increasingly urban society changed by industrialization and technological advances. At the national conference in 1866, the New Jersey delegation realized the advantages of organizing a tent revival in a pastoral setting patterned after the highly successful model of Wesley Park at Martha's Vineyard.

Upon return to Newark, a committee was formed, and its first camp meeting was held on rented grounds near Speedwell Lake in Morristown for 10 days in August 1866. It was a great success. A rigorous schedule of prayer and instructional meetings, along with strict rules forbidding intemperate behavior, ensured the sanctity of the camp revival. The quality of the sermons and the beauty of the surroundings kept enthusiasm high. When the camp meeting attracted 15,000 visitors the following year, it was decided that a permanent meeting ground was necessary. An exploratory committee was appointed, and an attractive parcel of land was located near Denville. Its central location and general accessibility gave it a geographical advantage.

Funding was subscribed for the purchase of 30.5 acres (another 100 acres would be added in 1872), and in 1869, the Camp Meeting Association of the Newark Conference of the Methodist Church was organized. A board of trustees was elected to manage the enterprise, and the location was named Mount Tabor, in homage to the traditional site of the transfiguration of Christ as recounted in Matthew 17:5.

With the example of the Martha's Vineyard camp meeting and its own experience at Speedwell Lake, the Camp Meeting Association was determined to establish the finest community imaginable. A unique charter was secured from the State of New Jersey empowering the board of trustees with the rights and privileges of a municipality. The camp at Mount Tabor was organized in a circular plan around three tabernacles in Trinity Park: the main tabernacle and the Bethel and Ebenezer pavilions. Sites were provided for society tents that allowed groups (such as the Women's Christian Temperance Union) to meet and worship separately. Parks and walking paths were designated. Significantly, the camp provided each subscriber with an individual tent site, far different from the dormitory-style accommodations provided at Martha's Vineyard.

In the first year, more than 300 tent sites were subscribed at prices starting at $20. Immediately, new occupants began improving their individual sites. Flower gardens and piazzas were soon added. The first permanent wooden house was built in 1870 on the corner of Simpson Avenue and Whitfield Place. Others quickly followed, and by 1890, more than 200 cottages had been erected. Architects such as Alexander Jackson Davis published widely available pattern books, the most common source of the cottage designs. Builders drew inspiration from the patterns and then accommodated them to meet the spatial limitations of the campgrounds. The theory supporting Davis's simple plans was that good architecture produces good people.

The natural beauty of the surroundings, with its magnificent chestnut groves, invigorating mountain breezes, and clean springwater, together with the improvements necessary to provide for the camp meeting, made Mount Tabor a very desirable summer residence. The strict behavior rules associated with the two weeks of camp meeting at the end of August were relaxed during the earlier part of the season, making Mount Tabor a wonderful place for mothers and children to spend the summer. The six o'clock train into Mount Tabor on Friday evening became known as the "Husbands' Train." Children's Day, an annual event still celebrated on the first weekend in August, was a highlight of the summer vacations. The board of trustees responded by expanding preaching services to include social activities before and after the camp meeting and by adding recreational facilities.

In 1881, the board of trustees reserved a park area for archery, lawn tennis, and croquet. The villagers organized the Tabor Field Club on that site and added a baseball diamond, tennis courts, and a golf course. In 1889, Dr. Henry Coit founded a free public library, although the original camp meeting rules did not allow reading novels.

The religious zeal that had inspired the camp meetings waned while Mount Tabor's reputation as a summer resort grew. Less time was spent in prayer and meditation as more time was devoted to golf, field hockey, and lectures on literature and social history. The amenities of a resort community were also becoming more obvious. By 1890, the village included two grocery stores, two butcher shops, a variety store, two bakers, a barber, a drugstore, a daily newspaper, a telegraph office, and a post office. The board of trustees recognized in 1909 that "the summer resort idea has modified the original character of our community." The Ebenezer pavilion, no longer used for sermons, was altered to house the public library.

The Great Depression brought even greater change. Few could afford to maintain both a summer and winter home. Families searching for inexpensive housing converted the summer cottages to all-season houses. Conveniently, a complete infrastructure was in place for all-season living, including water, electricity, stores within easy walking distance, and easy access to rail and bus transportation.

In 1939, the Mount Tabor Camp Meeting Association purchased an additional tract of 12 acres. Building on the tract was halted during World War II but resumed upon the return of the veterans. The new houses and the remodeling of cottages for all-season occupancy increased the trend in the direction of a year-round community, and by the mid-20th century, Mount Tabor's transition from the characteristics of a summer community to those of a year-round community was complete.

The charming Victorian houses and unique public buildings, clustered along narrow, hilly streets, stand today, much as they did in the late 19th century, as a reminder of the community life and neighborly goodwill envisioned by the founders of Mount Tabor. It is, after all, the spirit of the people that determines the character of the place.

One

CANVAS TO GINGERBREAD

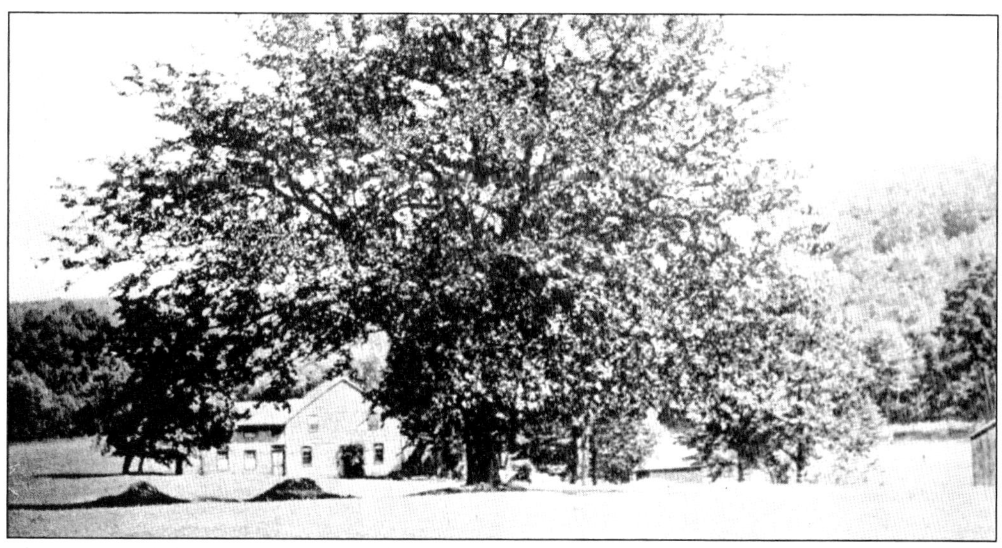

The origin of the Camp Meeting Association of the Newark Conference of the Methodist Episcopal Church dates back to the centenary of American Methodism in 1866. A committee was appointed to consider the possibility of a conference camp meeting, and on the closing days of August 1866, the first camp meeting was held at Speedwell Lake in Morristown. Bishop Edmund S. Janes gave the inaugural keynote sermon, preaching to an estimated 10,000 people. Subsequent meetings were hugely successful, and on August 31, 1868, a meeting was held to consider a permanent ground for camp meeting purposes. George Thomas Cobb, together with Rev. Jonathan Townley Crane, and Ichabod Searing, served on the exploratory committee, and on October 21, the site was selected. The first tract comprising 28 acres was purchased from W. H. Dickerson, and 2.5 acres was purchased from Nathaniel Dickerson. In May 1872, a farm of 100 acres was added to the original purchases. The Dickerson farm is pictured above. A massive mulberry tree, locally renowned, towers over the farmhouse. (Ron Dickerson.)

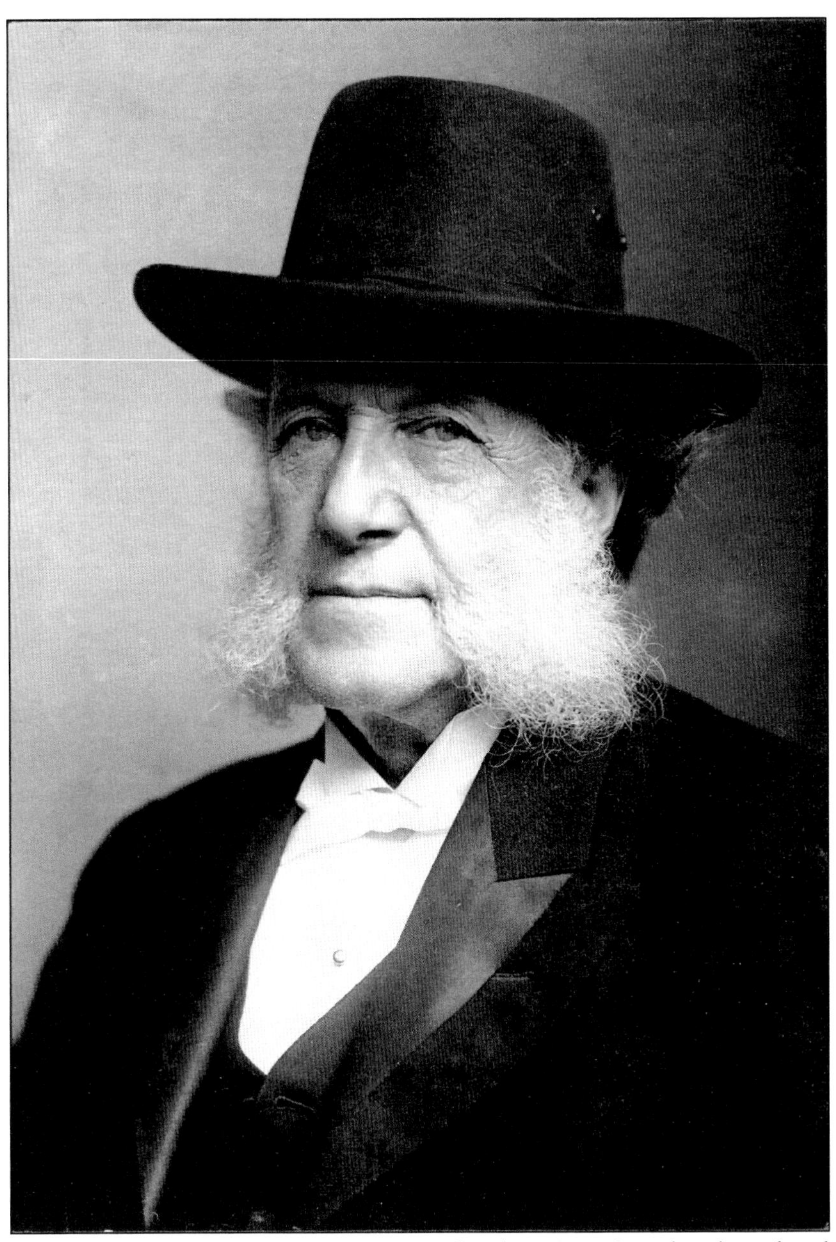

George Thomas Cobb was born in Morristown on October 13, 1813, and orphaned at the age of six. With little schooling, he amassed a fortune in foreign trade. After retirement he returned to New Jersey and was elected as a Democrat to the 37th Congress (March 4, 1861–March 3, 1863). He became affiliated with the Republican party in 1863 and as such was elected a member of the state senate in 1865 and again in 1868. He also served as mayor of Morristown from 1865 to 1869. Cobb, together with Rev. Jonathan Townley Crane and Ichabod Searing, had examined several sites for a permanent ground for camp meetings and served on a board of managers to create a "more perfect organization." On October 21, 1868, the Mount Tabor site was selected. Under the terms of the charter, the board of managers became the first board of trustees, with Cobb elected its first president. Cobb was killed in an accident on the Chesapeake and Ohio Railroad in Virginia on August 12, 1870. (Morristown Methodist Church Archives.)

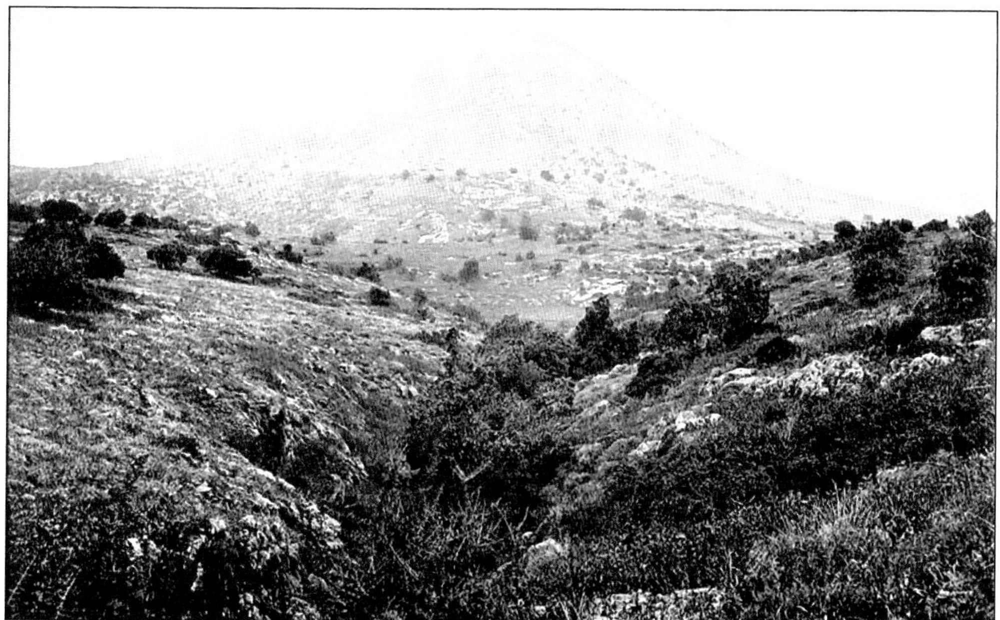

It is no small wonder that the exploratory committee searching for a permanent campground found themselves drawn to the Dickerson farm. The wooded mount bears close resemblance to the biblical Mount Tabor depicted above. Rev. C. S. Coit served on the first board of trustees and is credited with naming Mount Tabor, in homage to the traditional site of the transfiguration of Christ as recounted in Matthew 17:5. (Tom Nestor.)

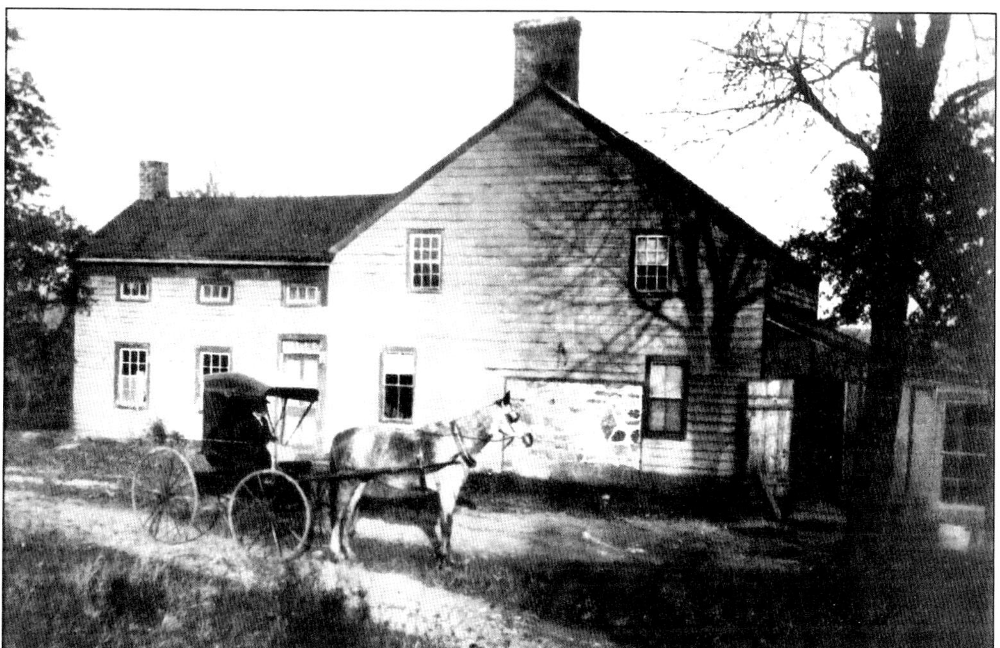

The Dickerson homestead stood near a spring where the fourth fairway of the Mount Tabor golf course is currently located. It replaced an earlier log cabin. Nathaniel Dickerson's descendant Claude Dickerson found a chimney stone from this building and incorporated it into his own house. (Ron Dickerson.)

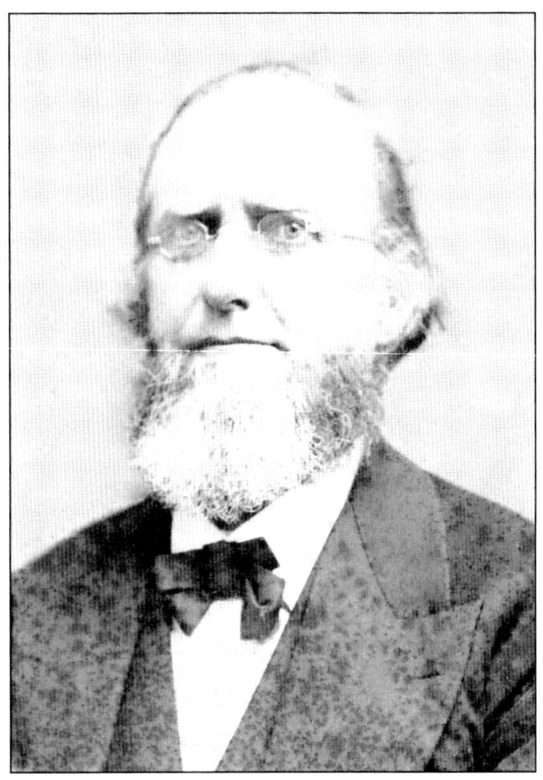

Rev. Jonathan Townley Crane, who explored permanent camp sites with George Thomas Cobb and Ichabod Searing, also served on the first board of trustees. He was instrumental in securing a unique charter for Mount Tabor, empowering the trustees with municipal rights and privileges. Novelist Stephen Crane was the 14th and last child of Reverend Crane and his wife, Mary. Young Stephen was a sporadic summer resident of Mount Tabor until his father's death in 1880. (Morristown Methodist Church Archives.)

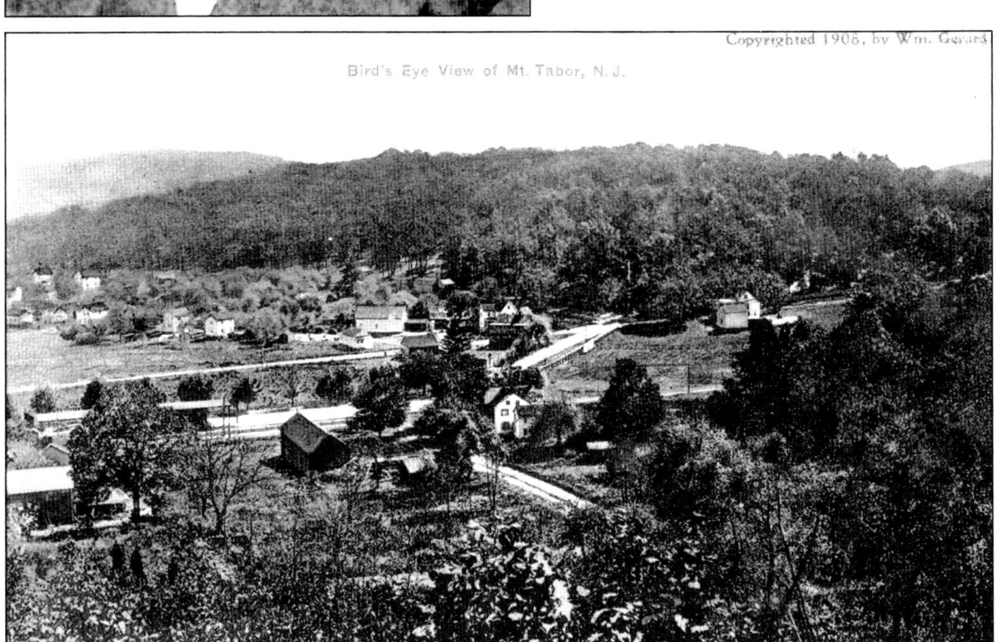

When the exploratory committee began its exploration for a permanent campground, it may have envisioned the biblical description of Mount Tabor, "a land of hills and valleys, and drinketh water of the rain of heaven." This bird's-eye view of Mount Tabor, copyrighted 1908, shows the hills and valleys, and the campground was renowned for its pure springwater. The railroad station, although far from biblical, was heaven sent. (Mount Tabor Historical Society.)

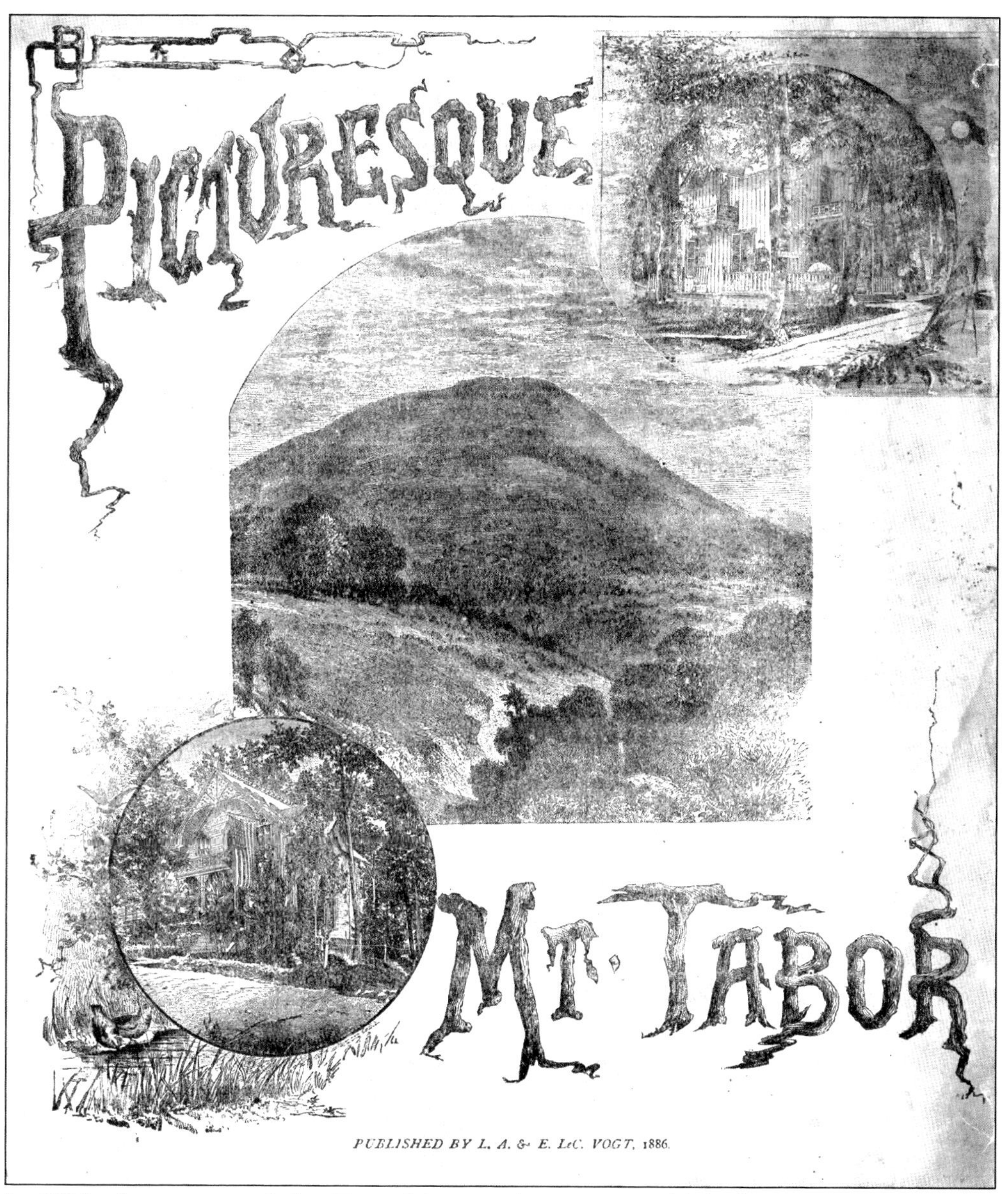

In 1886, the trustees of the Camp Meeting Association published *Picturesque Mt. Tabor*, a promotional booklet. In it, a fictional young couple begins a tour at a "beautiful wall of purple stone" and glimpses gleaming white tents "here and there" among the trees and people "scattered over the mountain." On the first level, the couple enters a wide avenue with stores, a police station, a telegraph office, a post office, boardinghouses, and so on. They pass through a gateway and enter Trinity Park, a grove of magnificent chestnut trees with a gentle descent to the tabernacle. The beautiful cottages and pavilions and a sparkling water fountain delight the couple. Night has fallen when the couple completes the tour, leaving one with this final image: "He who has never seen Mount Tabor lighted up at night can scarcely imagine the beautiful effect produced by countless lamps in the woods. In some respects it reminds one of a scene from a fairy tale." (Mount Tabor Historical Society.)

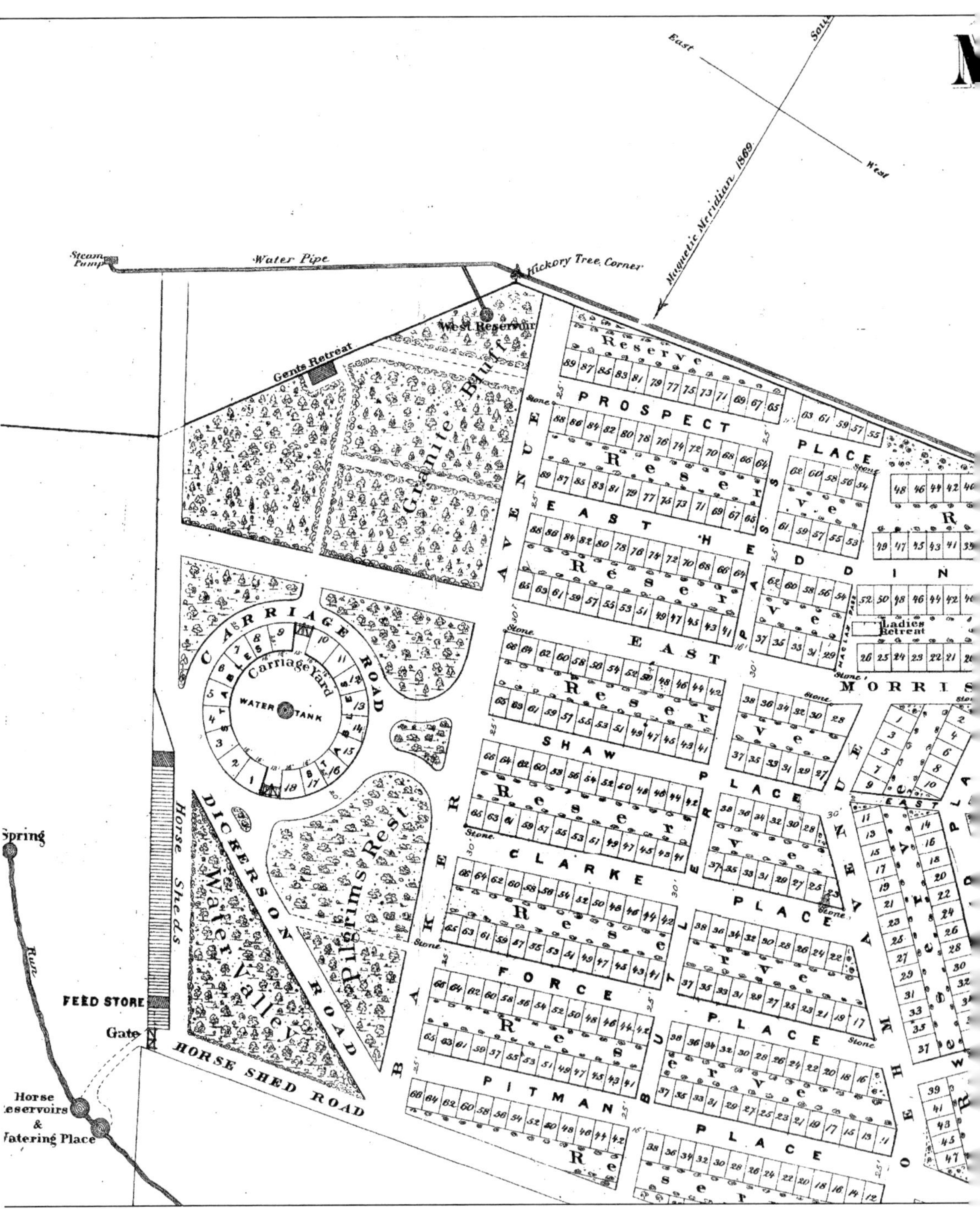

An early example of a planned community, the campground was laid out in tent lots separated by avenues and paths. At the center of the original ground was the tabernacle facing Trinity Circle. It was the nucleus around which the avenues wound, and could be reached from all directions by narrow passes. Trinity Circle was the focal point for all camp meeting activities. Fifteen-square-foot reserved areas behind each tent were provided for cooking. Small kerosene

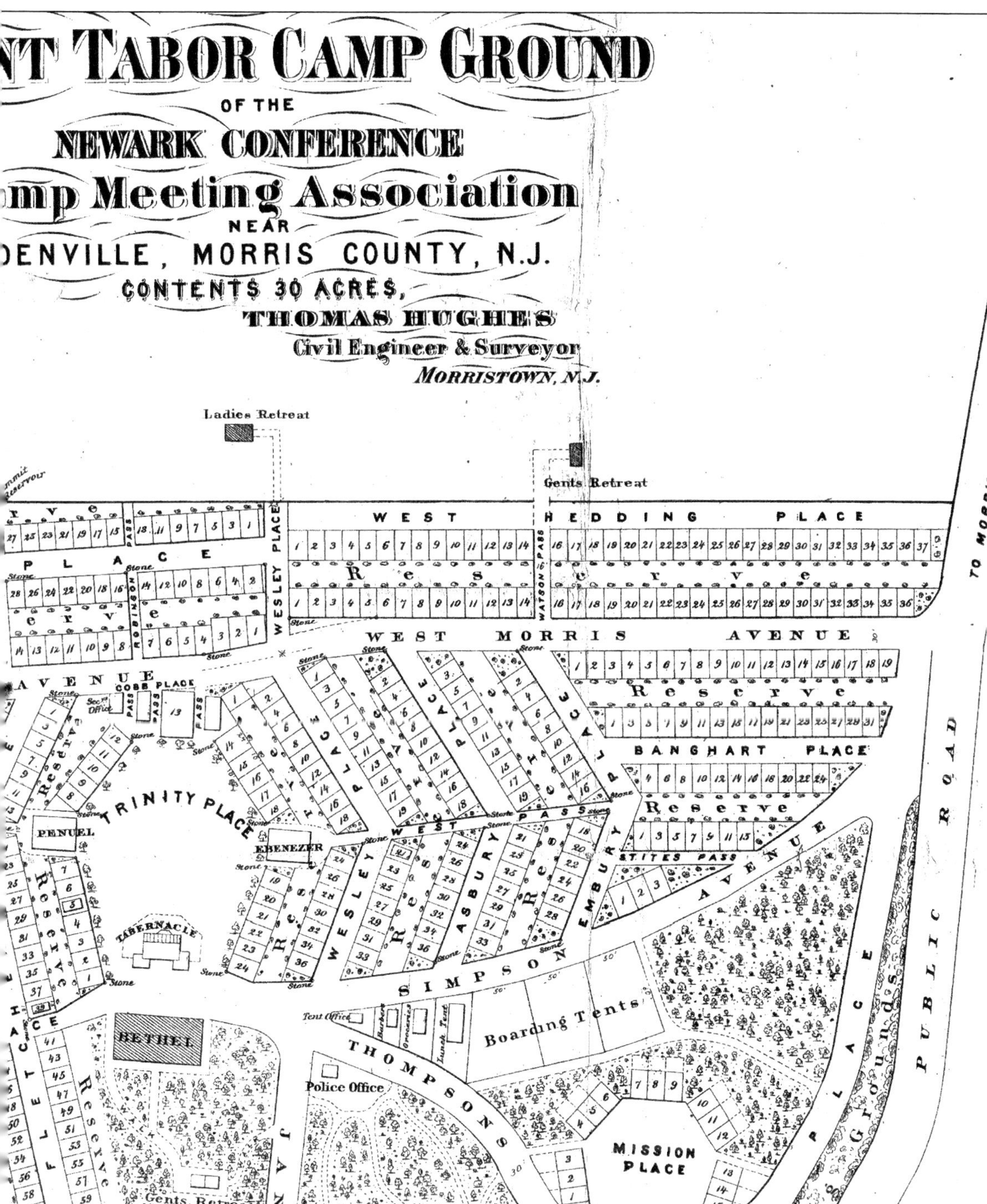

stoves or fireplaces built of loose stones were used to heat simple meals. Wealthier occupants could afford the luxury of prepared meals at boarding tents or the Arlington Hotel. Before indoor plumbing, private bathrooms were considered a luxury. Several facilities referred to as the "ladies' and gentlemen's retreats" were located along the outskirts of the camp. Bathing space and outhouses were located in these communal bathrooms. (Mount Tabor Historical Society.)

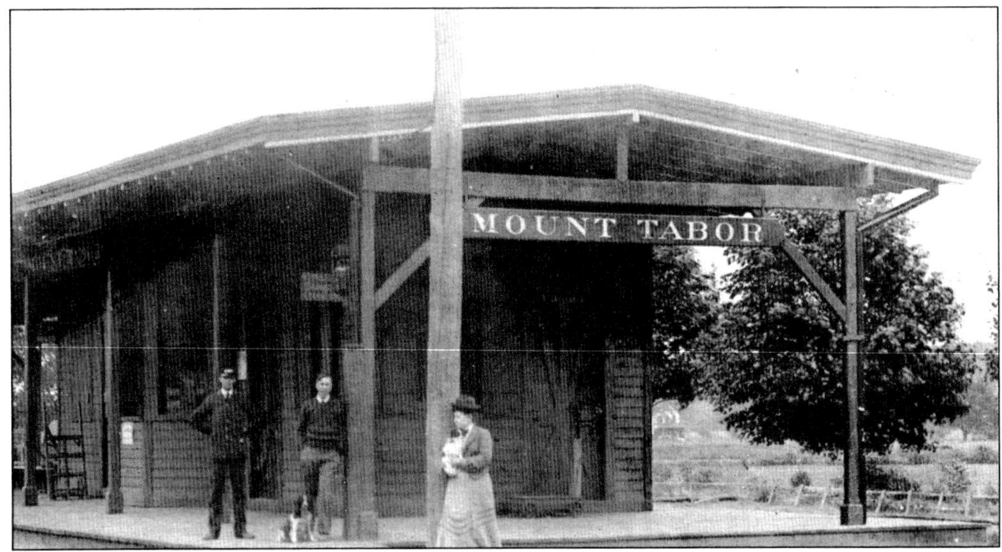

The minutes of the Camp Meeting Association dated August 19, 1881, state that "one of the greatest improvements made about the place in recent years is the new depot building." It was erected by the Delaware, Lackawanna and Western Railroad under the superintendence of John Scannell of Newark. The waiting room was 12 feet by 40 feet, and seats were arranged under the whole length of the platform roof. (Beth Shaw.)

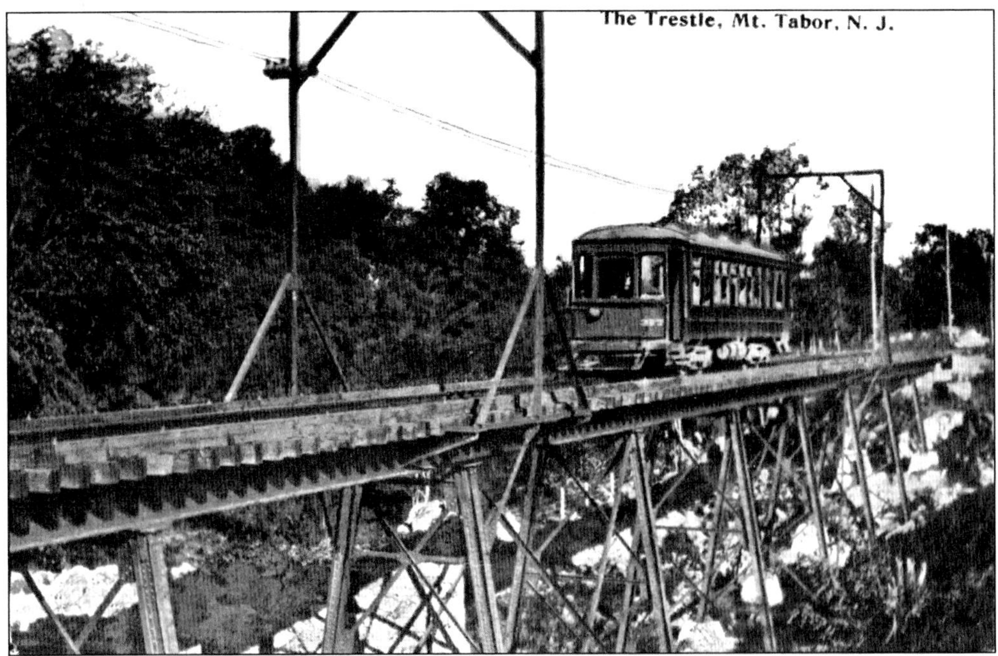

In 1900, the Morris County Traction Company requested the right to pass the association property. As the trolley approached Mount Tabor, it would make a nerve-wracking crossing on a narrow trestle over a steep ravine by the lake. Passengers could opt to forego this nail-biting leg of the journey by disembarking, hiking down and up the ravine on foot, and rejoining the trolley for the ride to Mount Tabor station. (Michelle LaConto Munn.)

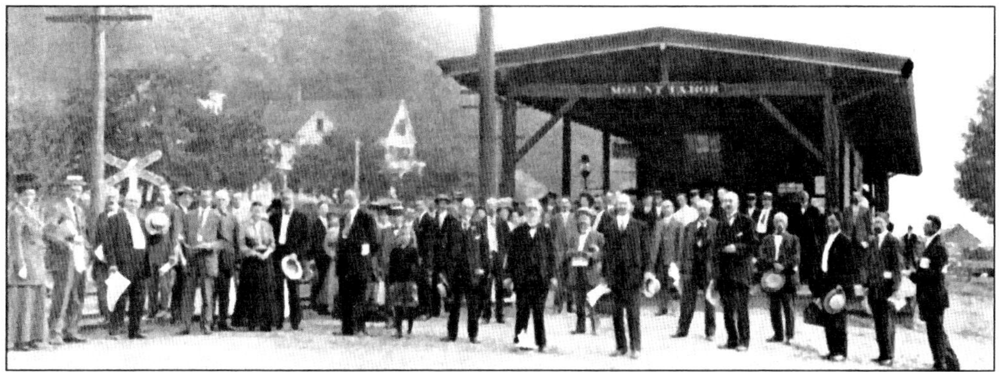

Commuters waiting at the Mount Tabor train station may have taken one last look toward the entrance of the campgrounds before boarding the train. If they did, they would have seen the Mount Tabor welcome sign arched over the main entrance of the wooded grounds. There is no documentation as to when it was erected, but on a postcard dated 1908, the writer informs that the arch image on the card was no longer standing and that most of the residents were glad because it reminded them of a "beer garden." The sign has been replaced through donations by the Mount Tabor Historical Society, the Camp Meeting Association, and a townwide fund-raising campaign. The dedication was on September 9, 2001. It is interesting to note that the six o'clock train into Mount Tabor on Friday evening became known as the "Husbands' Train," as husbands and fathers poured into the station for the weekend. (Mount Tabor Historical Society.)

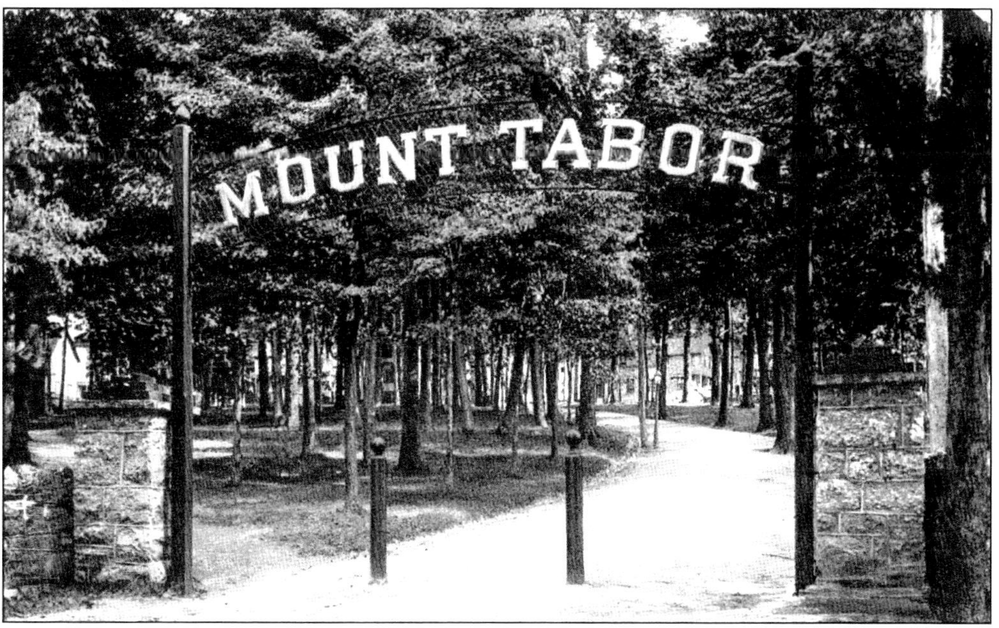

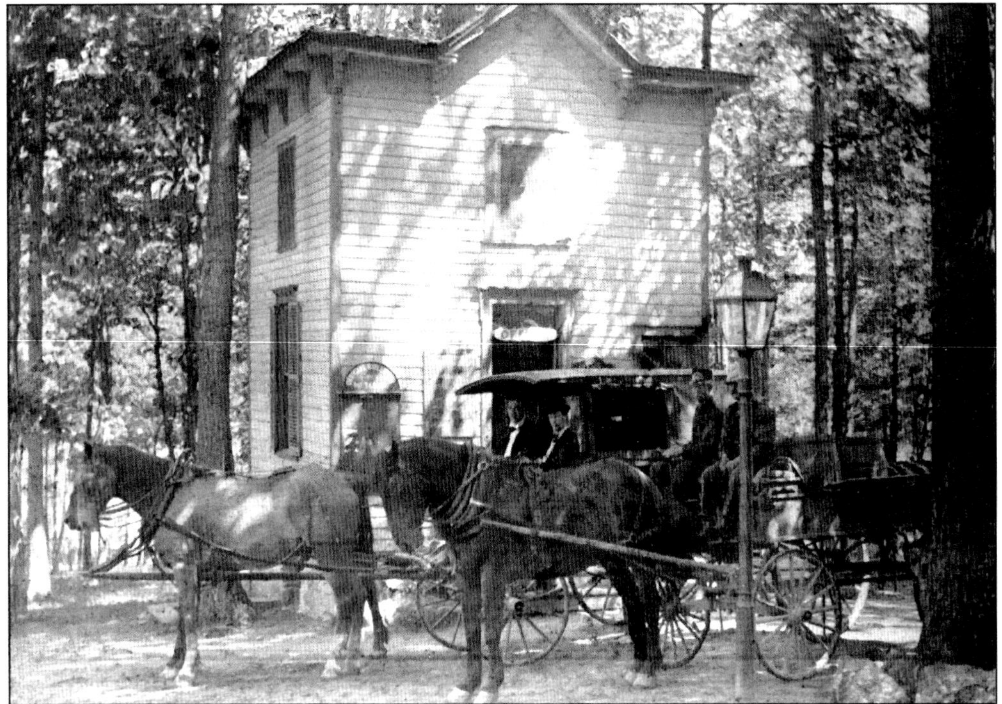

Two stages pause in front of the Camp Meeting Association office, located on the corner of Simpson Avenue and Durbin Avenue, across from the lower level of the tabernacle, around 1900. A stage service transported visitors and their baggage to and from the train station. At that time, the baggage express room was located in the association office. (Mount Tabor Historical Society.)

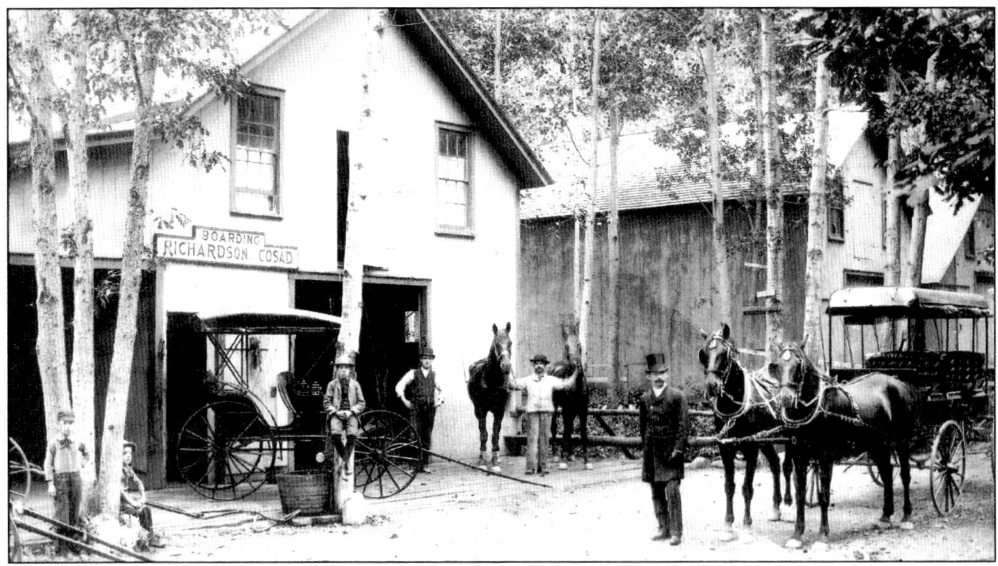

These barns, which are still standing, are located near the entrance of Mount Tabor. In the early days, many guests arrived by horse and carriage. The horses would board here during their stay at Camp Tabor. The caretakers of the barns, J. Smith Richardson and Dr. J. W. Cosad, lived in the triple cottage on Trinity Park. (Evelyn Clark.)

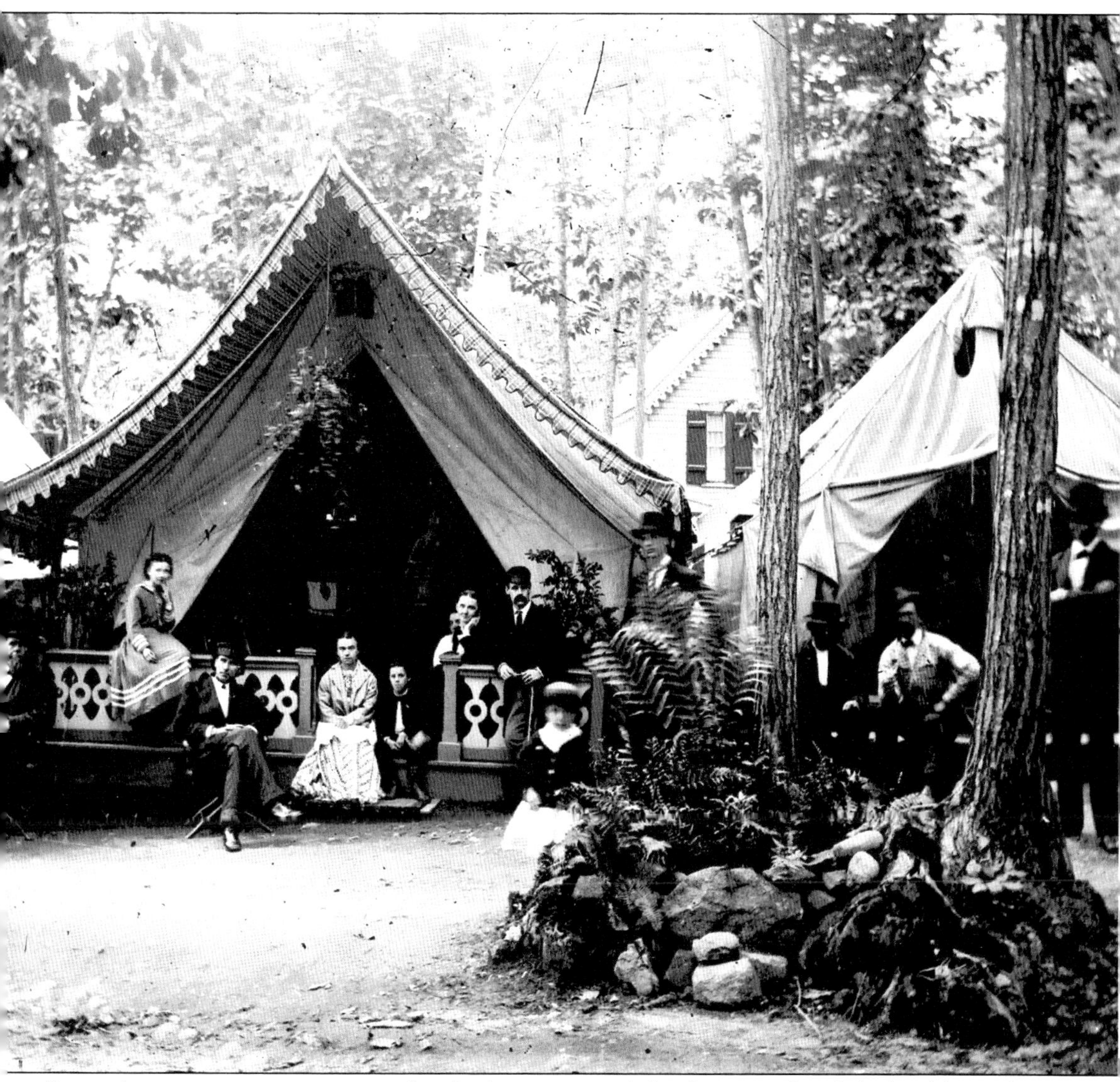

Original camp meetings were considered pilgrimages, and the devout endured the hardships of primitive tents rather than lush accommodations. Biblical stories of ancient Israelites played an important role in camp life. To defend the camp meetings, organizers recalled passages such as in the Feast of the Tabernacles: "Ye shall dwell in booths [tents] seven days, all that are Israelites born shall dwell in booths." Their sacrifice of worldly shelter placed the devout campers among the chosen people. Canvas tents were built on wooden platforms, which, along with the structural framework, comprised the only permanent parts of the shelters. Two rows of vertical beams, three in each, supported the canvas. The windows were holes along the ridgepole, and the tent flaps, which functioned as doors, were open in the daytime and tied together with string at night. The double doors of a cottage would later reflect these tent flaps. The scalloped tent edging would be translated into gingerbread. The interiors of the tents were divided into a front portion used as a parlor and a back portion used for sleeping quarters. (Mount Tabor Historical Society.)

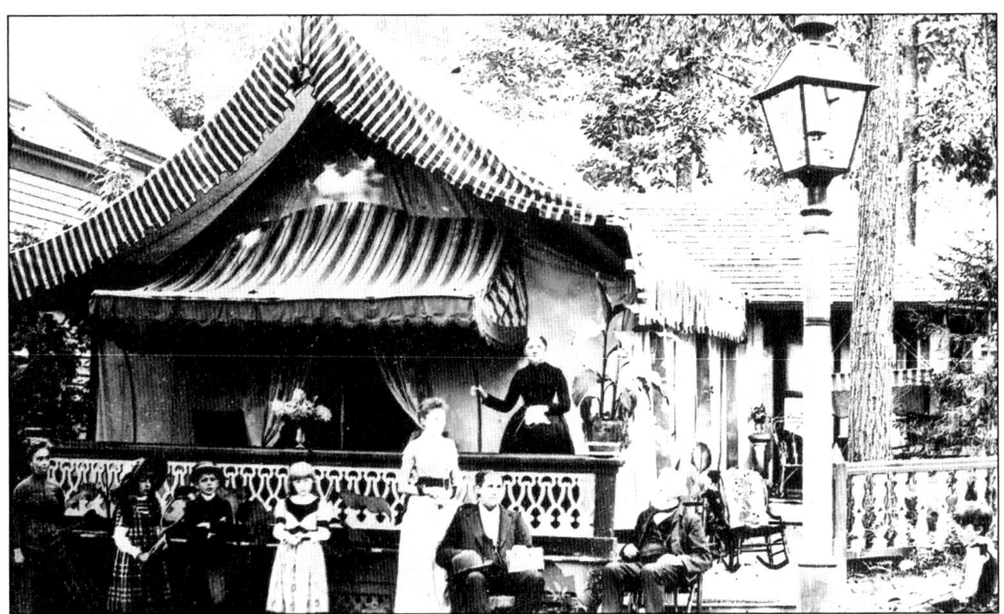

Erected in the mid-1870s for Daniel L. Lowrie, D.D., of Bloomfield, this "half tent-half cottage" included a parlor, study, dining room, modern kitchen, and sleeping rooms and was surrounded by a miniature lawn and gardens. Behind the tents were permanent structures with exposed beams for off-ground storage during the rest of the year. At the end of the summer, stacked furniture and rolled-up floor matting were securely stored in the "shed." Anything that could not fit was shipped back to the city. The tents were disassembled and left in the care of a year-round live-in superintendent. (Mount Tabor Historical Society.)

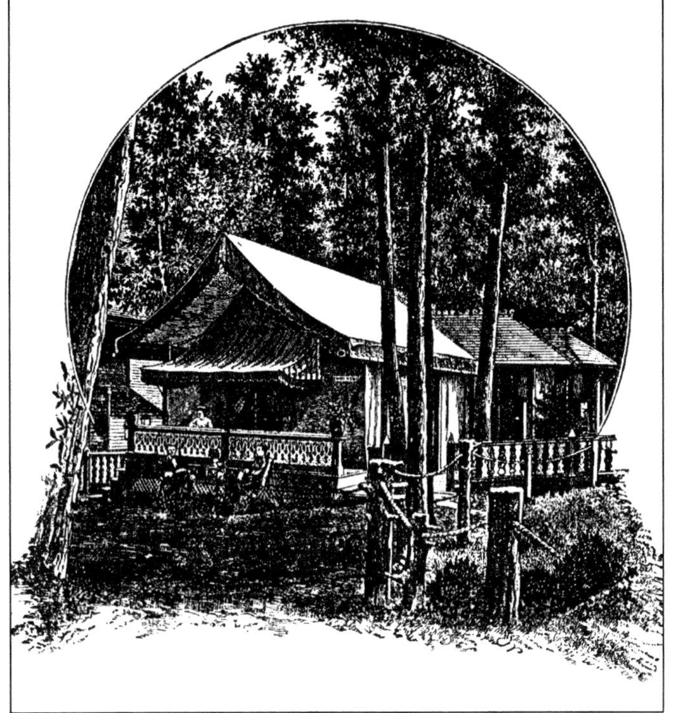

An excerpt from *Picturesque Mt. Tabor* eloquently describes this lovely etching of Lowrie's residence: "At the other side of the fountain is the delightful residence of Rev. Daniel L. Lowrie—a tent in the foreground and a cottage in the rear. It strikes one very pleasantly, especially with its suggestive name, 'Sweet Home.' There are other places on the grounds more pretentious, and some which are more elegant, but there is none more artistic than this." (Mount Tabor Record, 1880s.)

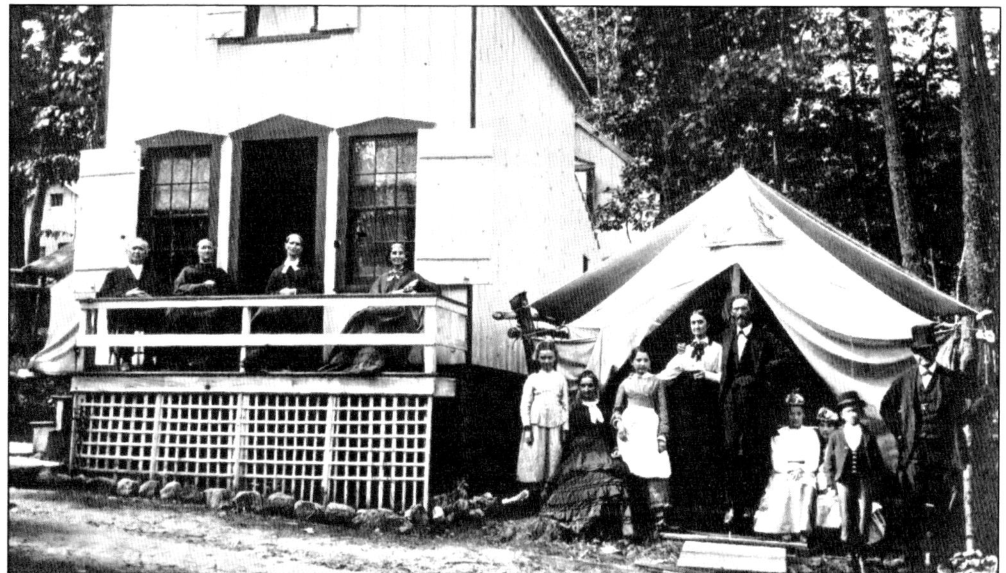

According to the *New York Times* on August 25, 1871, "Many of the friendly Methodists threw wide open the doors of their cottages and the walls of the tents in token that they would willingly receive the visits of the brethren in the Lord. Many people brought their servants with them to do the cooking and look after the tent while the inmates made the rounds of visits. But many ladies delighted at the opportunity to show off their housekeeping talents. These cooked boldly before the people at the side of their tents." (Tom Nestor.)

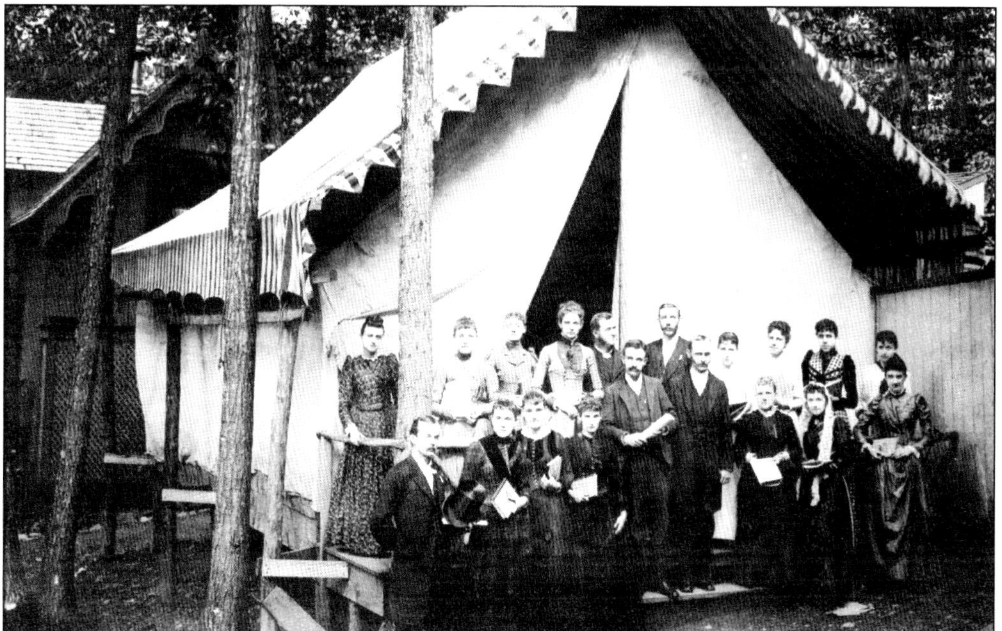

It was noted in the *Mount Tabor Record* in 1877 that a music tent was erected every year "for the accommodation of the people of the Methodist Episcopal Church of Mount Hope who may visit the grounds." Both the choir and band from the Mount Hope church participated in the activities of the early Mount Tabor camp meeting from 1872 through at least 1879. It is likely that the music tent had an appearance similar to the one pictured here. (Tom Nestor.)

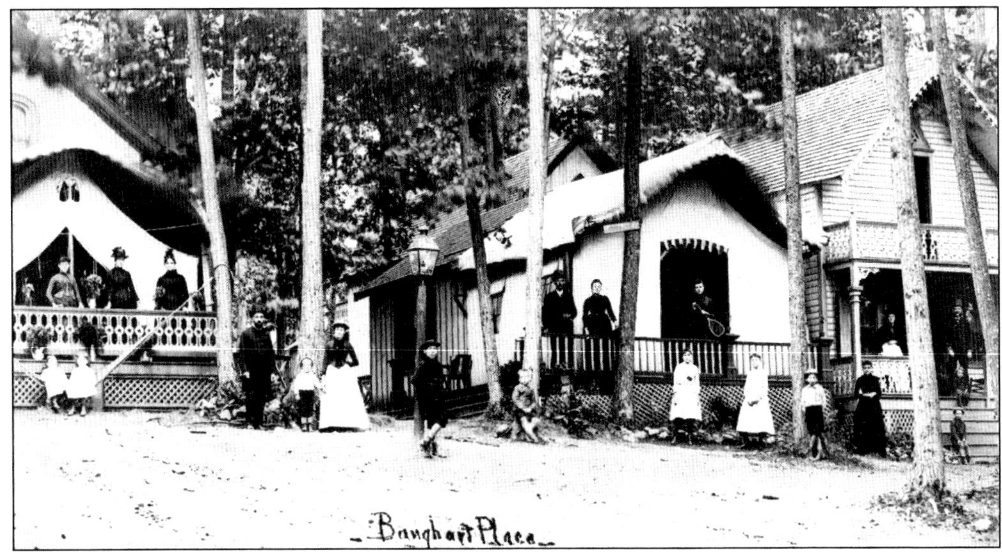

Banghart Place is one of the shortest streets in Mount Tabor. Only seven houses use this address today. The interiors of the tents were divided into a front portion used as a parlor and a back portion used for sleeping quarters. Due to space limitations furnishings were multifunctional. Sofas converted to beds, barrels doubled as chairs, and trunks became tables. Camp chairs and rockers also adorned the tents. (Tom Nestor.)

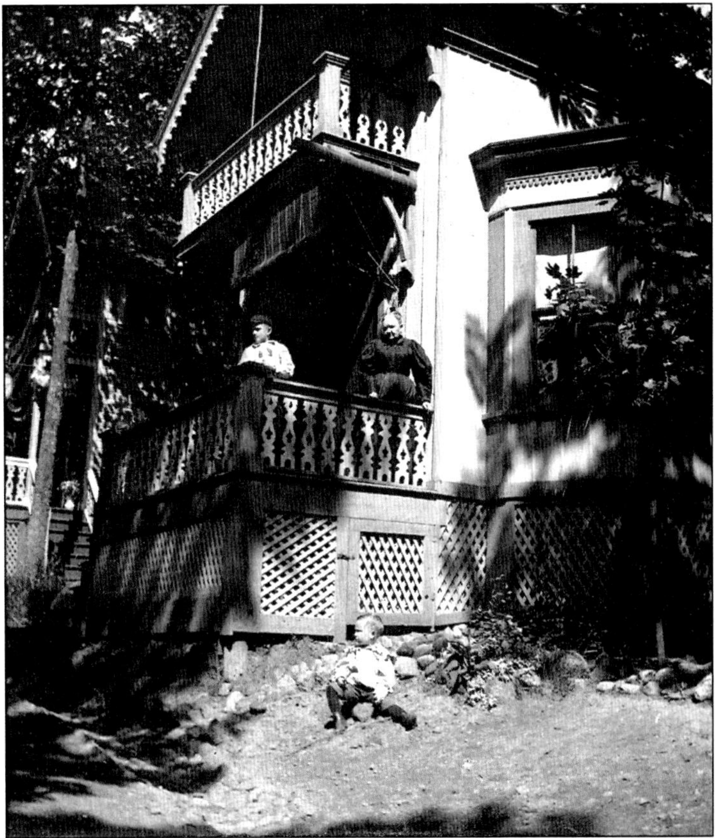

The Langstroth Cottage, located today at 12 Banghart Place, was built in 1871 by landowners in Glen Ridge. The cottage is similar in feel today, although it has undergone extensive renovation by its current owner. A pudding stone chimney with cherubs, foundation work with fountains, and double arched doors reclaimed from the Morristown library have been added to the house. The board and batten exterior has been returned to its original appearance. (Bud Knudsen.)

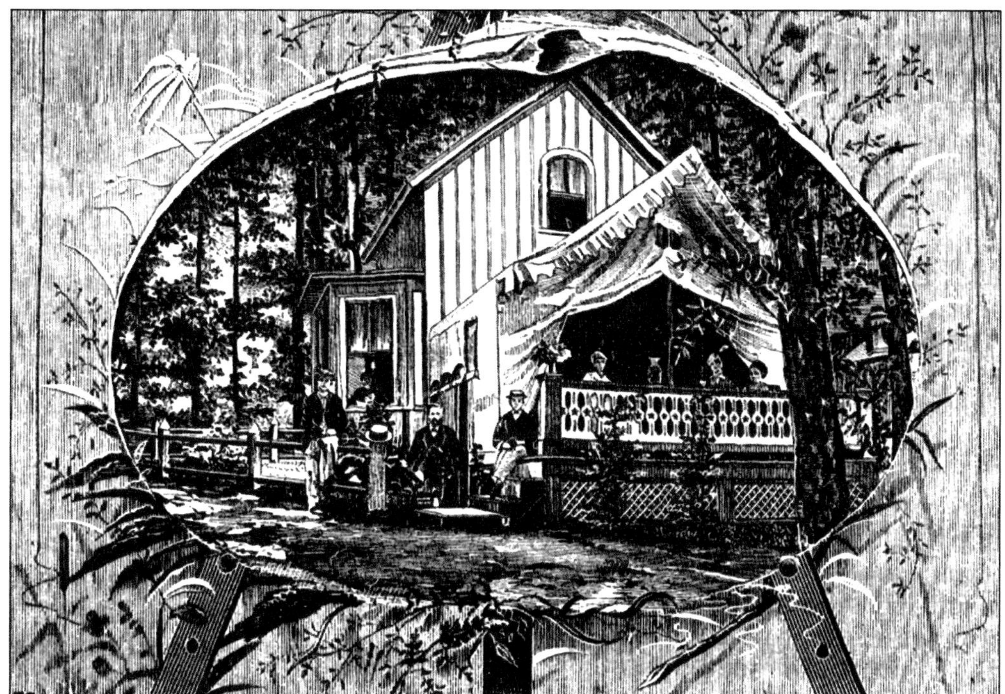

This combination tent and cottage illustration from the *Mount Tabor Record* depicts the residence of R. L. Chambers, Esq., of Newark. It is on the corner of Banghart Place and Asbury Place. "It embraces all the delights of tent life, yet offers the solid comforts of a cottage, built in the most substantial manner of the best materials." (Mount Tabor Record, 1880s.)

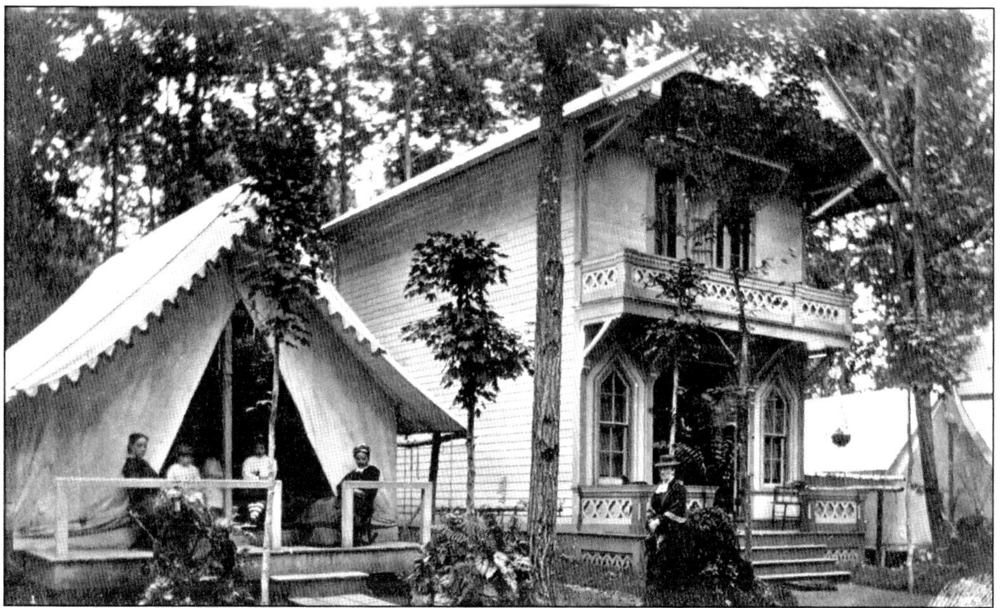

This early photograph is a wonderful example of harmonious tent and cottage living. Tent residents would have to close up their tent at the end of the season and transport their belongings home, while cottage residents could afford to stay longer into the season or year-round and decorate with more permanent furnishings. (Tom Nestor.)

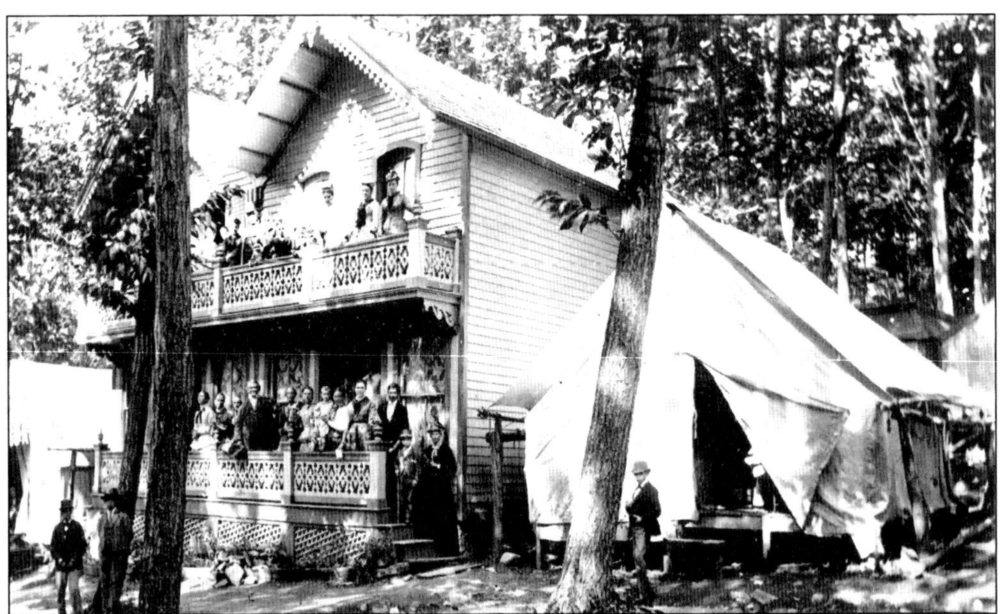

Lyon's Cottages and Boarding Tent was run by A. Lyon and his wife, Lavinia. Lavinia Lyon managed the double boarding cottage with accommodations for 60 boarders while her husband ran the restaurant in a large tent next door. An advertisement in the *Mount Tabor Record* of August 1878 publicized, "Meals available at all hours." Many tent dwellers took their meals at Lyon's boarding tent rather than cook outside over an open fire. A. Lyon, a Civil War veteran and member of the Grand Army of the Republic, spent most days in an armchair in front of his establishment next to a large sign that announced "Father Lyon Welcomes the G.A.R." (Above, Tom Nestor; below, Ann Britten Wilson.)

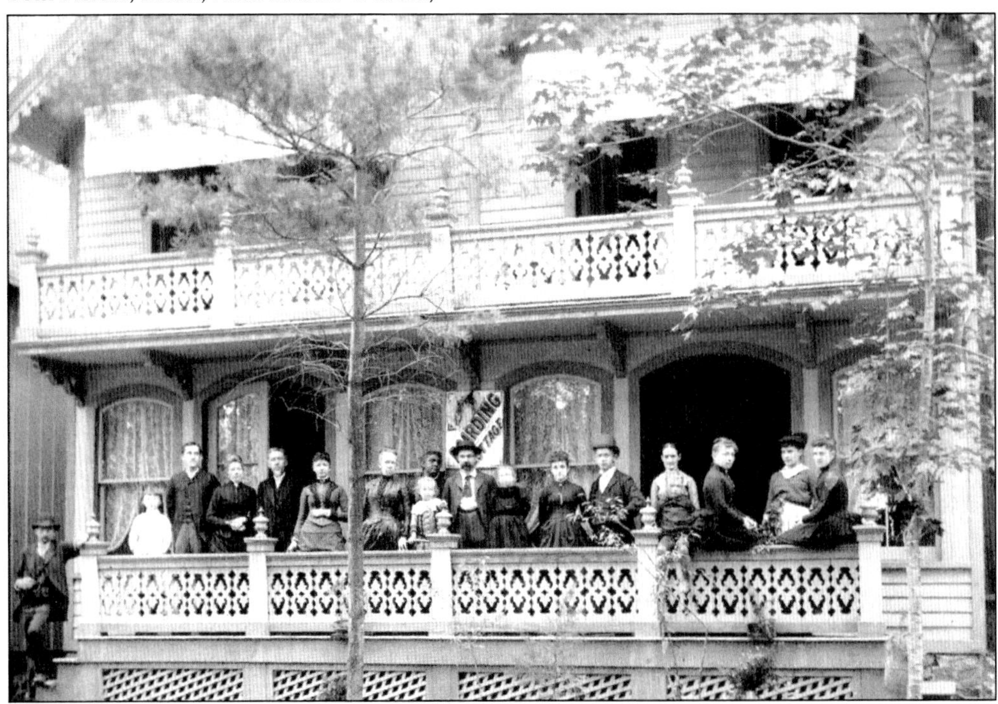

Two

TRINITY PARK

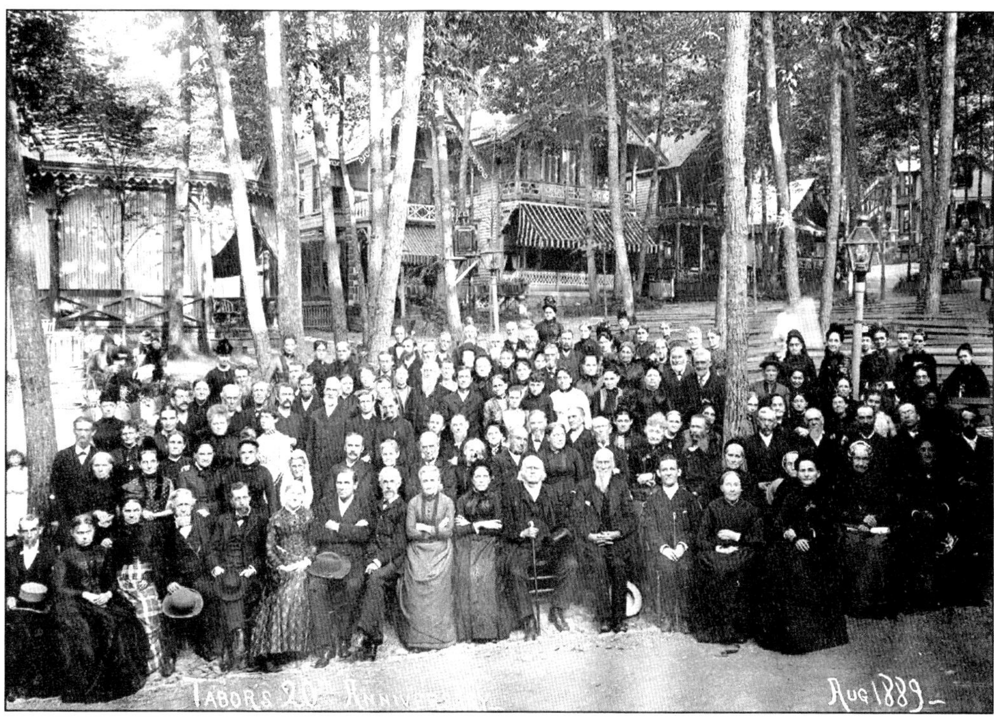

In August 1889, the faithful gathered in Trinity Park to celebrate the 20th anniversary of the founding of the Mount Tabor camp meeting. Just 20 years later on the occasion of the 40th anniversary, Rev. Rufus K. Boyd would laud the ladies and gentlemen pictured here: "Most of the generation which founded Mount Tabor have passed away. A few still live to tell of its early glory and rejoice in its present progress. Those who, year after year, come to enjoy its advantages and share its charming social and religious attractions, will not cease to hold in grateful memory those whose piety, devotion and sacrifice have made Tabor what it is; and will hold as a sacred trust the high purposes of its founders." This is one of the few photographs of the Ebenezer pavilion (at left) before it was enclosed. Here it is an open pavilion with canvas sides that could be rolled up or down. (Tom Nestor.)

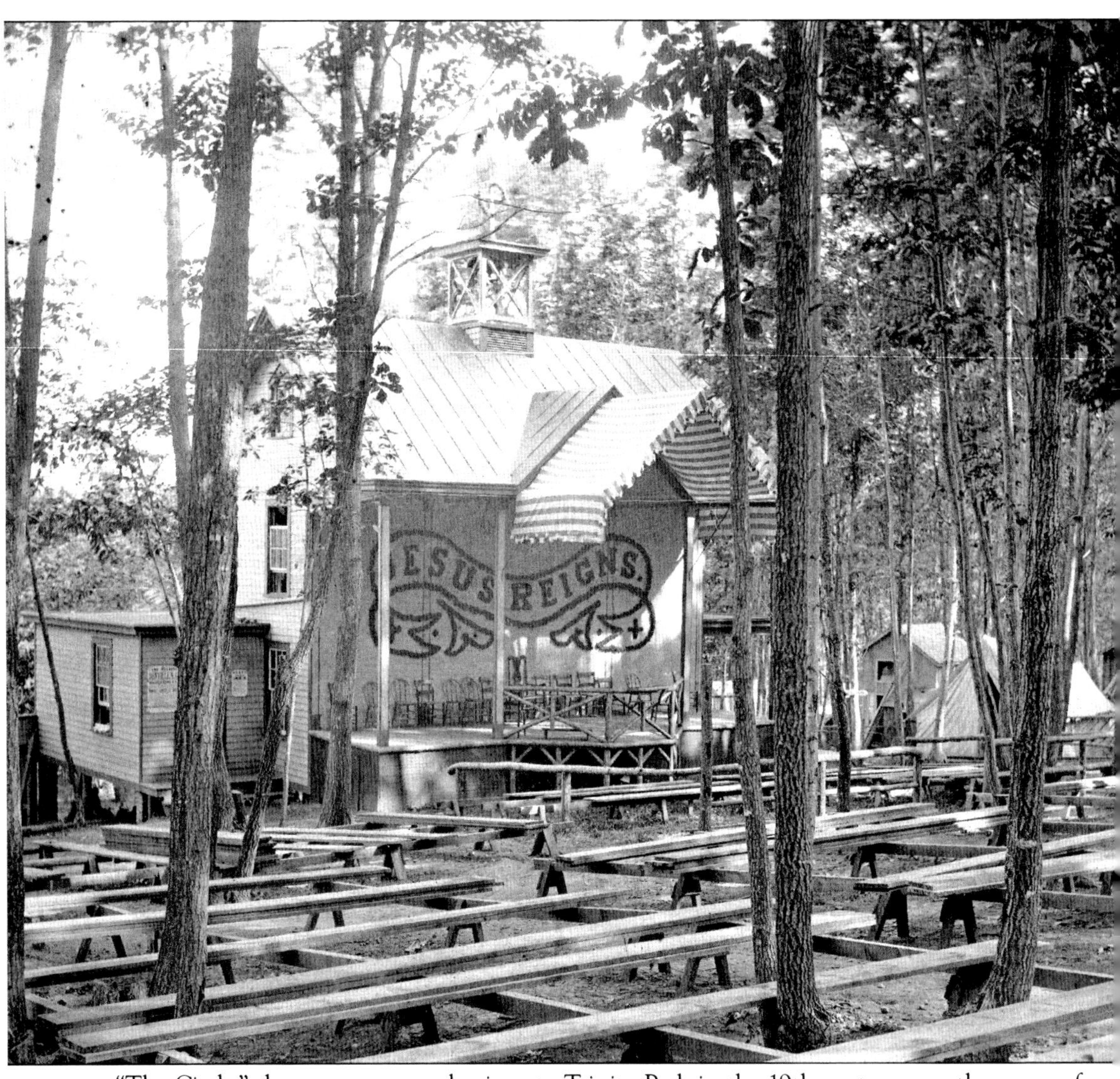

"The Circle," the name commonly given to Trinity Park in the 19th century, was the scene of large and enthusiastic camp meeting services. In 1877, it was reported that "the Circle will seat 4,000 people and within hearing of the services 8,000 people can congregate. There have been times in the past when no less than 12,000 people have been packed within this enclosure." Imagine these simple wooden benches as well as surrounding porches, both upper and lower, filled with attentive worshippers. The benches are facing the original tabernacle, around 1869. The preacher's stand and the famous Jesus Reigns sign are visible in this photograph. (Evelyn Clark.)

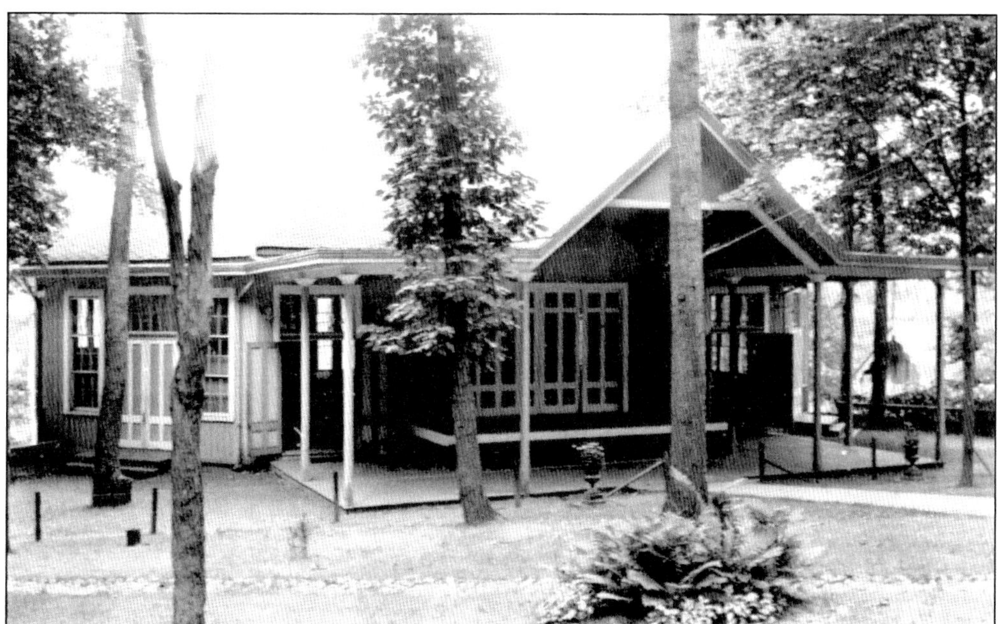

The present tabernacle, designed by John Post of Paterson and built by C. White, also of Paterson, was erected in 1885 on the site of the former preacher's stand and was paid for by contributions from residents and friends of the community. C. White's original bid was $4,030. Camp meeting notes on March 2, 1887, recorded the total amount paid as $7,281. The building has an elongated octagonal shape and tentlike characteristics. The preacher, by turning around on his platform, was able to face audiences inside and outside the tabernacle. Individuals with megaphones were stationed amid the throng to repeat the orators' words to the masses. Two such sermons were titled "The Doom of the Saloon" and "How to Catch and Train a Wife." An unidentified minister sits on the preacher's stand, at right. (Above, Tom Nestor; right, Bobbi Longstreet.)

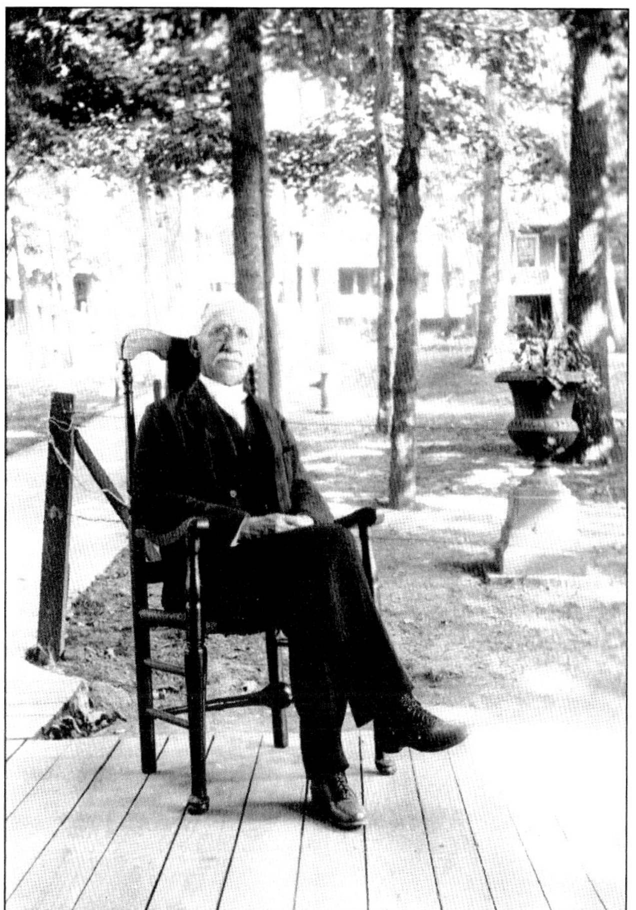

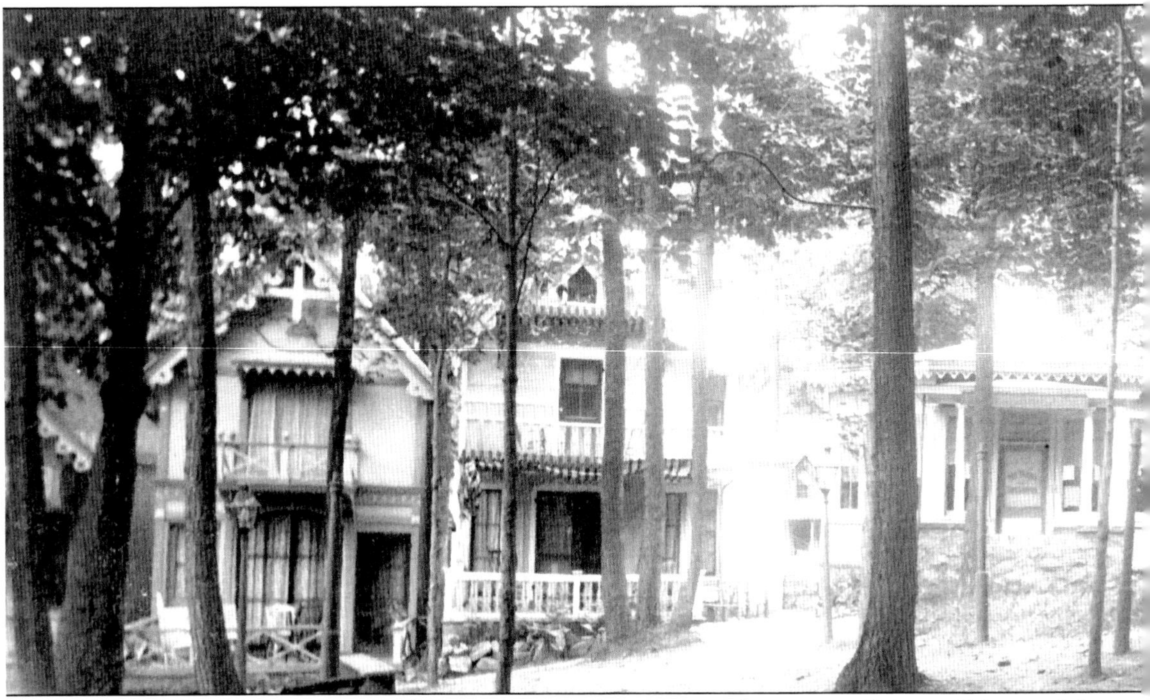

Trinity Park, or Trinity Circle, as it was once known, was the center of Mount Tabor and the hub of camp meeting activities. The earliest cottages were erected in close proximity to the park, and the cottages seen in the postcard above are early and fine examples of the esthetic and architectural details that continue to charm today. Clustered around Trinity Park, the cottages

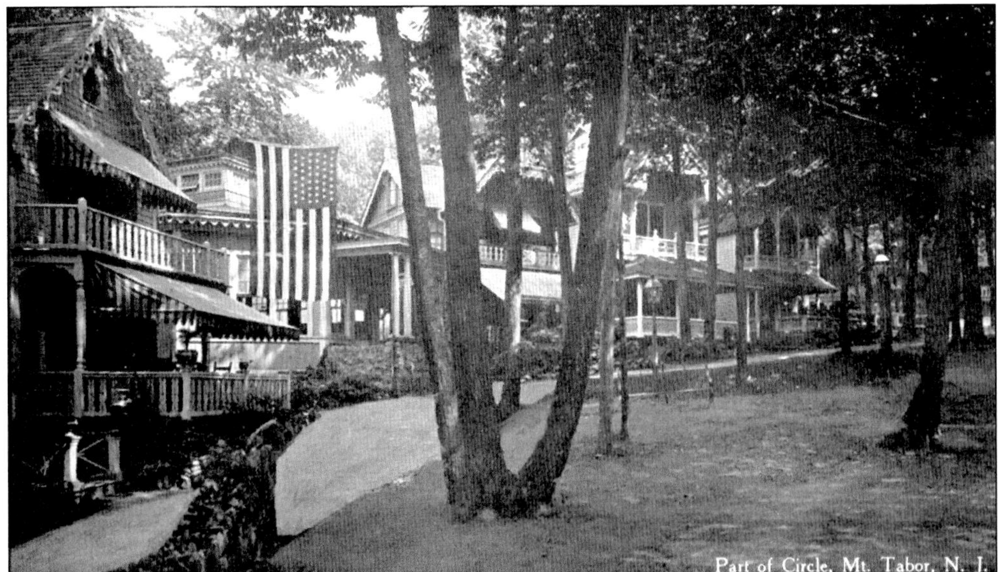

This sun-dappled view of the east side of Trinity Park has all the elements that characterize Mount Tabor cottages: narrow two-story Victorian houses, intricate gingerbread details, upper and lower porches, canvas awnings, and the ubiquitous American flag, proudly displayed by the residents, then and now. Following the gently ascending path leads one to the Golden Stairs, opposite the tabernacle, and presumably straight to heaven. (Mount Tabor Historical Society.)

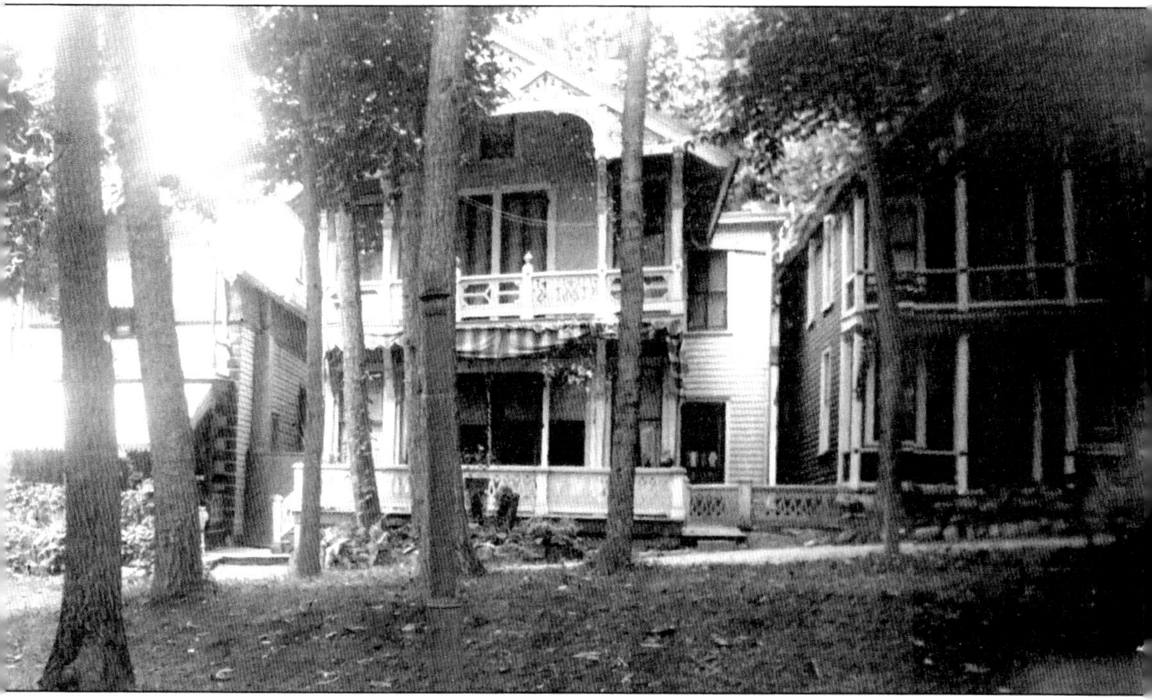

were anchored by the tabernacle, with its preacher's stand facing the park. Benches faced the tabernacle within the park. The octagonal-shaped Ebenezer pavilion, seen in the center of the postcard, with cupola and porch columns, today houses the public library. (Beth Shaw.)

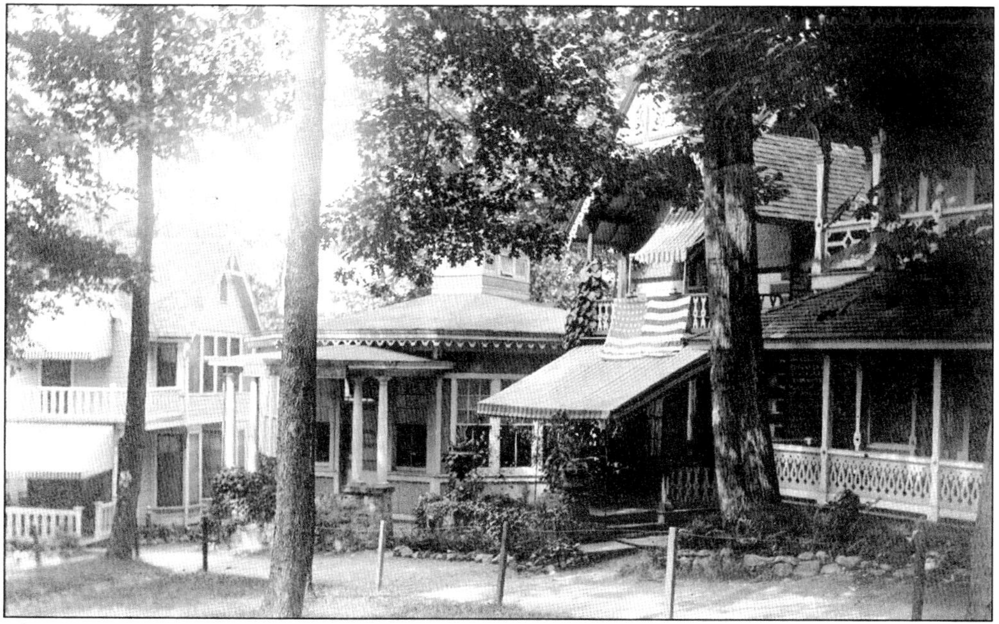

The same path is viewed on the descent from the Golden Stairs. Along the way, take note of the Allison cottage, far right, followed by the gingerbread encrusted cottage with the American flag draped from the upper porch, and a closer examination of the Ebenezer pavilion. (Mount Tabor Historical Society.)

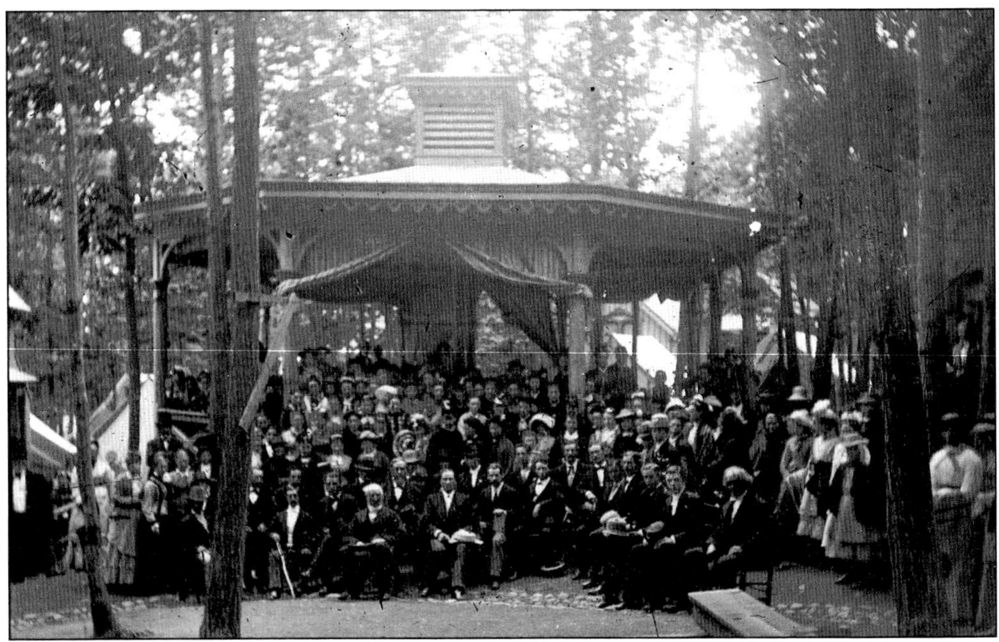

The Ebenezer pavilion, an octagonal structure with open sides covered by canvas flaps, was built in 1873 on the east side of Trinity Park. At one time, a large scale model of the Holy Land with topographical features worked in colored sand was on the pavilion floor. The structure was used for group gatherings, including the young people's meeting, which met every evening at 6:00 during the camp meetings. In 1889, Dr. Henry Coit, a Newark pediatrician who owned a drugstore in Mount Tabor, donated his private lending library to found the Mount Tabor Free Public Library, which was housed in the pavilion. Enclosed in 1901, the library was open only during the summers until the 1950s, when the porch was enclosed and a heating system installed. Still in the same location, the library is now a branch of the Parsippany–Troy Hills Public Library. (Mount Tabor Historical Society.)

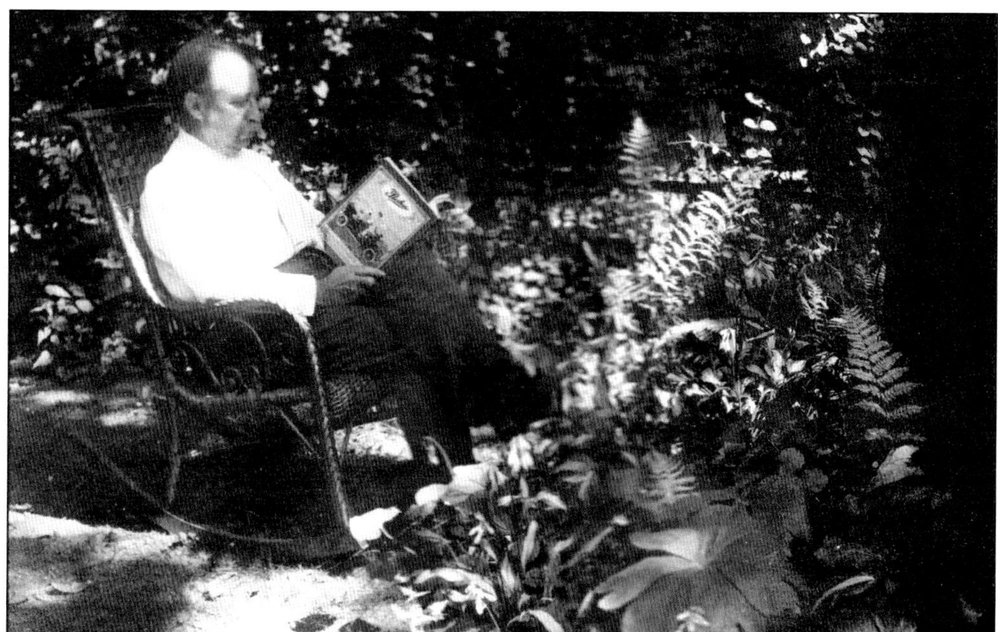

Franklin N. Barrett served as president of the library association for 21 years. Upon Barrett's death in 1921, the association issued a resolution that stated, "The Board of Trustees of the Mount Tabor Free Library has sustained a severe loss in one, who has worked so diligently and successfully in building this institution of entertainment and instruction, and in years to come, we will appreciate the keen interest he took in its welfare." (Jeanne Apgar.)

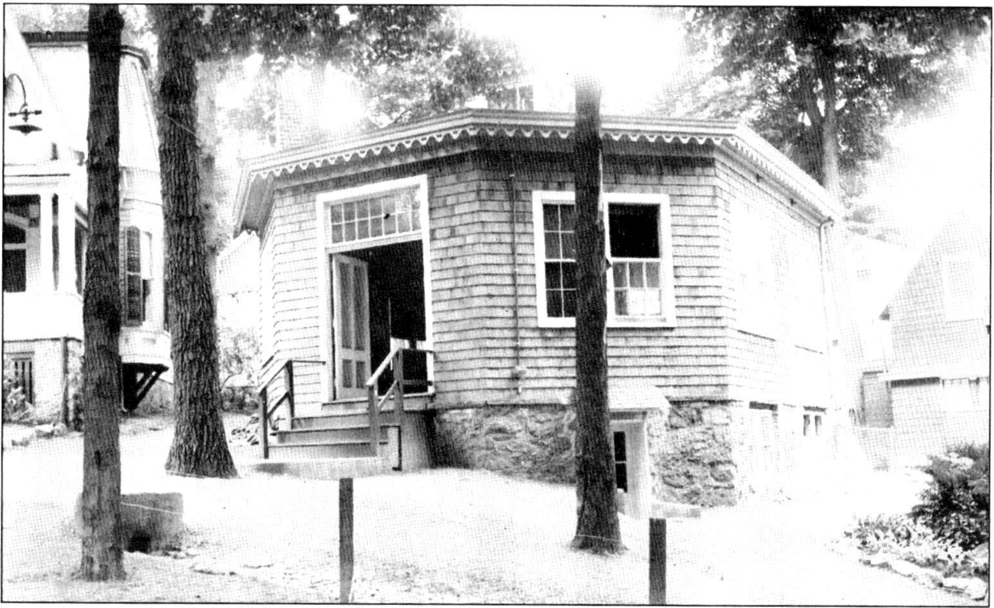

This photograph shows the Bethel in 1938. The Bethel was originally an open-sided prayer pavilion with canvas flaps that could be closed when it rained. Its octagonal shape mirrored the Ebenezer pavilion, now the library, on the opposite side of Trinity Park. In 1886, the Bethel was enclosed and rededicated as the Children's Temple. Further improvements were made in 1938, including a new vestibule, basement, kitchen, and heating system. (Mount Tabor Historical Society.)

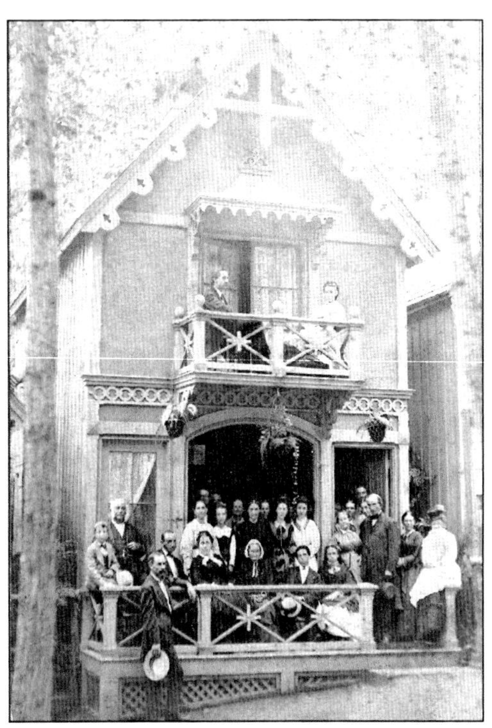

Dated 1877, this photograph shows one of the earliest cottages on Trinity Park, built in 1873 for Rev. C. S. Coit, an original member of the board of trustees. The lease was transferred through the Coit family from 1869 through 1961. Exterior details include the ornate cupola on the roof, finial and pendant ornaments, decoratively carved bargeboards with a dove motif, and tent fringed hood over the second-story balcony. (Camp Meeting Association.)

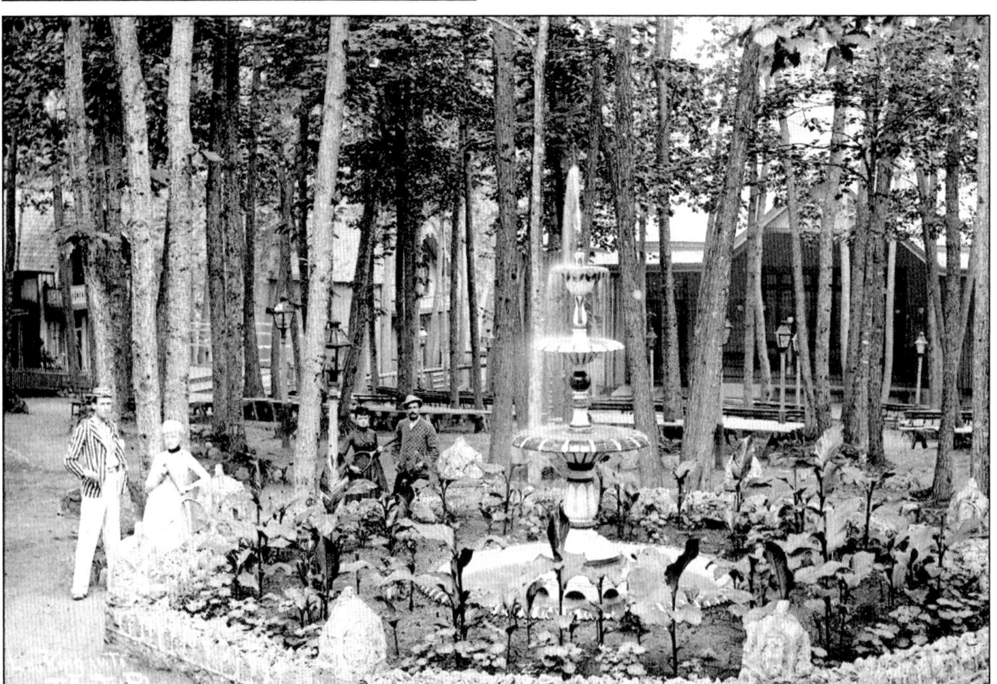

An ornate triple-tier, cast-iron fountain was placed at the top of Trinity Park in 1875, at a cost of $225. The Delaware, Lackawanna and Western Railroad provided delivery of the fountain to the grounds at no charge. A lovely addition to the campgrounds, the fountain was described in *A Story of Camp Meeting*, by Mary Harriott Norris, as "tossing aloft its sparkling waters, refreshing the ferns and flowers which clustered around its basin." (Mount Tabor Historical Society.)

This house is just above the library on Trinity Park. It has wonderful gingerbread trim and corner quoins. The peak trim has small acorns hanging from the scrollwork and a larger acorn in the center. With ample room for seating on both upper and lower porches, there is no doubt this family and its guests heard every word of the sermons. (Tom Nestor.)

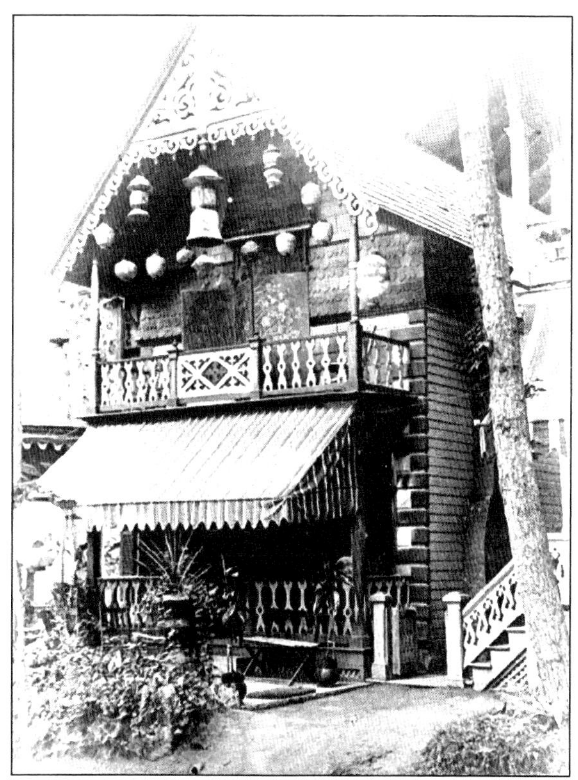

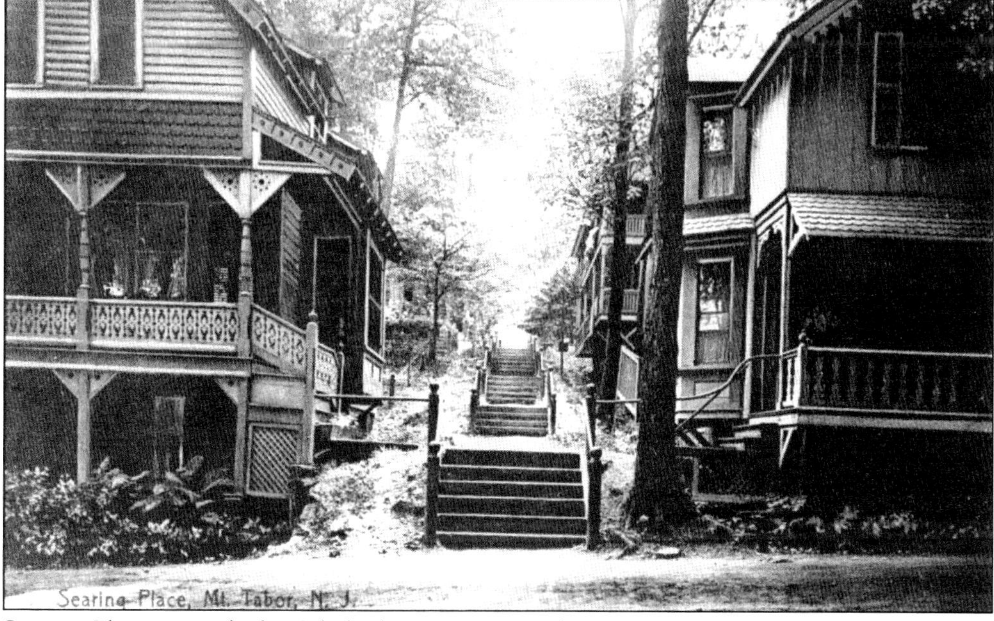

Searing Place, named after Ichabod Searing, an early camp leader, was originally mapped as a street. Because it was so steep, it was altered with a series of steps for easier navigation to St. James' Park. Perhaps it became known as the Golden Stairs because the residents felt they were ascending a golden stairway to heaven, since a panoramic view of rolling green fields and lush woods awaited them at journey's end. (Mount Tabor Historical Society.)

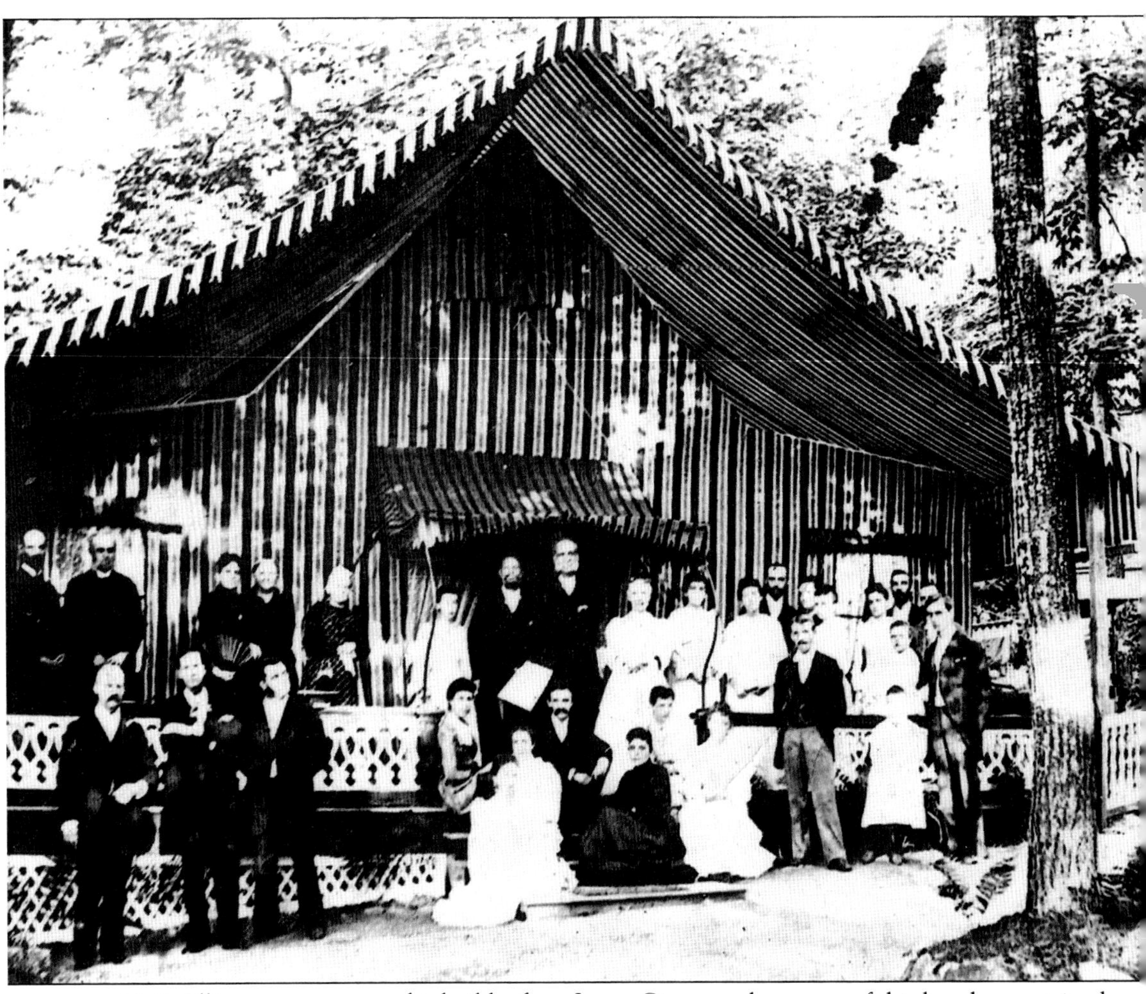

M. S. Allison, a prosperous shipbuilder from Jersey City, was the owner of this handsome striped tent. The double-wide tent covered two standard 16-feet-by-20-feet tent sites. The convenient location on the east side of Trinity Park allowed the Allison family and friends to hear the sermon at the preacher's stand in front of the tabernacle from the comfort of their porch. As grand as this tent was, it was replaced in 1877 by an even grander cottage. Jersey City builder and Mount Tabor resident Samuel Cosgrove was responsible for the design and construction of the Allison cottage, which is featured on the facing page. (Davis family.)

A stunning survival today, this cottage was no less remarkable in its infancy. In 1877, the year of its construction, the *Mount Tabor Record* published a description of the cottage. "This is perhaps the finest single cottage upon the grounds, having recently been completed at a cost of over $2000. It is in fact a substantial residence, occupying two lots, built in a becoming order of architecture, and with a view to comfort and convenience in its interior arrangements. Upon the first floor are parlor, dining room, and kitchen, and upon the second seven sleeping apartments." There is a small gable roof cupola, and elaborately turned knee braces support the balcony and the projecting gable. (Right, Mount Tabor Record, 1880s; below, Mount Tabor Historical Society.)

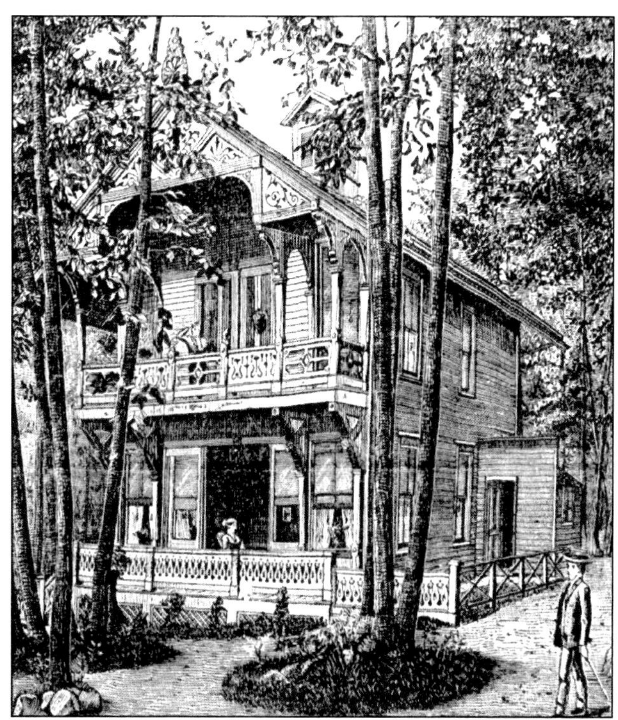

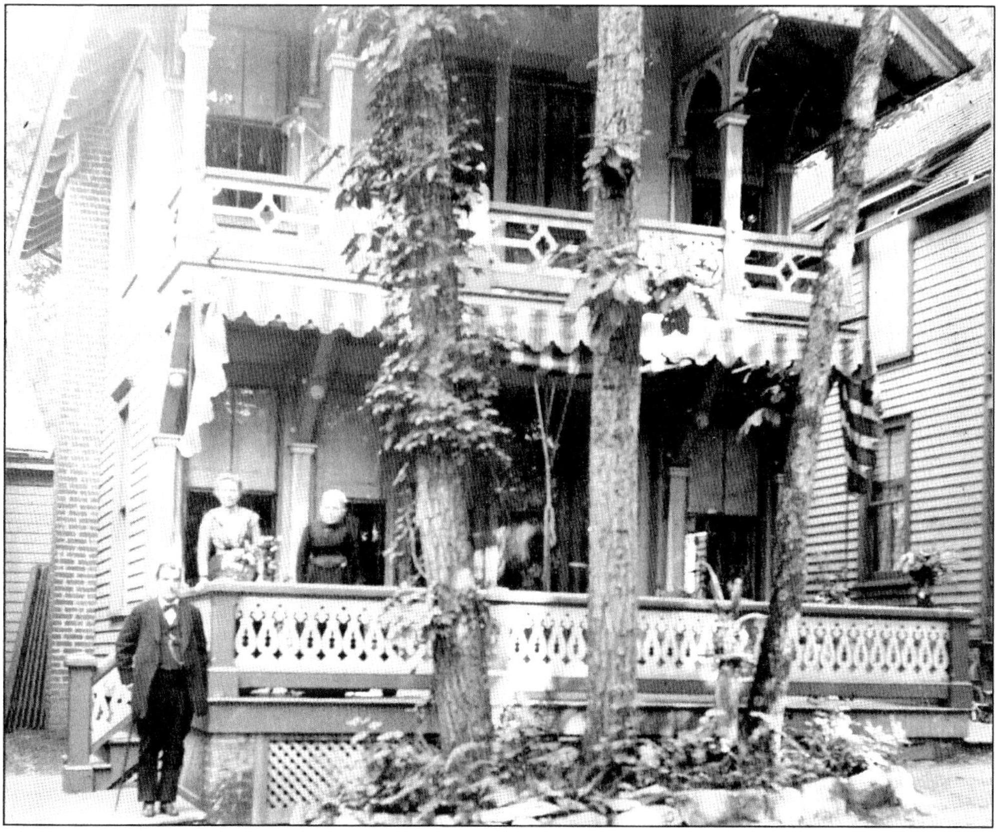

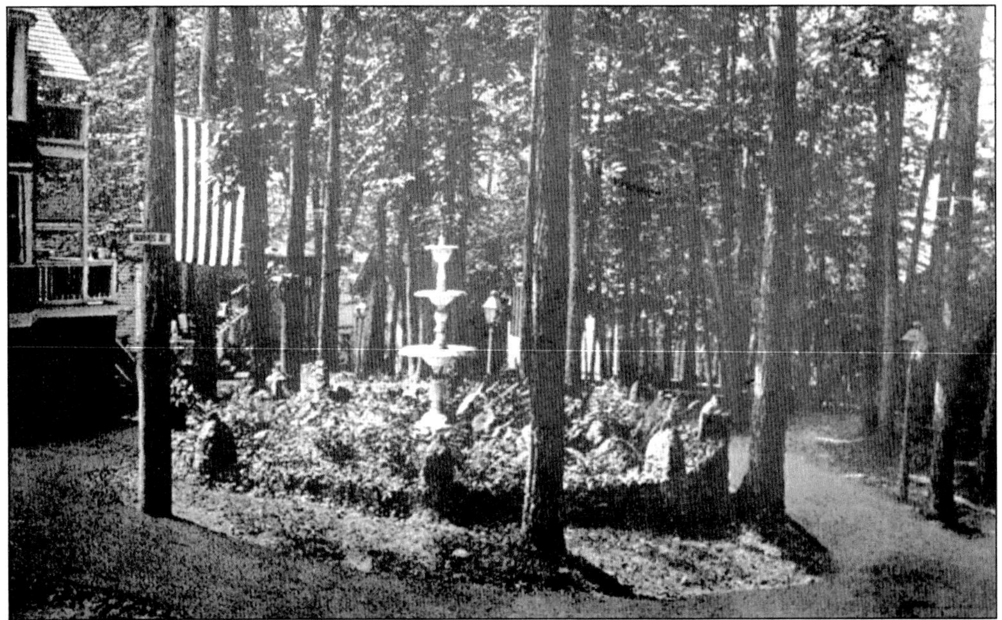

This view from Morris Avenue at the top of Trinity Park faces the tabernacle, hidden by the grove of towering chestnut trees. Osee Fitzgerald's cottage is shown on the left. The cottage afforded an ideal location to hear the sermons from the comfort of the rear balcony that faces the preacher's stand. (Mount Tabor Historical Society.)

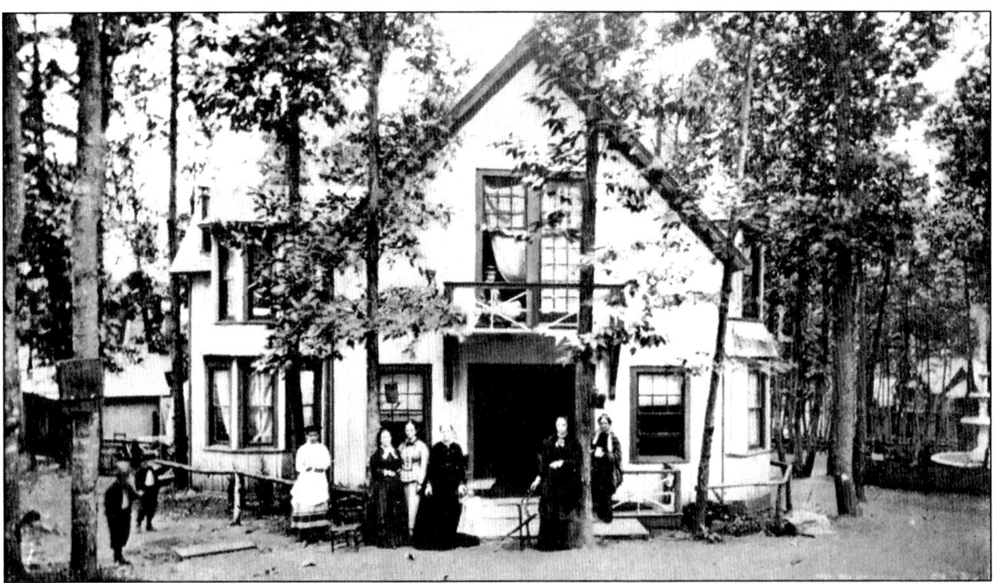

The Fitzgerald cottage is located on the corner of Morris Avenue and Wesley Place. The August 17, 1877, *Mount Tabor Record* states, "Mrs. Fitzgerald . . . takes up her residence in the upper story, and devotes the lower part to special public meetings upon the subject of holiness." In 1883, it was reported, "The Holiness meetings of Mrs. Fitzgerald are well attended, the audience frequently filling the room and the standing room about the doors." (Tom Nestor.)

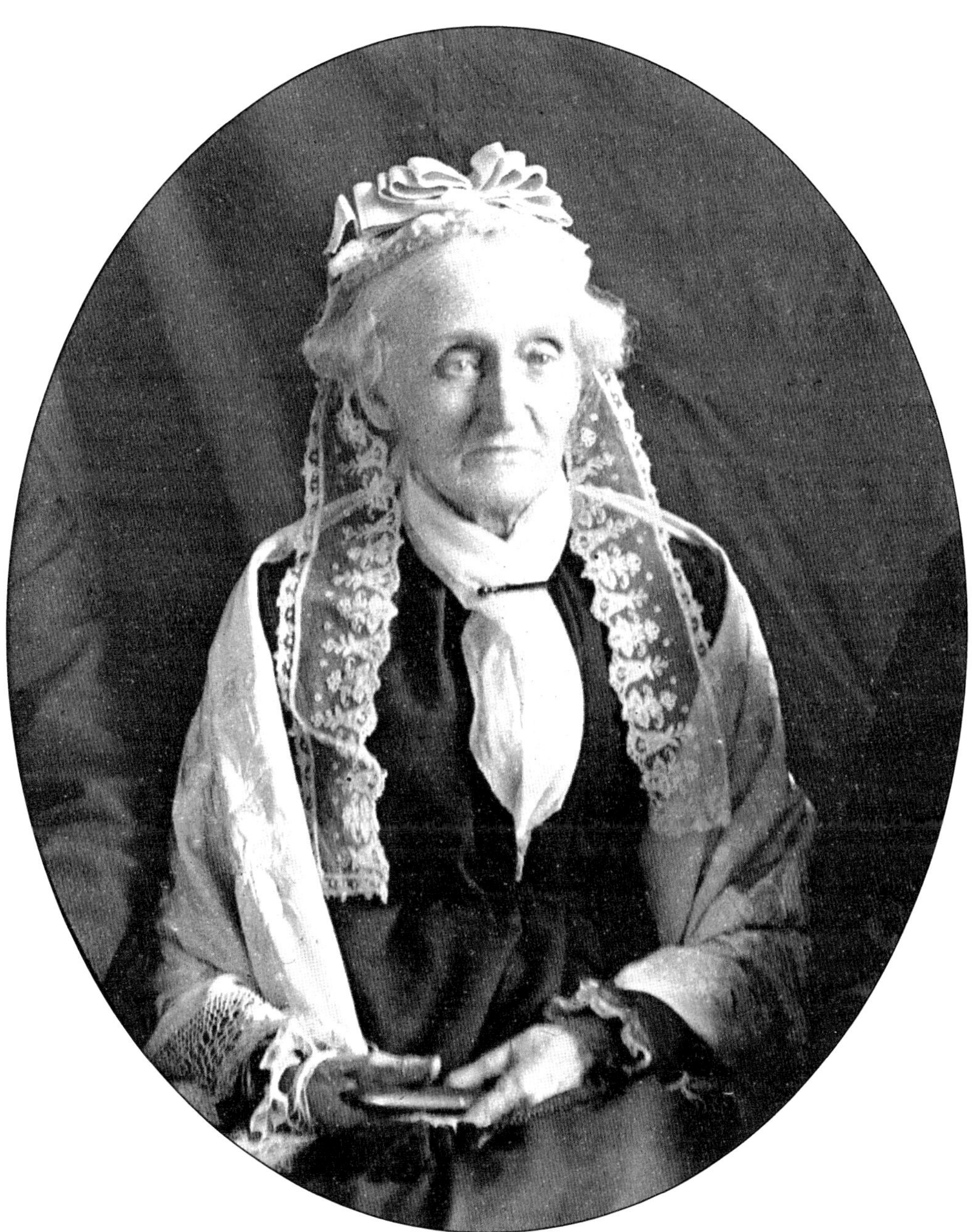

In the mid-19th century, a large group of eastern American Methodists formed the national holiness movement, which organized and sponsored revivals and camp meetings. Osee Fitzgerald, the mother of Methodist bishop James Fitzgerald, lived and held camp meetings in Mount Tabor. Her evangelical beliefs placed her in high regard in the holiness movement, and she held a leadership position within the community. Women were given the unusual opportunity to become spiritual leaders by holding prayer and class meetings, offering testimonies, and participating in revivals. The spirit of camp meeting evangelism had ebbed by 1891; only the holiness meetings under the leadership of Osee continued to express the old camp meeting fervor. When Osee died in 1909, these meetings ceased. Usually identified by a white lace scarf on her head, Osee was a pillar of the Mount Tabor religious community. (Mount Tabor Historical Society.)

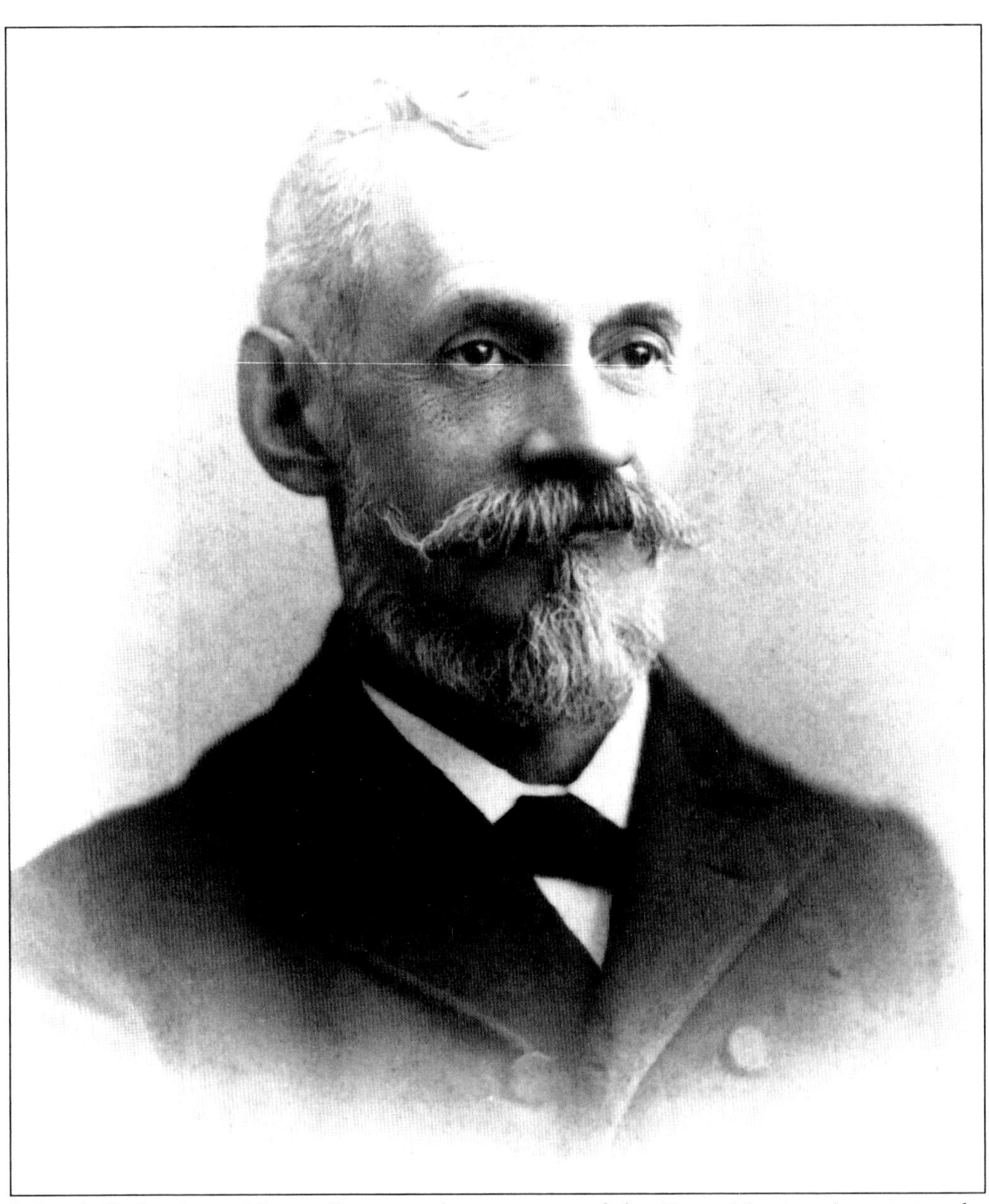

J. Smith Richardson of Jersey City served as treasurer of the Camp Meeting Association for 22 years, ending in 1907. On his retirement, the Camp Meeting Association issued a resolution stating, "He has held this position and served the Association as its treasurer continuously with such great efficiency and satisfaction; therefore be it resolved that while most reluctantly acceding to his request we desire very heartily to bear record for the entire present board as well as for many who have preceded us, of our high estimate of his Christian character and unswerving loyalty and devotion to our church, to his great concern in all that related to the best interests of the Association to his unquestioned fidelity in the discharge of his official duties, enjoyed the fullest confidence of all, and to his special ability and adaptation of the work imposed. And further be it resolved that while retiring from his official position as treasurer we trust that he will long retain his relation as a member of our board, thus giving to us the benefits of his long experience, wise counsels and personal influence." (Tom Nestor.)

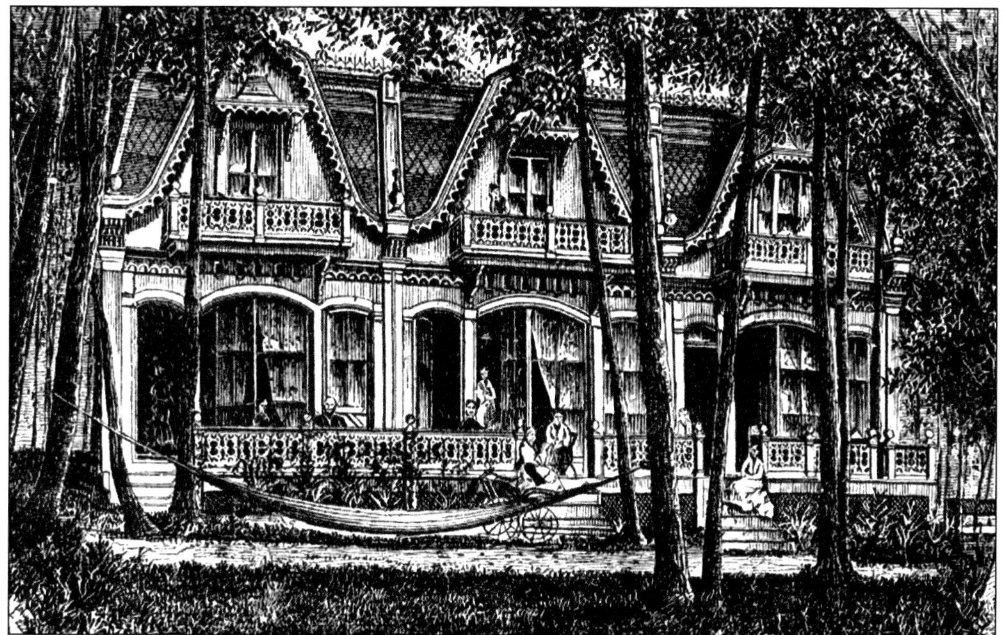

In 1873, Richardson and Dr. J. W. Cosad had three cottages built under one roof for approximately $2,700. Richardson and Cosad occupied the end units, and the center one was sold to Rev. Alexander Craig. The *Mount Tabor Record* described it in 1877 as "one of the prettiest buildings on the grounds; its very appearance denotes taste and refinement." (Mount Tabor Record, 1880s.)

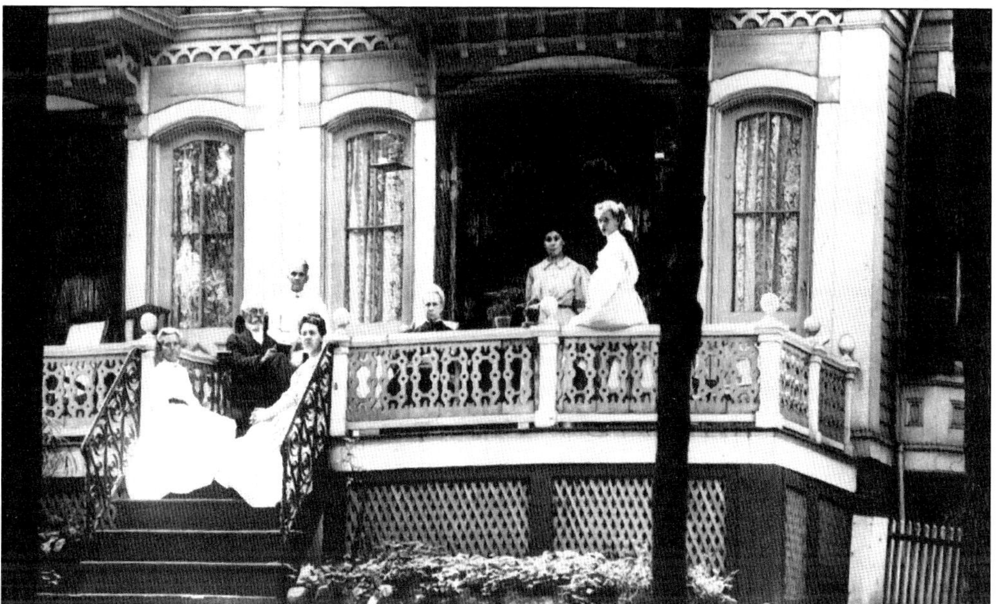

Pictured here, around 1904, is the lower third of the triple cottage owned by Richardson. From left to right are Lizzie Jones (daughter of J. Smith and Lydia Richardson), J. Smith Richardson, Lydia Richardson, Sue C. Blackford (niece), Martha "Honey" Blackford (Sue's mother), the maid, and Edith Jones, (granddaughter of J. Smith Richardson). Note the beaded curtain in the doorway that was strung to form a flower pattern. This was an effective way to allow air to flow but keep out the insects. (Evelyn Clark.)

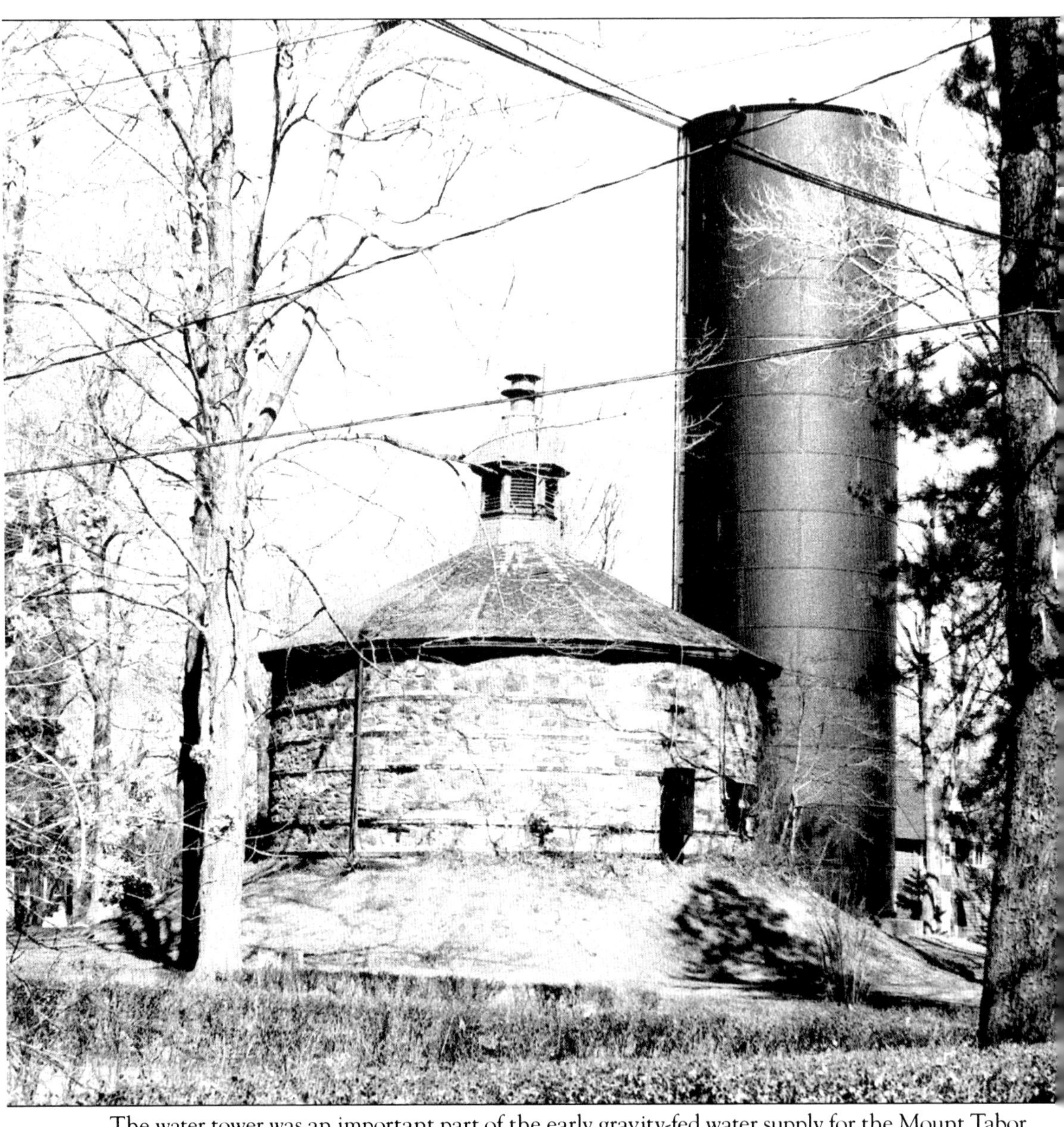

The water tower was an important part of the early gravity-fed water supply for the Mount Tabor summer community. Situated in the center of St. James' Park, the rubble stone water tank has a 12-sided roof with hexagonal pointed roof cupola and louvered side vents. In 1878, the reservoir replaced an earlier and much smaller tank. The original dimensions of this tank included a 90-foot circumference and 12-foot-high walls. It was extended eight feet in height in 1885 and another six feet in 1892. There are five metal girding bands and cross-shaped iron anchor beams that help support the curved walls. Water was pumped up to the reservoir from springs at the east end of the grounds and then gravity-fed from the tank to the cottages and public taps. The newer water tower on the right was removed in 1987. (Jo Campbell.)

Three

COTTAGE LIVING

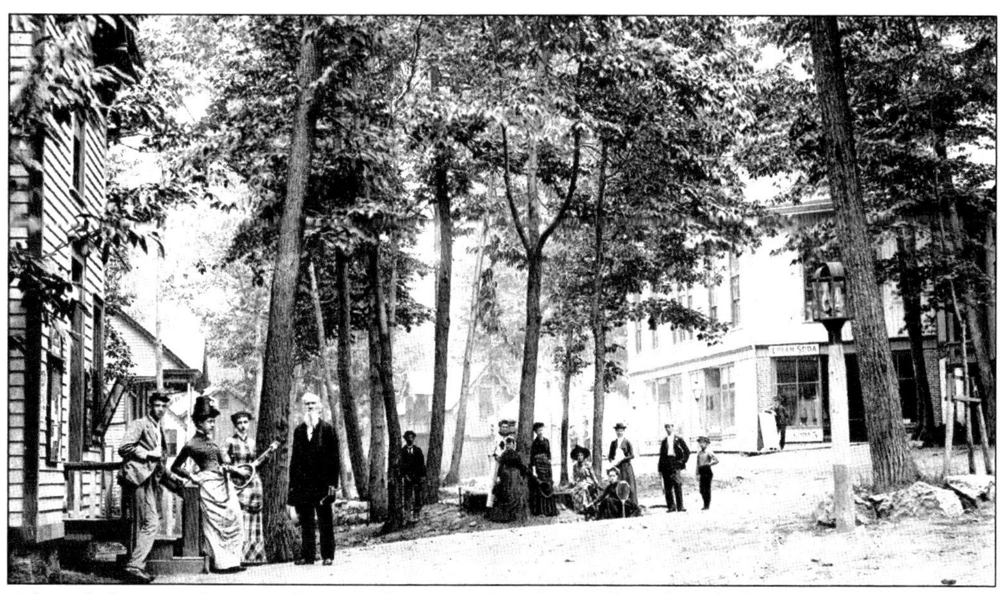

A bearded patriarch peers through the years. A girl in a plaid dress holds a tennis racquet, as a young twosome casually rest against a stair rail. Young people seek shelter from the summer sun under the stately chestnut trees. The tabernacle stands watch over the lighthearted scene. This 1885 photograph perfectly captures the transition from a religious colony to a summer resort. Cream soda is sold on the main street that evolved on Simpson Avenue as small businesses leased space in the tabernacle. The building where the young couple pauses to rest no longer exists. The small business establishments no longer exist, but Simpson Avenue continues to wind its way across the first level of Mount Tabor, and residents now gather at the post office housed in the tabernacle where cream soda was sold. Canvas tents were replaced with narrow gingerbread-laced cottages. The cottages remain, rich with the history of lives longing for rest and peace. Their stories are told through the community they left in future generations' care. (Mount Tabor Historical Society.)

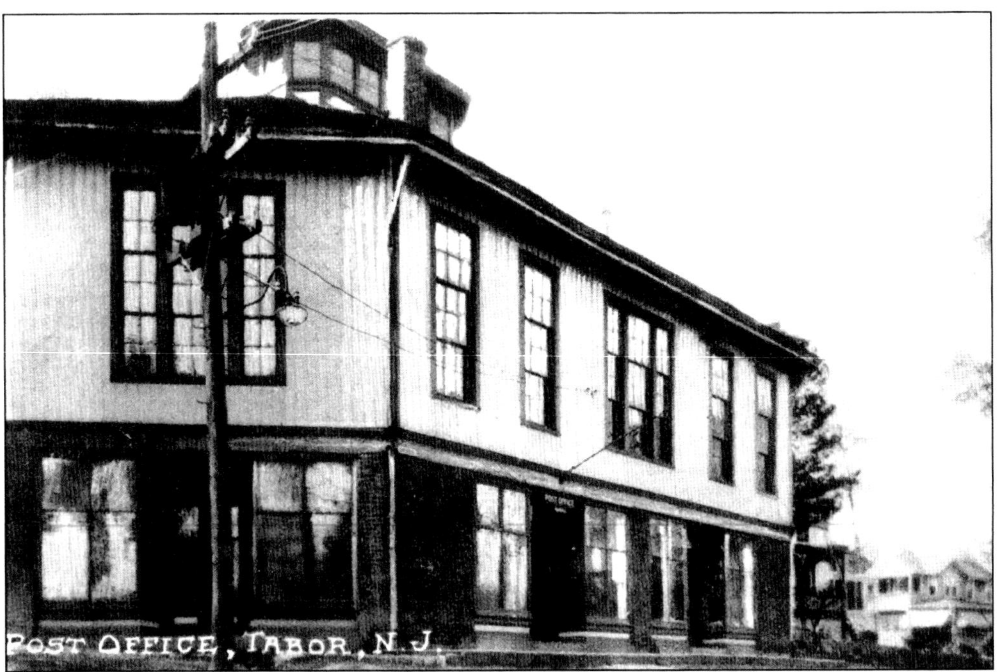

While the tabernacle auditorium and preacher's stand faced Trinity Park, the lower part of the building, under the sanctuary and facing Simpson Avenue, was used for commercial purposes. Over time, space was leased to a post office, barbershop, fancy goods bazaar, ice-cream vendor, and drugstore. Today the Camp Meeting Association office and fire department occupy the two spaces on the lower left of this postcard. (Tom Nestor.)

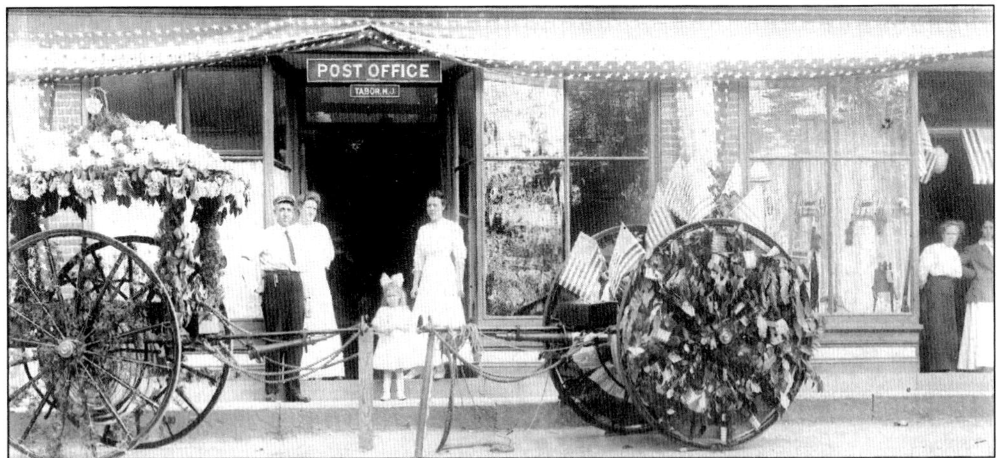

In 1882, the United States Post Office Department authorized the establishment of a fourth-class post office in Mount Tabor. E. B. Earles, the first superintendent of Mount Tabor, was also the first postmaster, and it was in his house that the post office was initially located. Later it was moved to the middle bay under the tabernacle as shown in the picture above. Note the fire hose carts decorated for Children's Day. The post office moved again in 1952 to its current location on the south side of the building. Mount Tabor was offered a new post office in the 1960s, but the residents said they liked things the way they were and the government should save its money. There is no house-to-house mail delivery, and all residents must have a post office box. Today the post office is the gathering place for the community. (Mount Tabor Historical Society.)

42

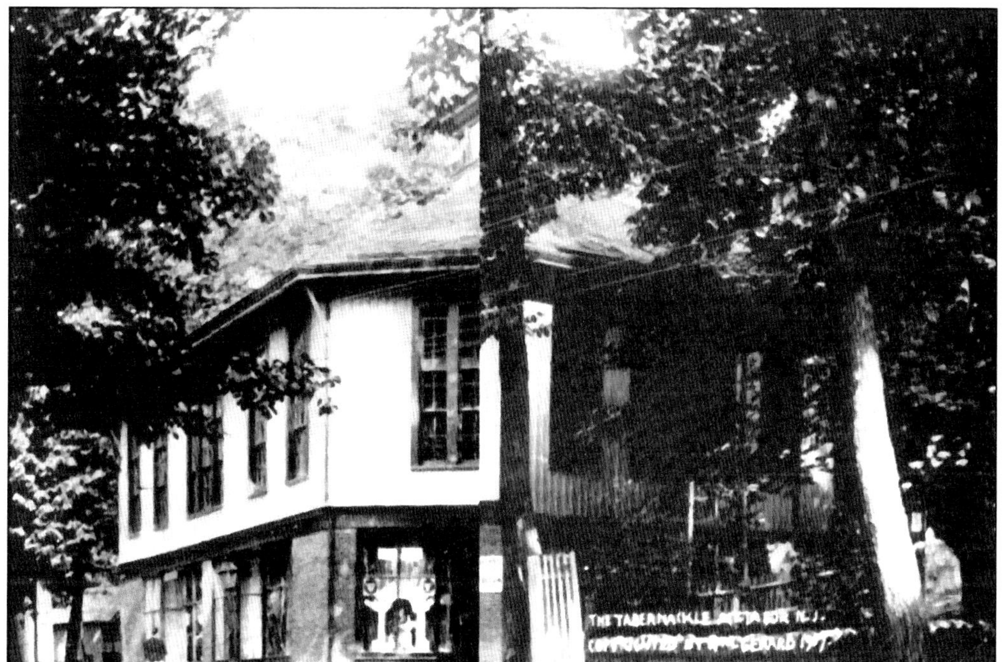

An ice-cream vendor advertises on the shop window shown here on the right around 1907. Windows were later replaced by doors in the center space of the lower tabernacle to accommodate the Mount Tabor Volunteer Fire Department. (Tom Nestor.)

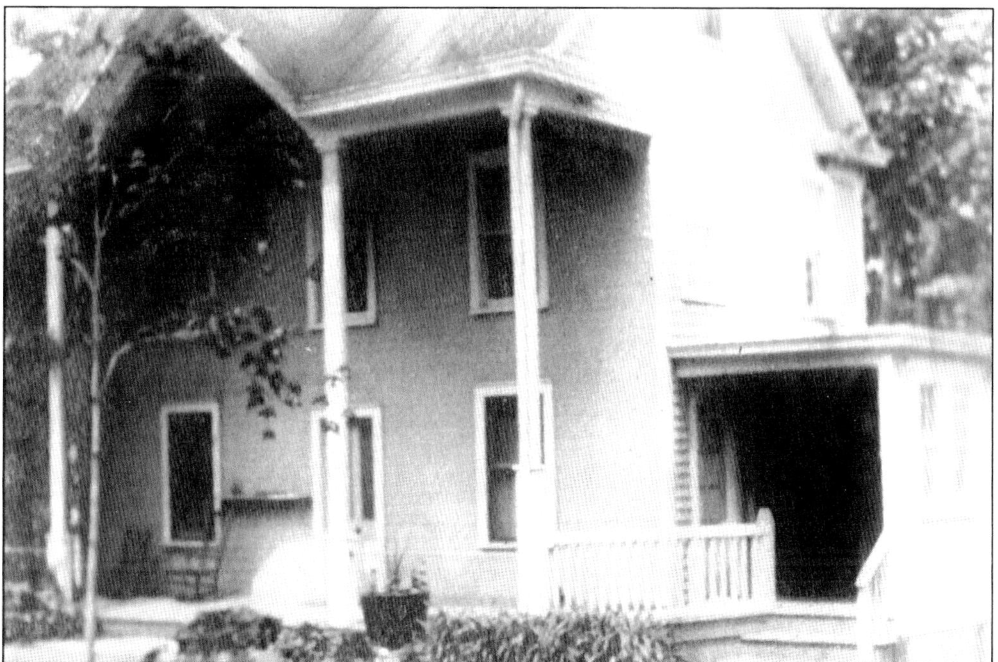

The manager's house shown in this early photograph was the original tabernacle in Trinity Park. In 1885, when the new tabernacle was erected, the building was moved across Simpson Avenue to its present location. Recently the Mount Tabor Historical Society has used the building for museum exhibits. (Bobbi Longstreet.)

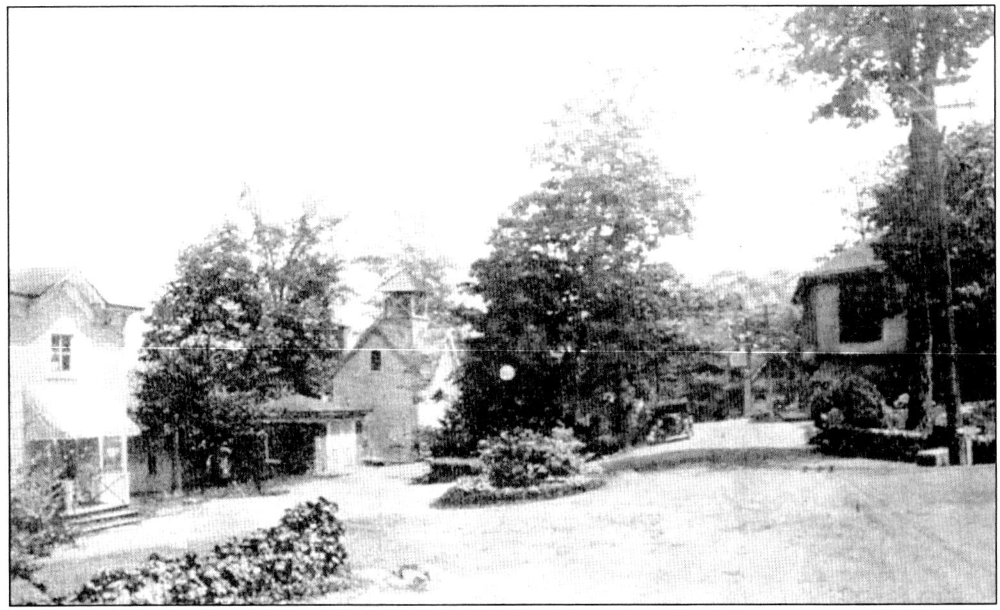

Both of these postcards show the main thoroughfare of Simpson Avenue. Above is a view looking north, showing the tabernacle on the right side and the Camp Meeting Association office, the stone house, and the old firehouse on the left. In the middle of the street is an oval planted with small trees, bushes, and flowers. The scene below looks south showing two houses on the left that are still standing today and the Arlington Hotel in the distance. The grocery store in the foreground is no longer standing. (Camp Meeting Association.)

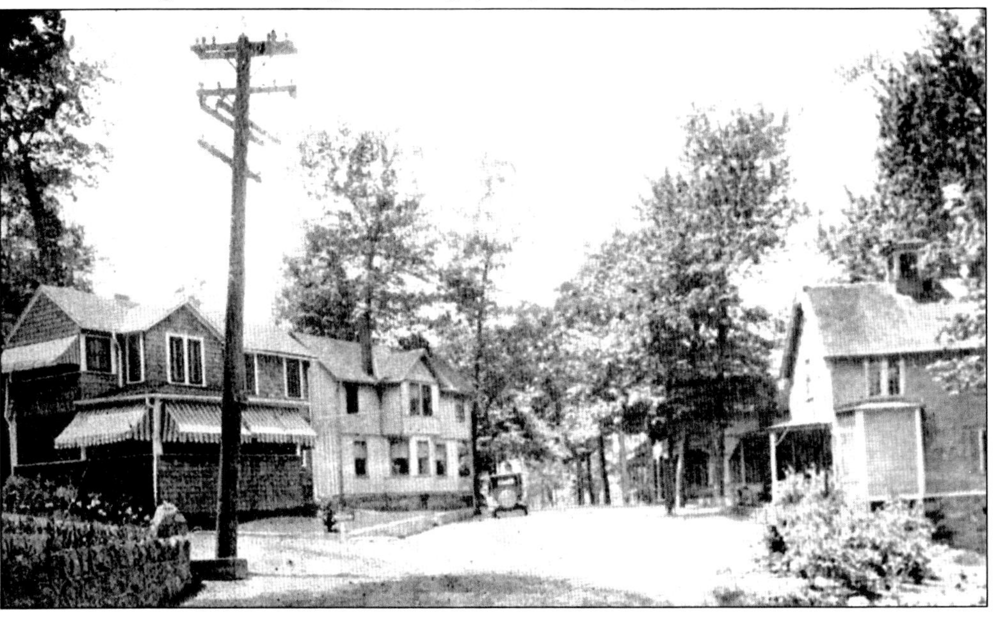

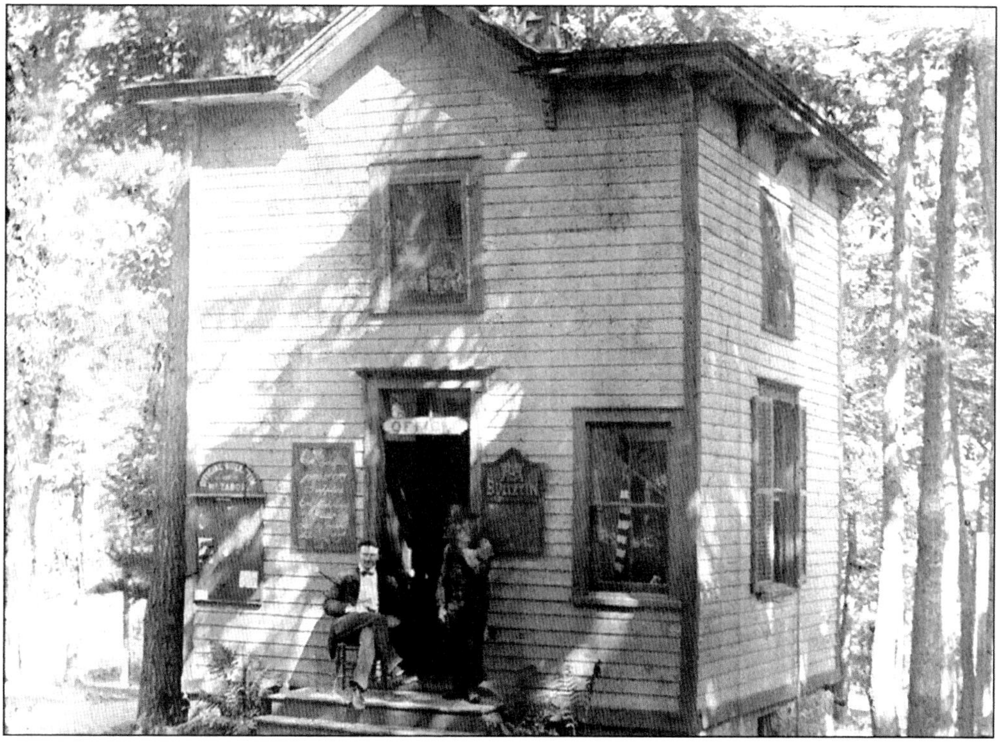

This building, shown around 1910, was located on the corner of Simpson and Durbin Avenues. Originally built as police headquarters, it also housed the first post office and telegraph office. In the basement was a jail that seldom, if ever, held prisoners and for several years was used to store ice. In 1883, the police moved to new quarters and the building became the Camp Meeting Association treasurer's office. That same year, the first public telephone in Mount Tabor was installed. Eventually the Camp Meeting Association office was moved to the lower level of the tabernacle. Remarkably, a large safe, purchased in 1886, is still in use in the present Camp Meeting Association office. (Above, Tom Nestor; right, Ron Dickerson.)

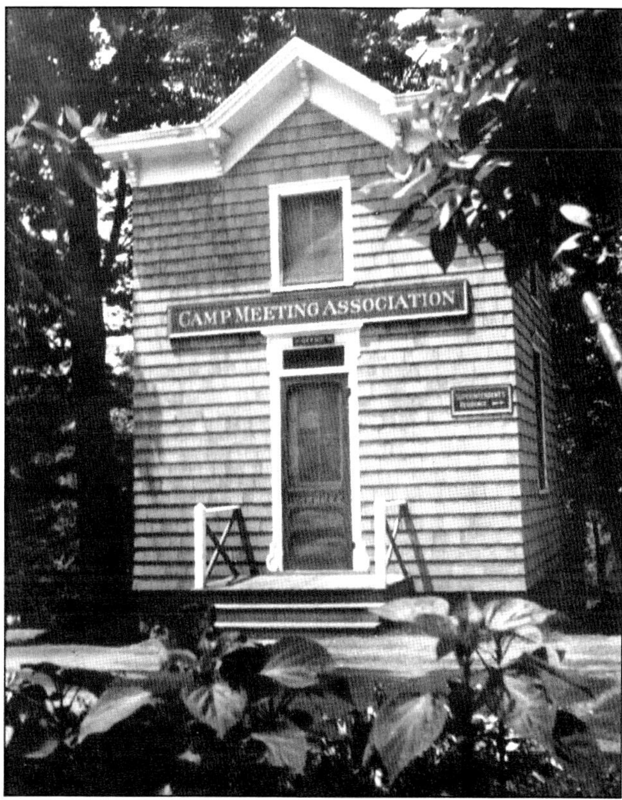

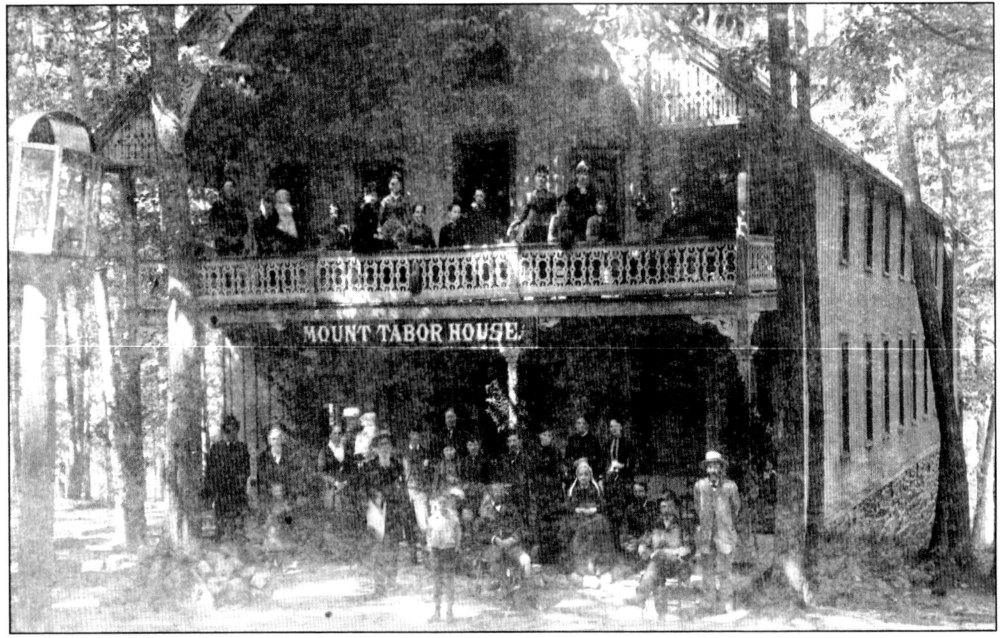

In 1877, Mount Tabor House, later named the Arlington Hotel, was built by David Campbell for the trustees with the understanding that after he reimbursed himself from the income, the building would become the property of the association. During their ownership, the trustees enlarged the building twice. (Evelyn Clark.)

At left is the bill of sale from Cornelius White, a lumber dealer from Paterson, dated August 20, 1887, and listing supplies purchased for the expansion of the Arlington Hotel, totaling $176.25. The ornate design and careful penmanship are a far cry from the computerized receipts of today. (Camp Meeting Association.)

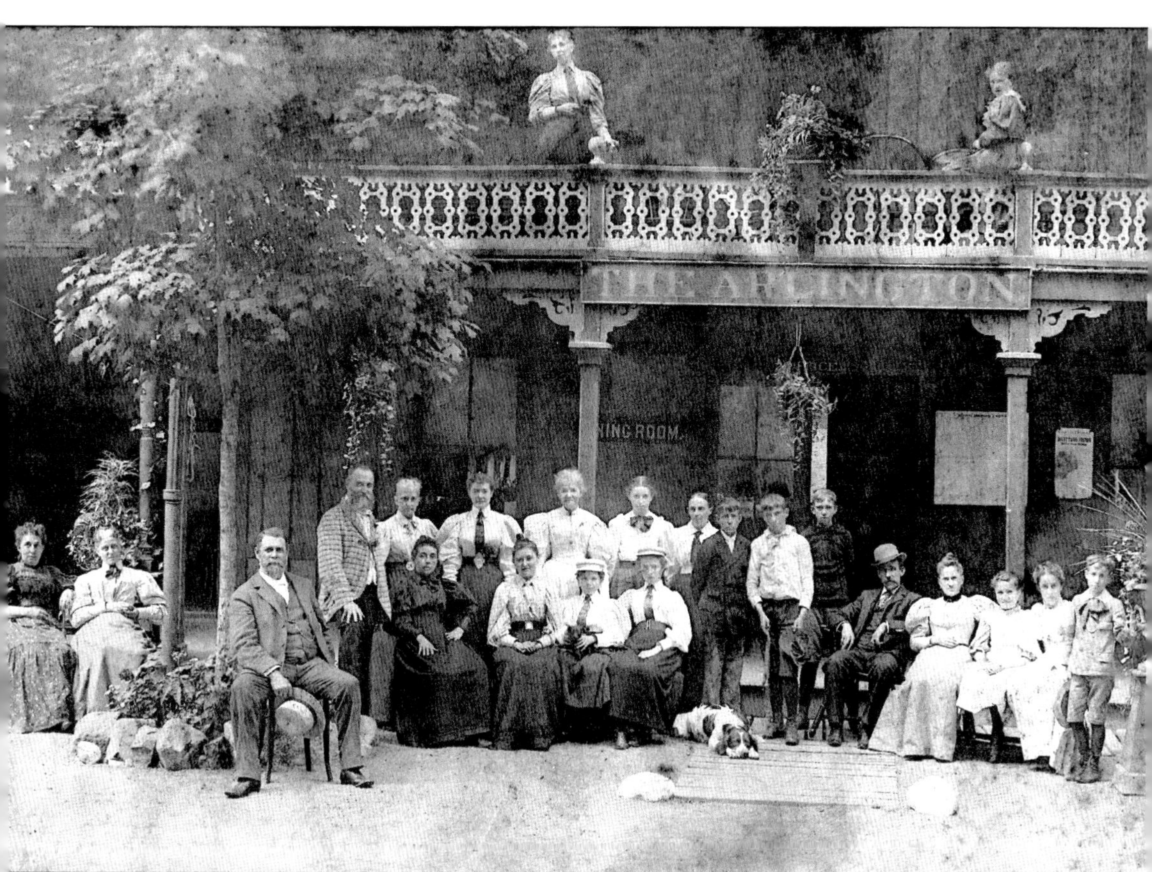

The Arlington Hotel offered extensive parlors, dining rooms, and verandas, and guests could choose from an American or European plan. The hotel served as a gathering space for guests, as well as a restaurant for those who could afford it. Visiting ministers often stayed at the hotel. An Arlington Hotel advertisement in the *Mount Tabor Record*, dated August 20, 1892, offered reduced rates for September, boasting that "the Hotel is located, according to the report of scientific statisticians, on the most healthful mountainous range in the United States, and thousands of invalids have already received great benefits, and many of them have been entirely cured by the invigorating and Health Restoring Qualities of the Air and Water." The attractive group posing in front of the hotel appears to be made up of happy recipients of the restorative qualities advertised. (Mount Tabor Historical Society.)

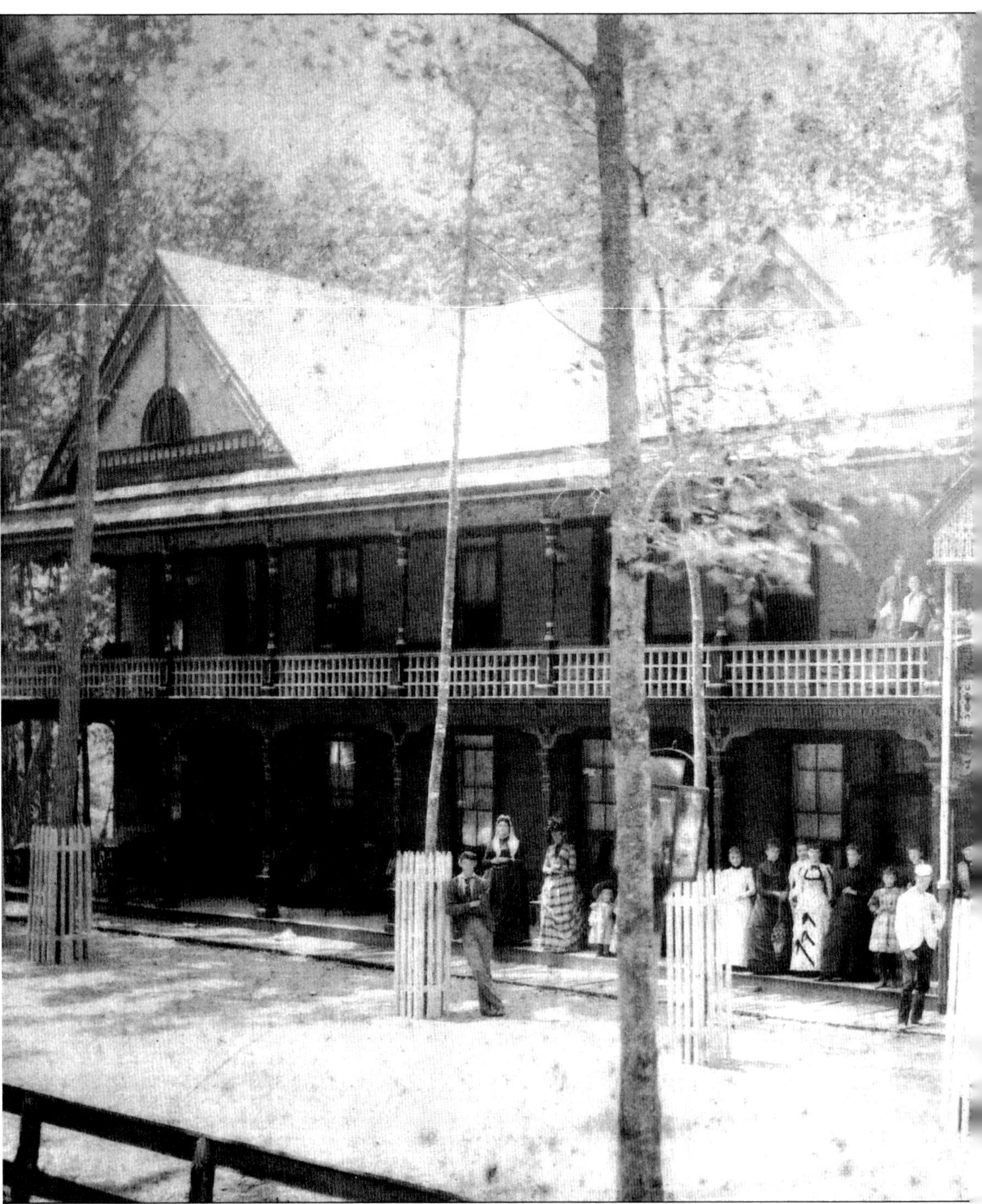

This lovely photograph captures the beautiful details of the Arlington Hotel's facade. The upper and lower porches are filled with vacationers, here posing for a group portrait. The first floor opened to a barbershop, grocery store, drugstore, and ice-cream shop. In her book *Camp Meeting*, Mary Harriott Norris writes about two young friends enjoying a plate of ice cream. Young Bentie says, "I really don't know, Ben, what we would do in warm weather without cream." As the

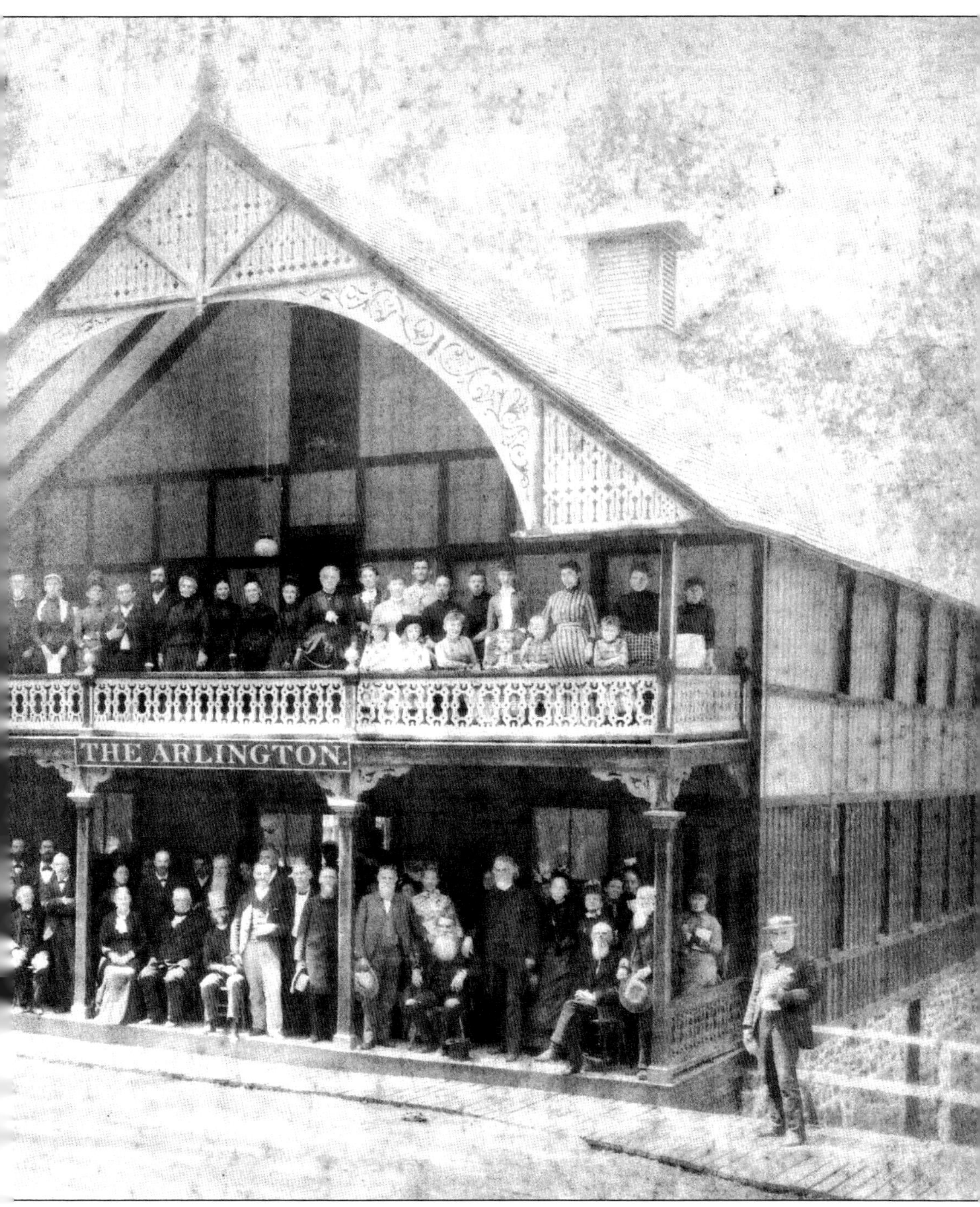

popularity of Mount Tabor grew so too did the demand for housing. The Arlington Hotel, the only hotel on the grounds, offered 14 bedrooms on the second floor. In 1895, two water closets were added (at a cost of $50). Although many boardinghouses served the ever-growing numbers of vacationers, the Arlington Hotel, with its extensive parlors, dining rooms, and verandas, was "unexcelled in this part of the State." (Mount Tabor Historical Society.)

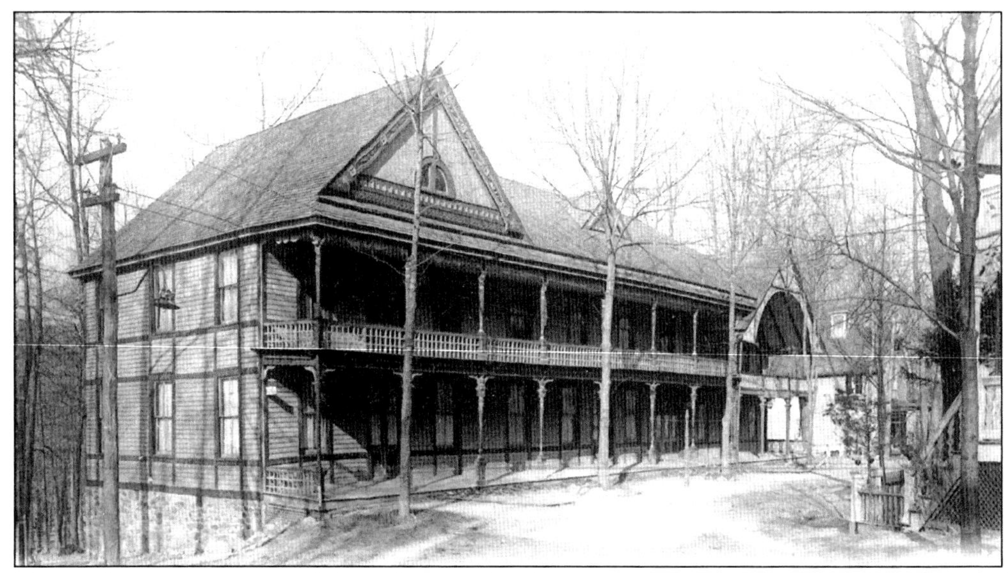

This stark winter postcard of the Arlington Hotel offers a unique view of the side and rear of the building. A section of the stone foundation of the hotel remains today, serving as a retaining wall along Simpson Avenue. (Tom Nestor.)

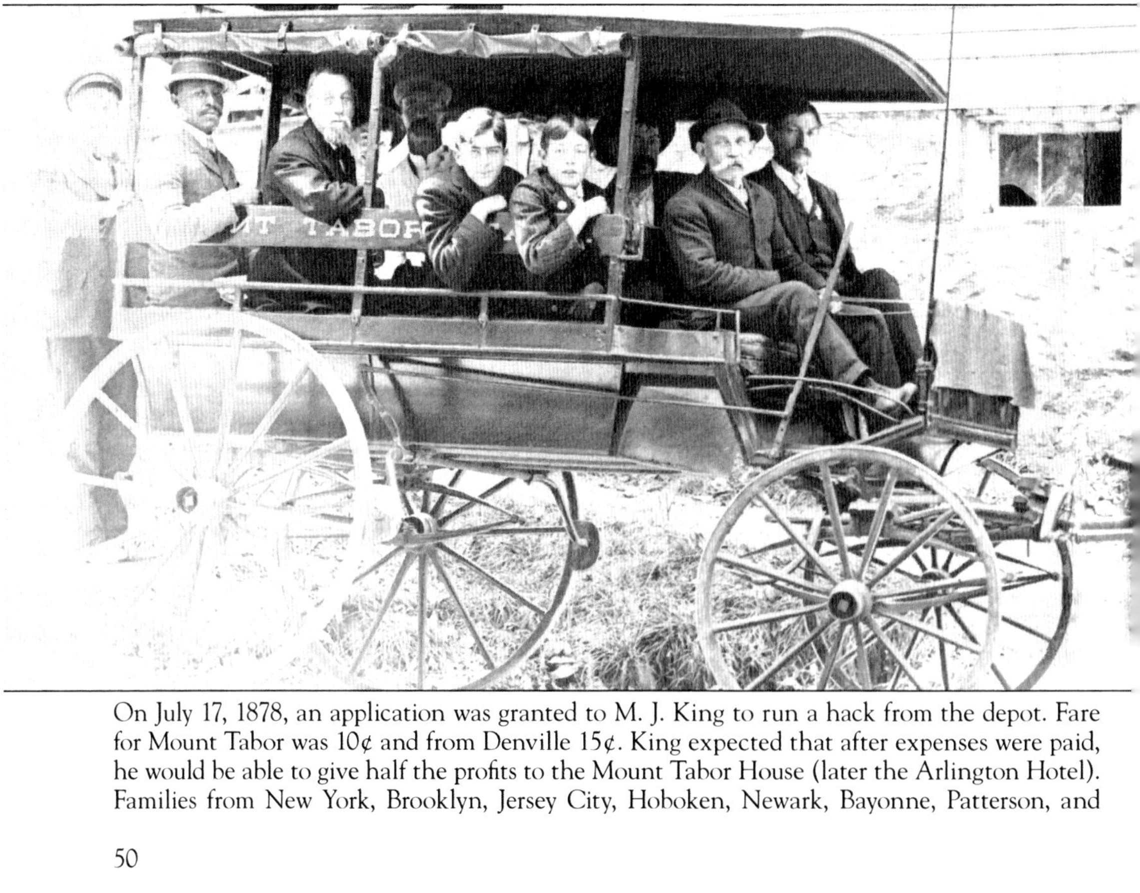

On July 17, 1878, an application was granted to M. J. King to run a hack from the depot. Fare for Mount Tabor was 10¢ and from Denville 15¢. King expected that after expenses were paid, he would be able to give half the profits to the Mount Tabor House (later the Arlington Hotel). Families from New York, Brooklyn, Jersey City, Hoboken, Newark, Bayonne, Patterson, and

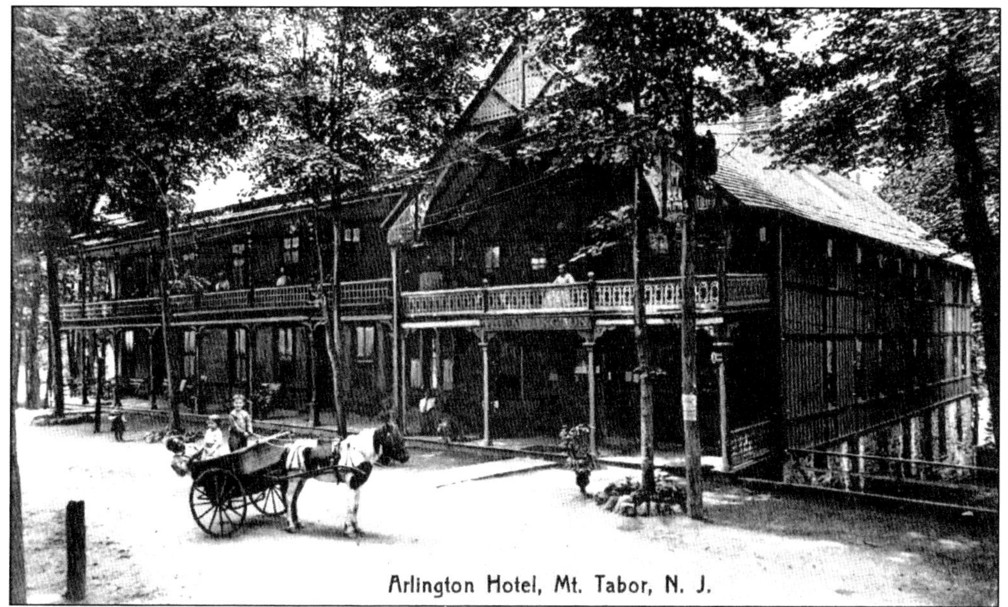

The Depression and the automobile signaled the end of Mount Tabor as a summer community, and with fewer and fewer guests, the Arlington Hotel was eventually torn down. Photographs and postcards showing the gingerbread details and intricately carved wooden balustrades are the only portals to its past. (Tom Nestor.)

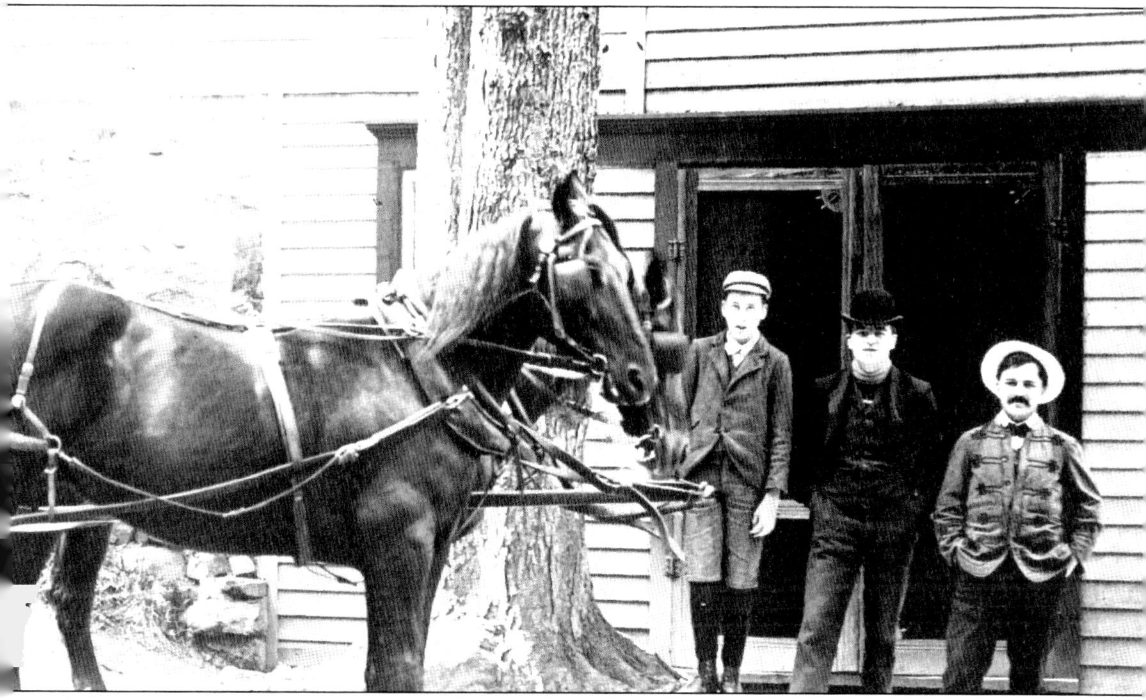

other cities spent the summer in Mount Tabor. While the women and children enjoyed the healthful atmosphere and the mountain breezes of Morris County, the men commuted weekly to their businesses in the cities. In this view, from around 1910, the Mount Tabor stage pauses at the lower level of the Arlington Hotel. (Tom Nestor.)

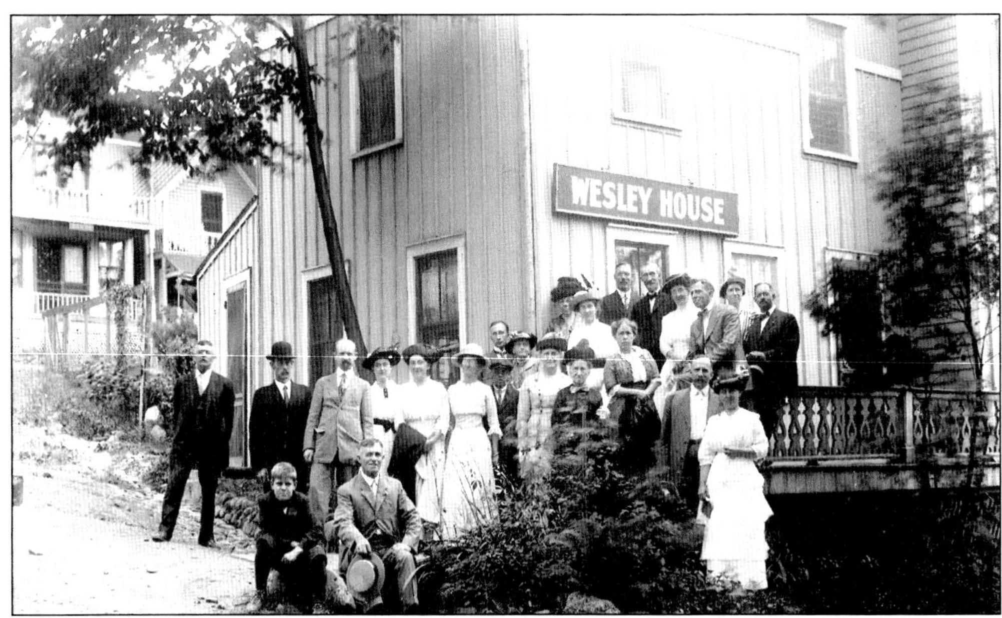

This photograph shows Wesley House, a boardinghouse that was situated on Embury Place between Simpson Avenue and Banghart Place. The west pass easily accessed it from Trinity Park. Boardinghouses were needed for those who came to camp meeting and did not lease a tent or cottage. The assembled group here includes some of the 60 boarders this cottage could accommodate. In 1880, a rate of $1.25 per day was charged for meals and lodging or $5 for the week. Although the boardinghouse no longer remains today, a few glass slides document its earlier days. Below is an old sign advertising a house to let. The beautiful handwriting and pen and ink crosshatch lettering surely would catch one's eye. (Mary Ellen Cheasty.)

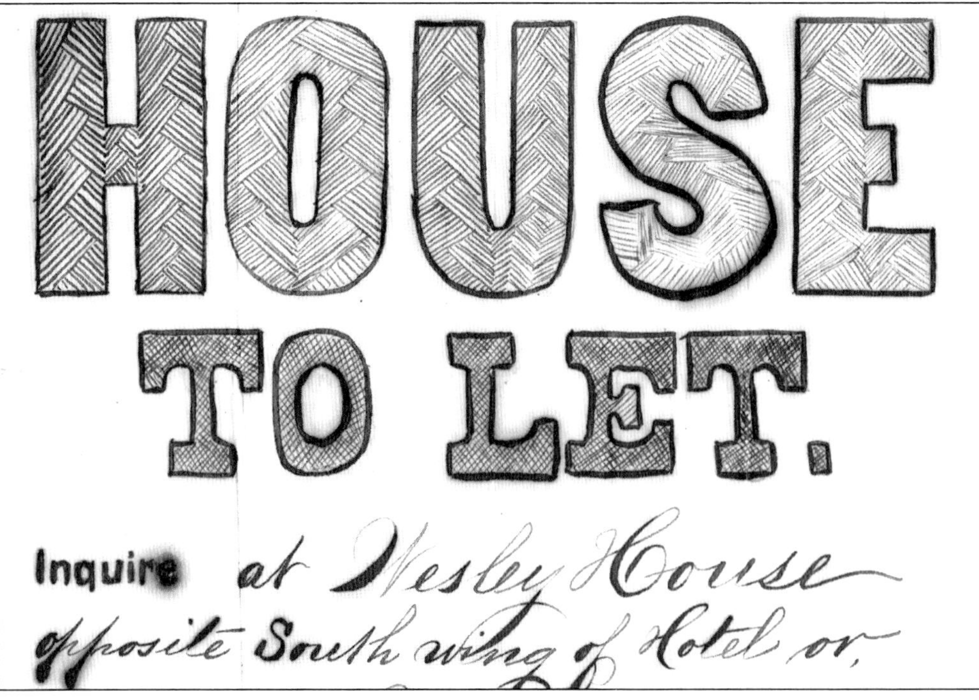

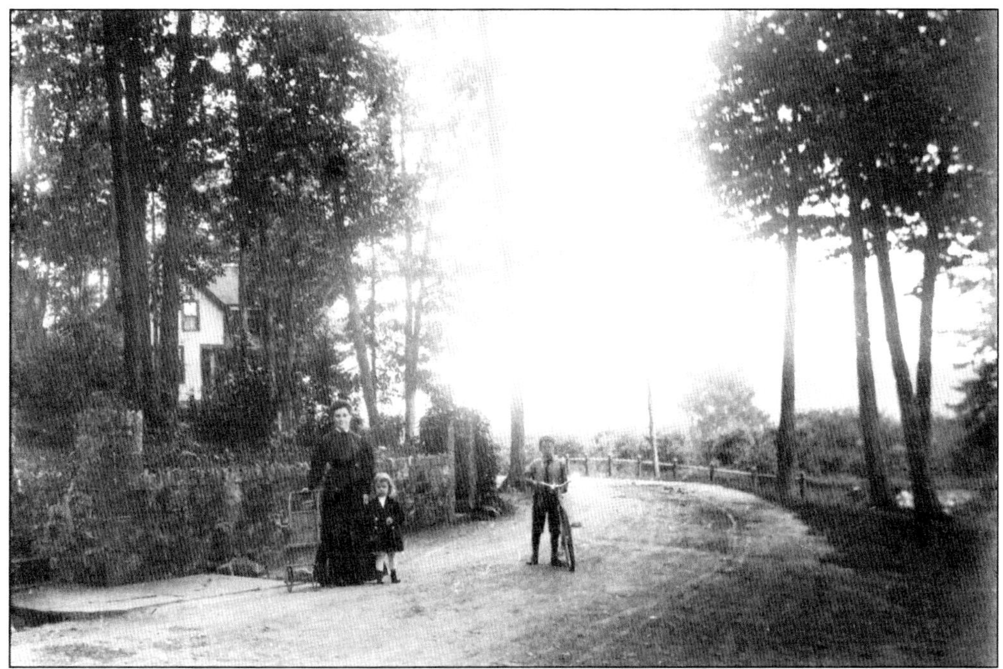

This view of Simpson Avenue, named after Bishop Matthew Simpson, a national Methodist leader, is the main avenue on the first level of Mount Tabor. The young mother and her two children shown in the photograph above are probably on their way to the town center. The stone wall still borders Simpson Avenue, and the house shown remains today much as it appears in the photograph below. The chestnut trees shading the walkway were destroyed by an Asian blight. If one looks closely, the Arlington Hotel can be seen peeking through the trees just before the road slips out of view. (Above, Tom Nestor; below, Mount Tabor Historical Society.)

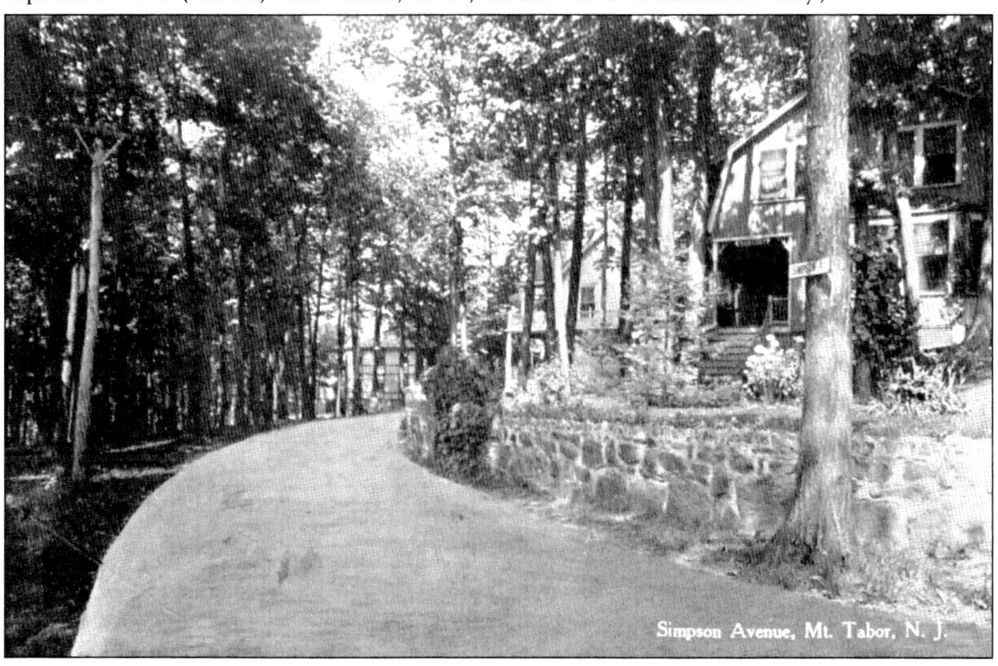

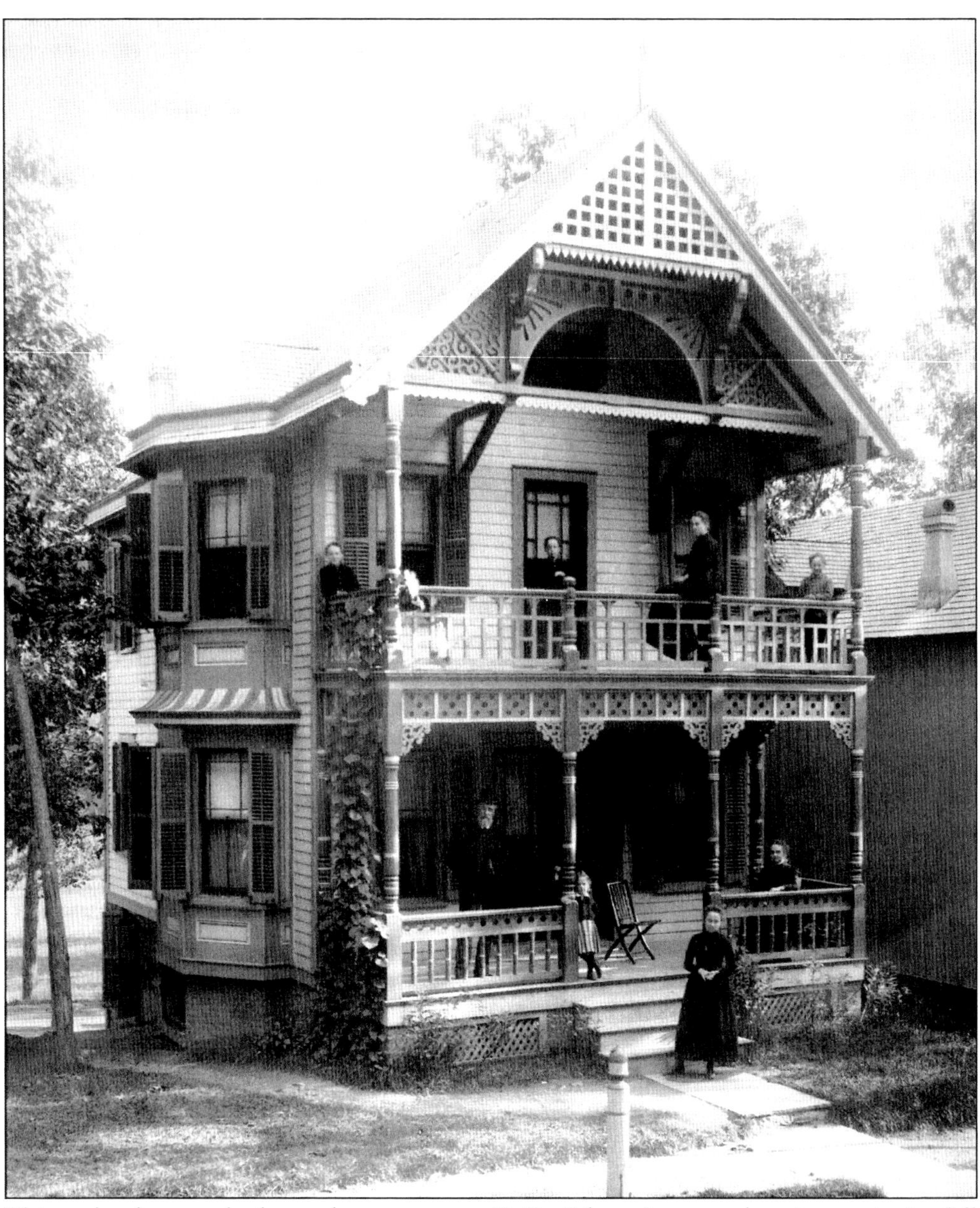

This early photograph shows the cottage at 46 St. Johns Avenue when it was in its full Victorian/Carpenter Gothic glory. The combination of three lots enables the property to border on two streets. Camp chairs on the porch were the furnishings most often associated with the camp meetings. They were found in every tent and cottage. Lightweight, simple in design, and collapsible, the camp chair, or stool, was easily moved from inside the tent to the porch and then to the meeting circle. Machine mass production of the chair made it affordable to all classes. The quality of the upholstery and ornamentation dictated the final cost. The convenience and comfort of the camp chair made it an easy alternative to the discomfort of the rough-hewn benches around the tabernacle. As porches or piazzas took on more importance in Mount Tabor, portable furnishings made it possible to move the parlor outdoors, the porch replacing it as a formal gathering space. (Mount Tabor Historical Society.)

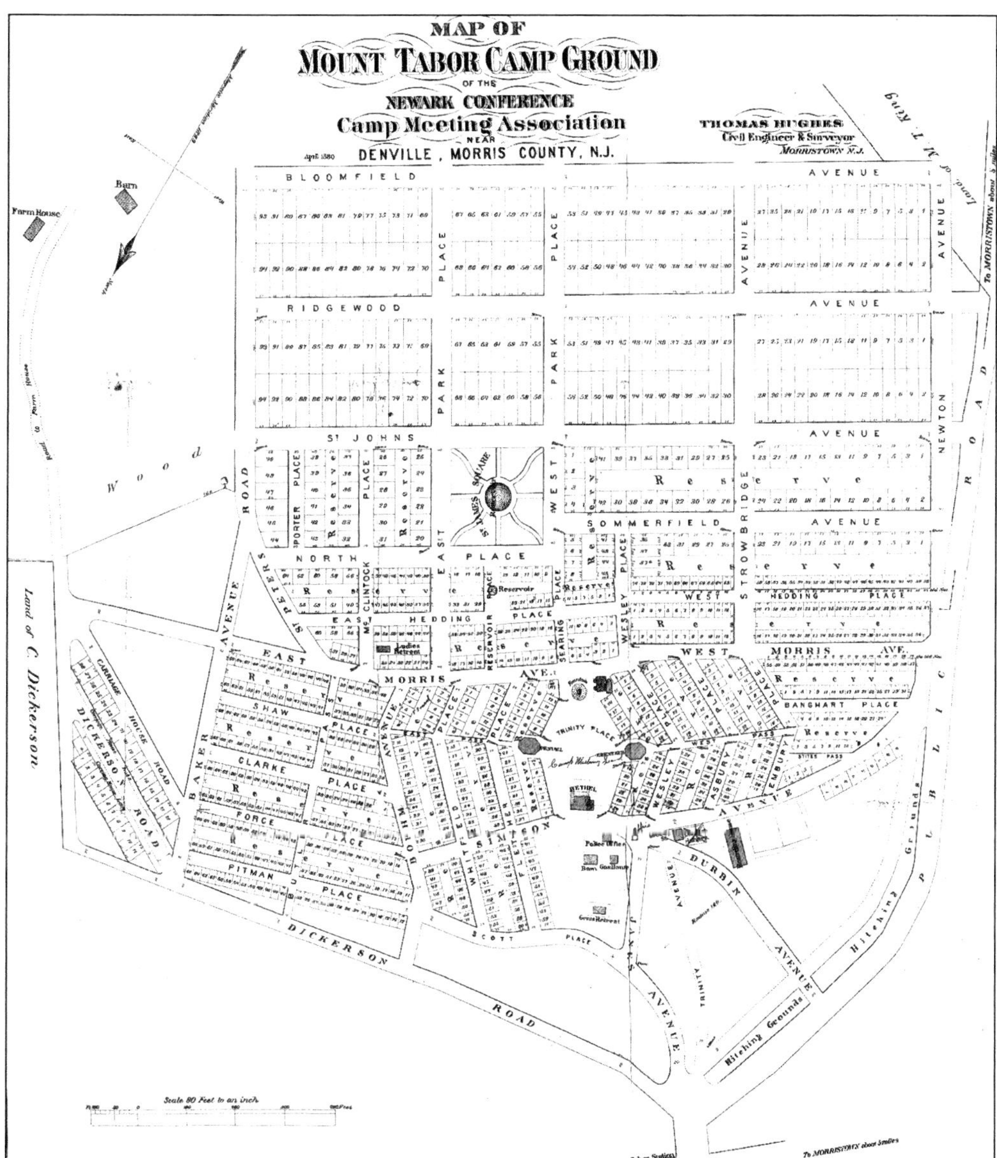

Within the new community's first three years, a second land acquisition greatly expanded the area of Mount Tabor. In May 1872, the purchase of an adjoining farm of about 100 acres was authorized by the board of trustees at a cost of $10,000, including a donation of $1,000 from the Delaware, Lackawanna and Western Railroad. "Improvements were at once commenced upon the new property, prominent among which was the laying out of a new park," known today as St. James' Park, which contained a large water reservoir. "Since then the work of improvement has gone steadily forward at a pace that has been remarkable. A personal visit is necessary to obtain an adequate idea of the beauty and splendid proportions of this encampment," told the *Mount Tabor Record*. The new streets, which extended along the higher elevation south of the original campgrounds, followed a regular grid pattern. These lots were significantly deeper and the rear reserve, a feature of the earlier plotting, was absent. Even though the map shows lots laid out between Ridgewood Avenue and Bloomfield Avenue, the area eventually became part of the country club. (Mount Tabor Historical Society.)

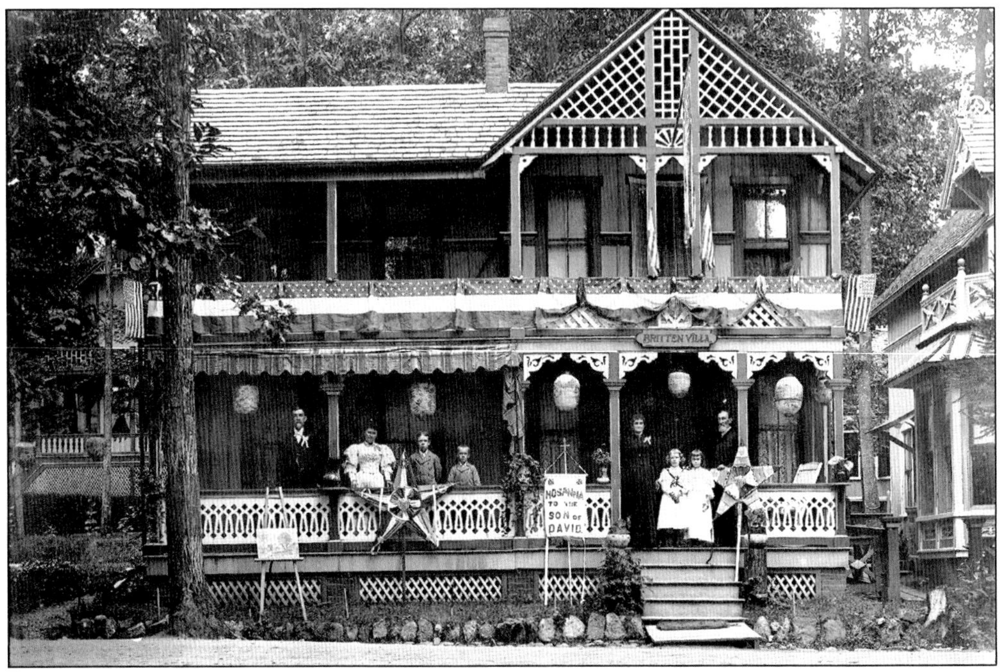

Benjamin Foster Britten (1837–1912) of Jersey City was one of those who purchased lots when they were first offered in 1869. Britten Villa, 28 West Morris Avenue, was one of several houses he and his family owned. In 1892, he stands on the right of the entrance with his family nearby. The house is decorated for Children's Day with patriotic and religious symbols as well as Chinese lanterns. (Ann Britten Wilson.)

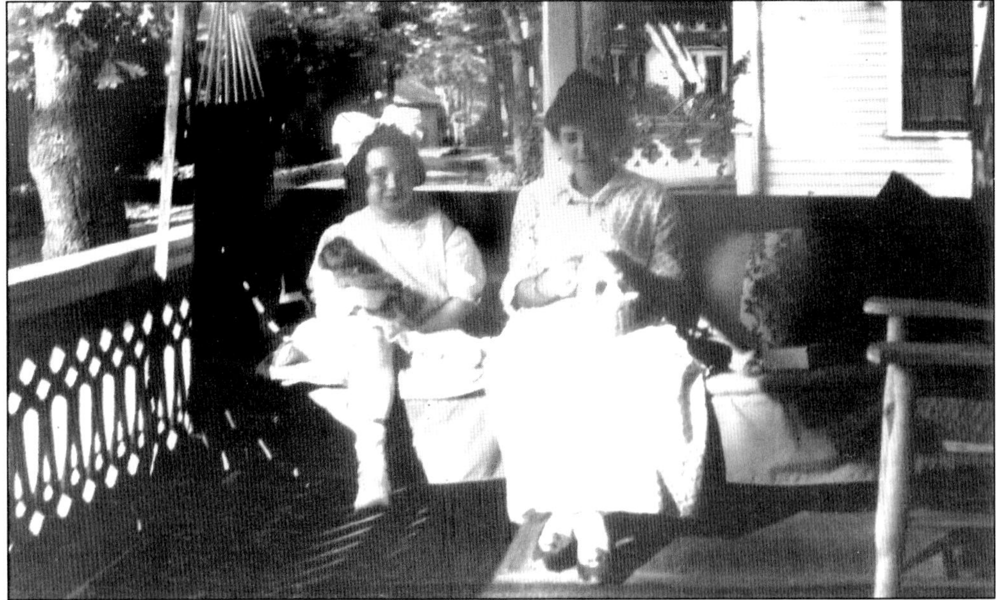

Mary Shelley, left, and Anna Okie sit on the porch swing at 28 West Morris Avenue. The porch was a favorite place for family and friends to watch the Children's Day parade. In 1914, Anna Menagh took this picture of two of her best friends. She was especially close to Mary, who was her only cousin near her in age. (Ann Britten Wilson.)

Ann Britten Wilson; her mother, Anna Menagh Wilson; and Bobby Roberts share refreshments in the backyard at 28 West Morris Avenue during the summer of 1936. Roberts lived next door at 30 West Morris Avenue. Note the shed attached to the house. The icebox stood inside the shutters. Ice was delivered regularly, and it was Ann's job to empty the water in the pan under the icebox. (Ann Britten Wilson.)

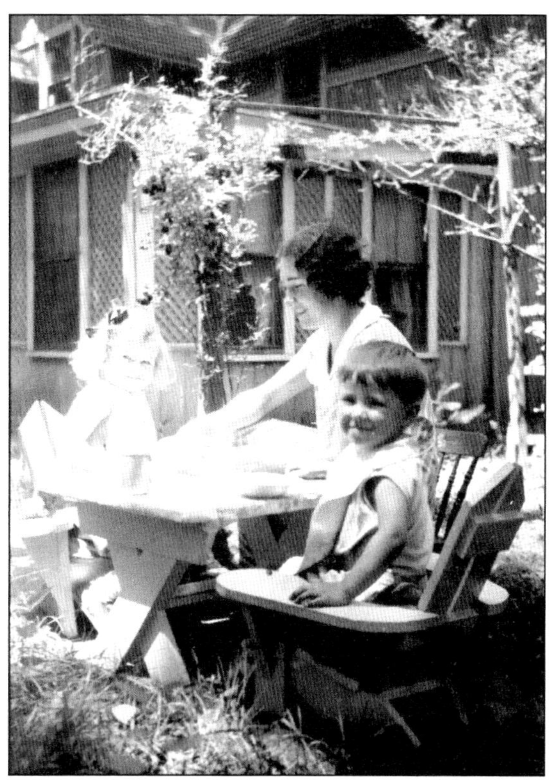

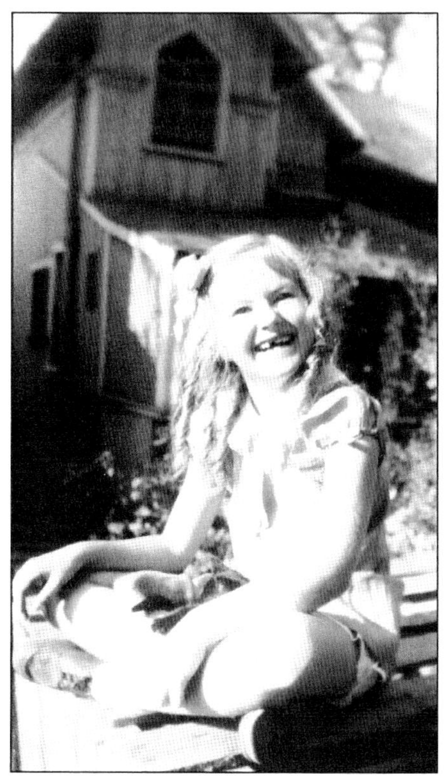

Ann Britten Wilson was always happiest during summers at Mount Tabor. She often went to the playground behind the clubhouse but also played in the yard behind her house at 28 West Morris Avenue. In 1938, she plays with a neighbor's cat. Note the unusual shape of the bathroom window upstairs. (Ann Britten Wilson.)

Cora Day Britten (1865–1957) married Louis Randolph Menagh Sr. She inherited 28 West Morris Avenue from her father and spent every summer there from the earliest days until the 1950s. Her diaries relate her adventures on worldwide cruises during the 1930s. Her son Louis R. Menagh Jr. became president of the Prudential Insurance Company of America in 1962. (Ann Britten Wilson.)

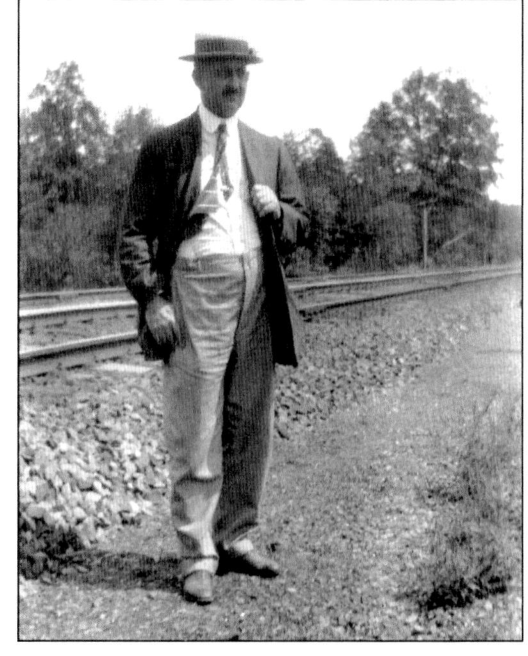

Louis Randolph Menagh Sr. (1860–1947) of Mendham visited the earliest camp meetings with his relatives and became a permanent summer resident in 1880. He remembered Mount Tabor when cooking was done outside the tents by means of pots hanging from iron cranes over a coal or wood fire. One Sunday, walking in pouring rain, he saw many of the ladies standing unprotected except for waterproof garments, busily engaged in preparing their Sunday dinners. In August 1914, he stands near the railroad tracks that run to Denville. (Ann Britten Wilson.)

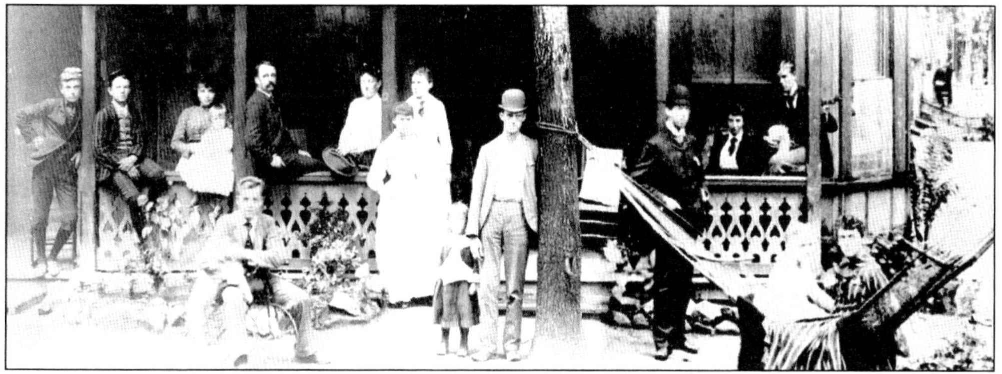

This photograph, dated summer 1888, shows the porch of the cottage owned by Mary and Drucilla Mockridge. The cottage was built for them in 1877 at the corner of what became Morris Avenue and Asbury Place. For many years, the Mockridge sisters ran a boardinghouse at this location. (Mount Tabor Historical Society.)

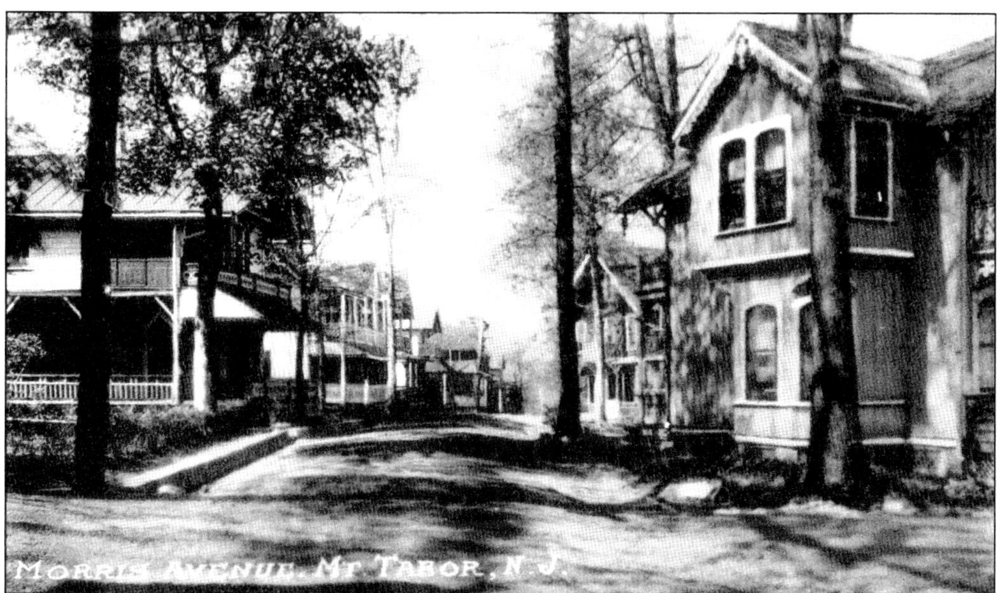

This postcard places the viewer in the intersection of Morris Avenue and Wesley Place. All the houses in this scene remain today with little change. Morris Avenue, one of the longest and broadest thoroughfares in Mount Tabor, was originally planned to be the main street through the town. It was supplanted in that role by Simpson Avenue as the merchants housed in the tabernacle began to draw the traffic along that route instead. (Mount Tabor Historical Society.)

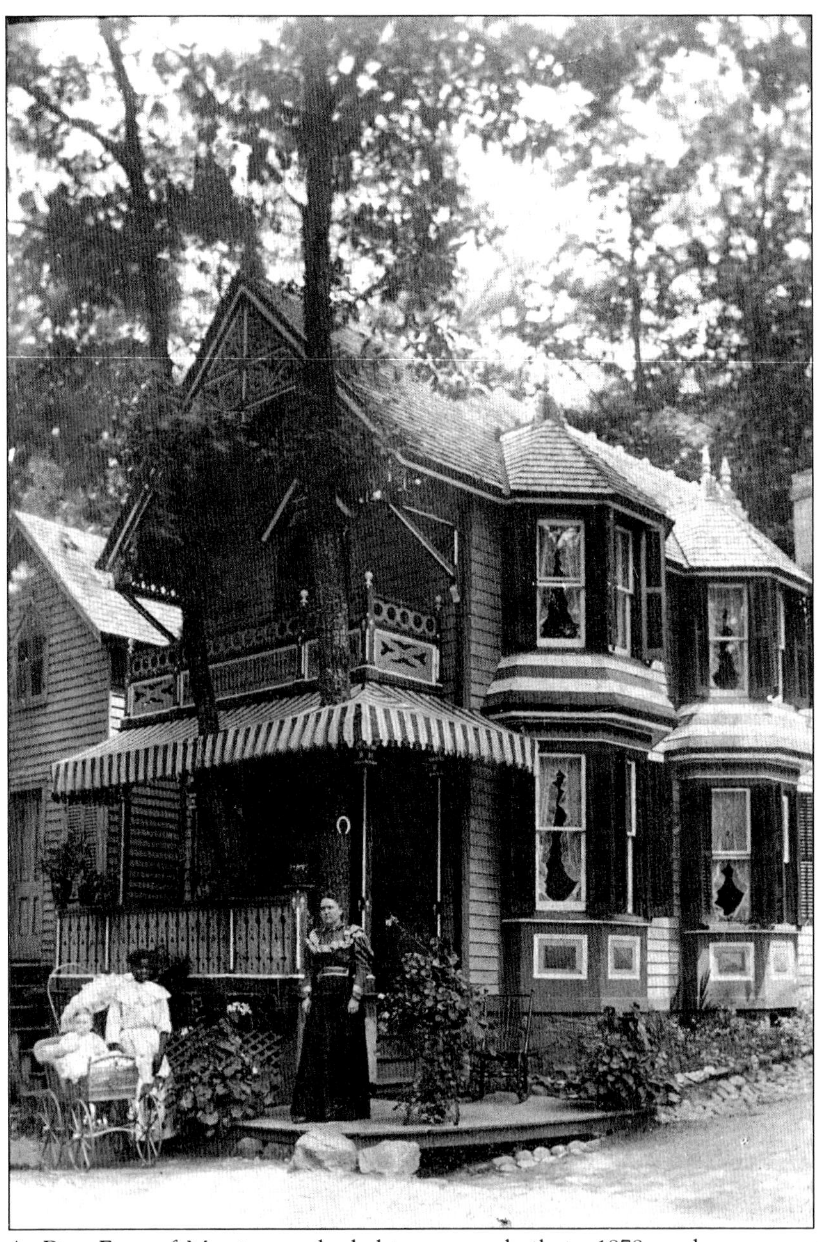

Frances A. Day, Esq., of Morristown had this cottage built in 1878 at the corner of Morris Avenue and Wesley Place. In 1882, the *Mount Tabor Record* reported, "It is in one of the most desirable locations, being just about centrally located among the improvements of the grounds, and while ornamental enough to please the eye was built more with a view to economizing space, and thus securing comfort, than from an esthetic standpoint. This building was the first cottage on Tabor finished in lath and plaster or 'hard finish.' It has a cellar beneath the whole, two two-story bay windows give added light, room and the beauty of curved lines, water on both floors, and of course the modern improvements." In this photograph from around 1898, an unidentified African American nanny is standing with the Hedden family. Harold R. Hedden is in the carriage. Nearby is his mother, Isabelle Hedden. It was common for African Americans to live both independently and as live-in servants in the community. (Marc Miller.)

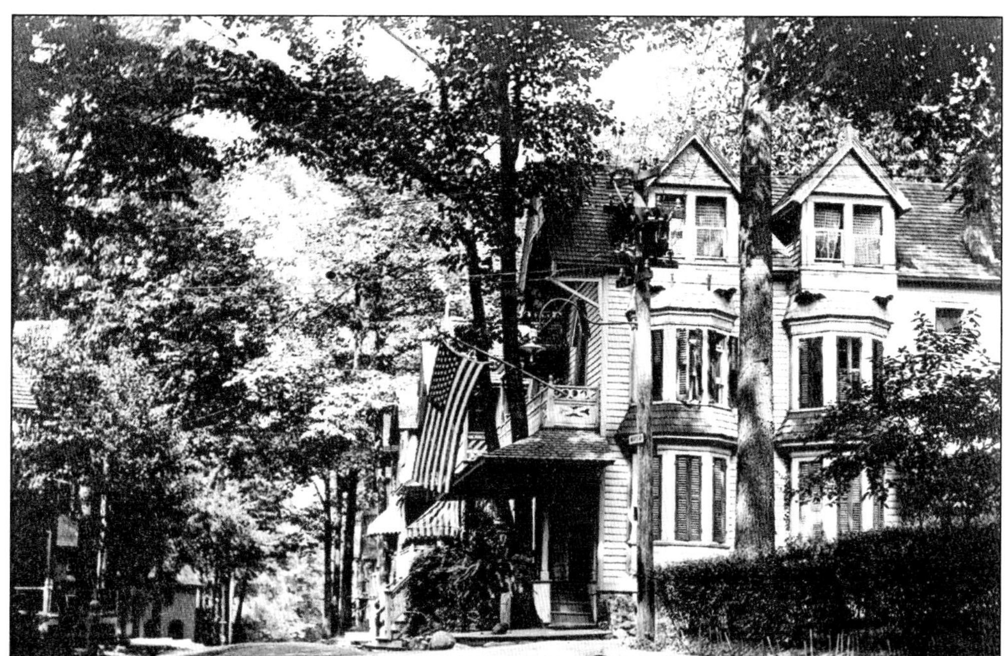

This house at 36 Morris Avenue was originally built as two small cottages. The projecting gable roof, supported by diagonal brackets, faces Morris Avenue and determines the width of the original cottage. The owner, Dr. J. W. Hedden, had a second cottage joined to the east side of the building to make up the present "double" width. A third floor was added at a later date, best illustrated by the addition of bracketed window heads above the existing double bay windows. The bay windows retain their original raised panels. When built, the front porch was shallow, and when the deeper porch was added, high priority was given to the trees that occupied the desired porch space. The builder paid careful attention to the circumscribing of the trees, and allowance for the growth of the trunks has brought to the present day a whimsical joining of man-made structure and nature. (Above, Marc Miller; right, Mount Tabor Record, 1880s.)

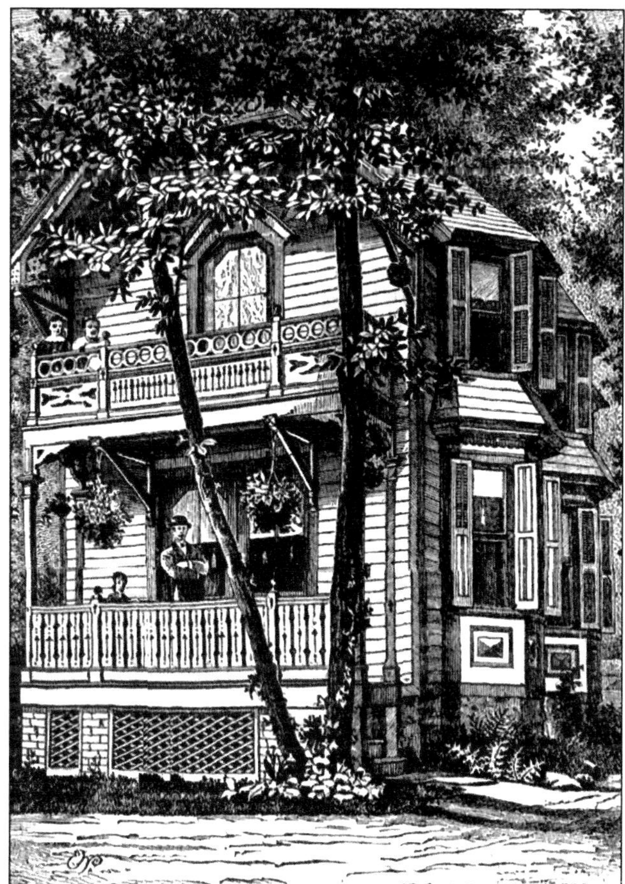

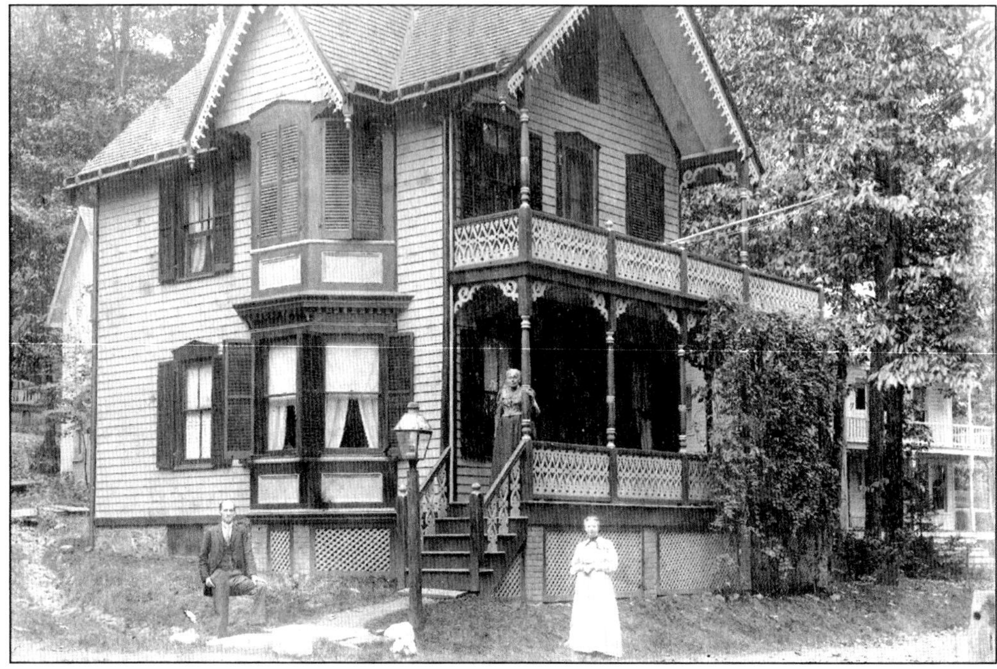

The house in the photograph above, dated 1900, was built for Dr. G. W. Eddy on Simpson Avenue. In January 1895, according to the minutes of the Camp Meeting Association, Eddy was given permission to widen his porch so that the cottage would be better suited for boardinghouse purposes. (Rothman family.)

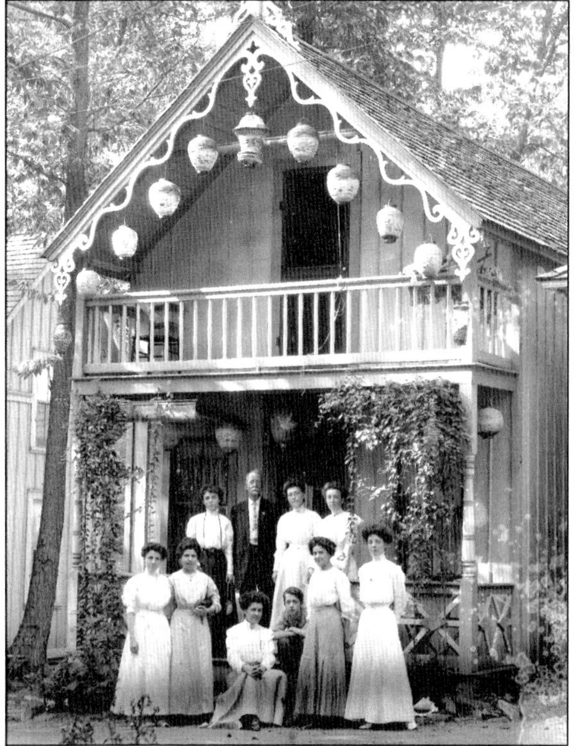

This house at 35 Embury Place, proudly decorated for Children's Day in this photograph, stands today, although the only recognizable remaining feature is the turned porch column on the right side of the house. The house on the left, 33 Embury Place, remains unchanged. The house to the right, 37 Embury Place, now has two stories. (Mount Tabor Historical Society.)

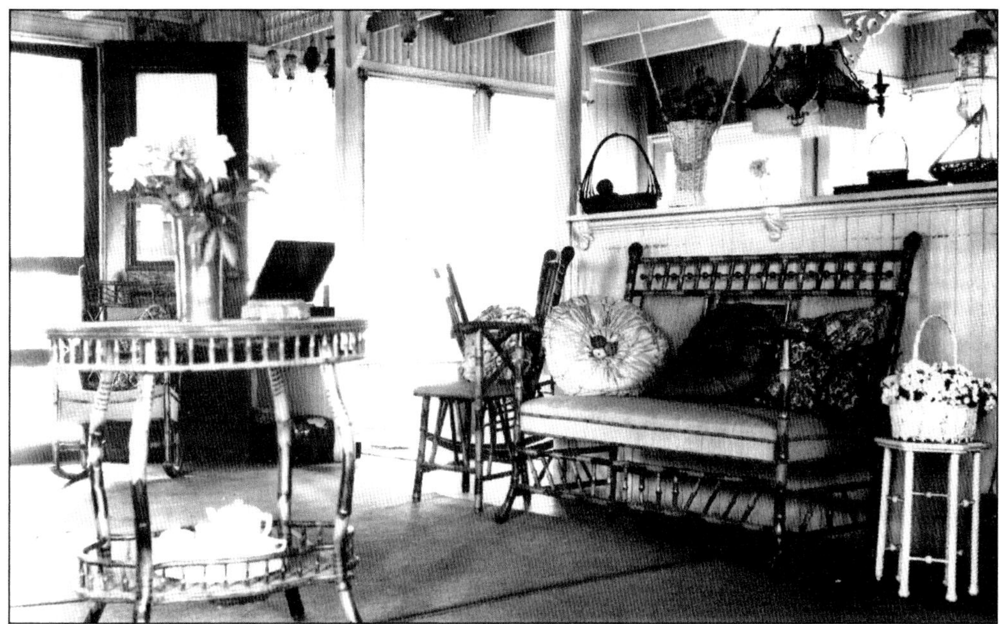

The Victorians were enamored of the newly emerging Asian market, and Mount Tabor residents were not immune to the American craze for exotic Asian-inspired decorative arts. One early description of a cottage notes that the house is decorated "inside and out with Chinese lanterns, a variety of fans and several unique frames to pictures made of ferns and cat-tails." These early interior photographs of 88 St. Johns Avenue capture the eclectic decorating style found in many of the cottages. The Asian influence is evidenced by the Chinese lanterns hanging from the exposed beams and the lovely wicker furnishings. The fresh flower–filled vases and baskets complete the enchanting scene. (Margaret Findley.)

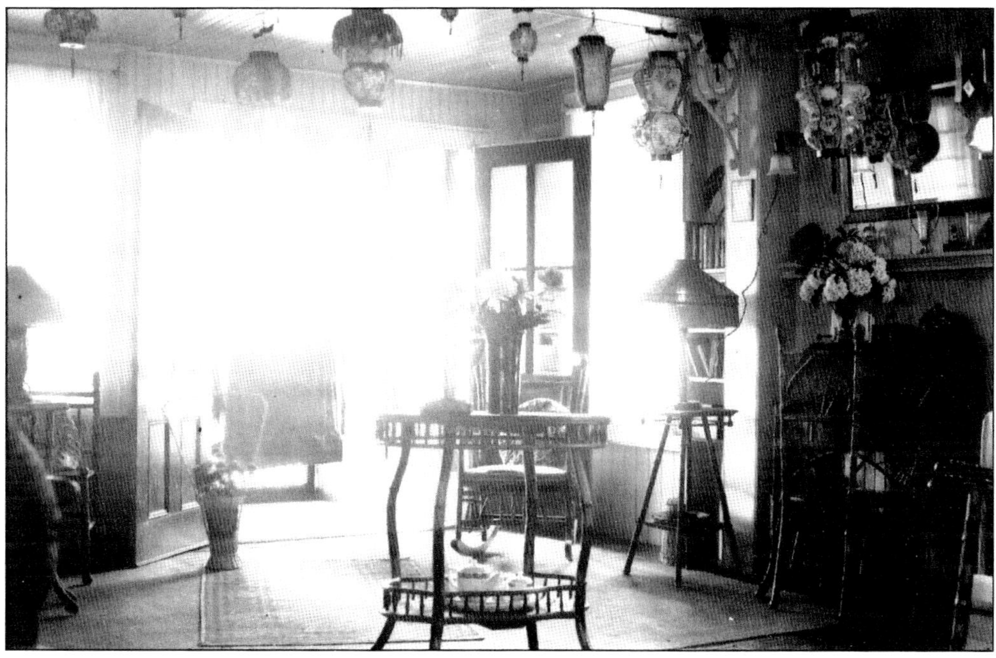

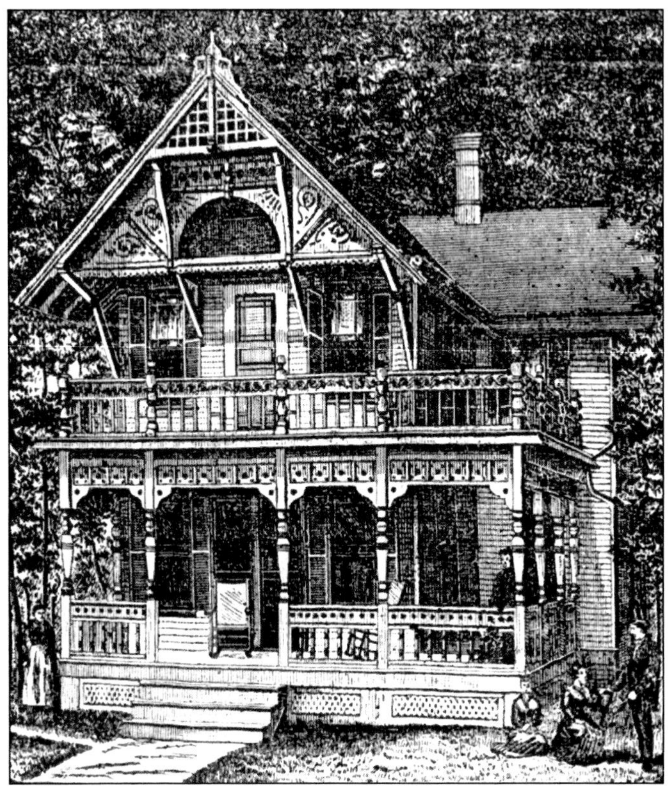

This etching from the *Mount Tabor Record* captures the exquisite piazzas of the Alfred C. Getchius residence on Sommerfield Avenue. It is described as "roomy but not so large that the cares of housekeeping become a burden: of original and pleasing architectural design, but not so covered with 'gingerbread' work that it becomes tiresome to even a critical eye." (Mount Tabor Record, 1880s.)

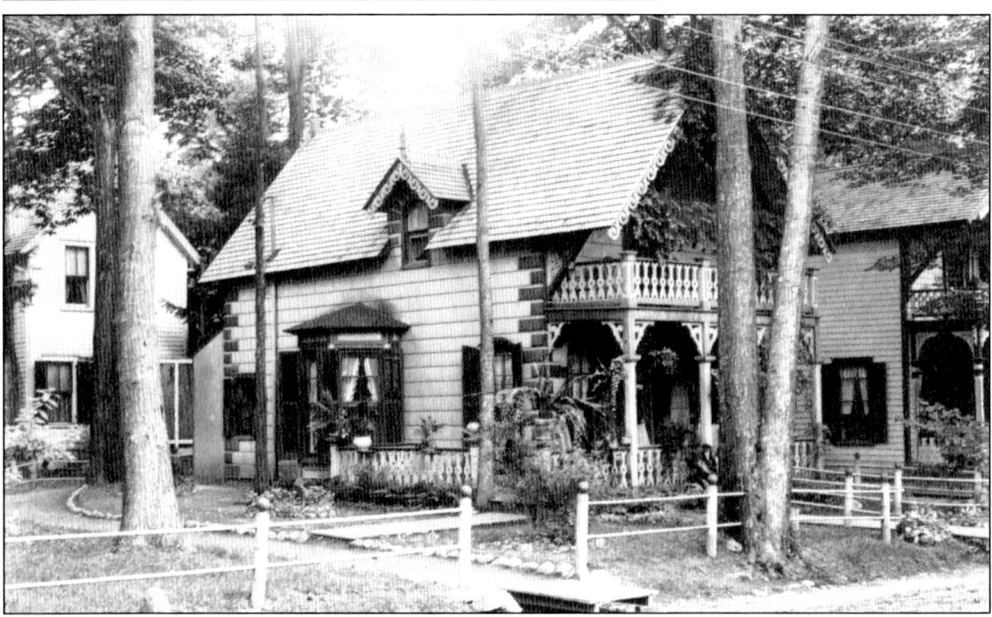

This cottage, also on Sommerfield Avenue, was built in 1877 for Rev. A. L. Brice, D.D., a leader and prominent participant in early camp meetings. Note the wood block details and treatment of window caps in imitation of cut stonework usually found in much larger buildings. The same treatment can be seen on the Sommerfield Avenue cottage shown on the opposite page. Only three houses in Mount Tabor are known to have this detailing. (Tom Nestor.)

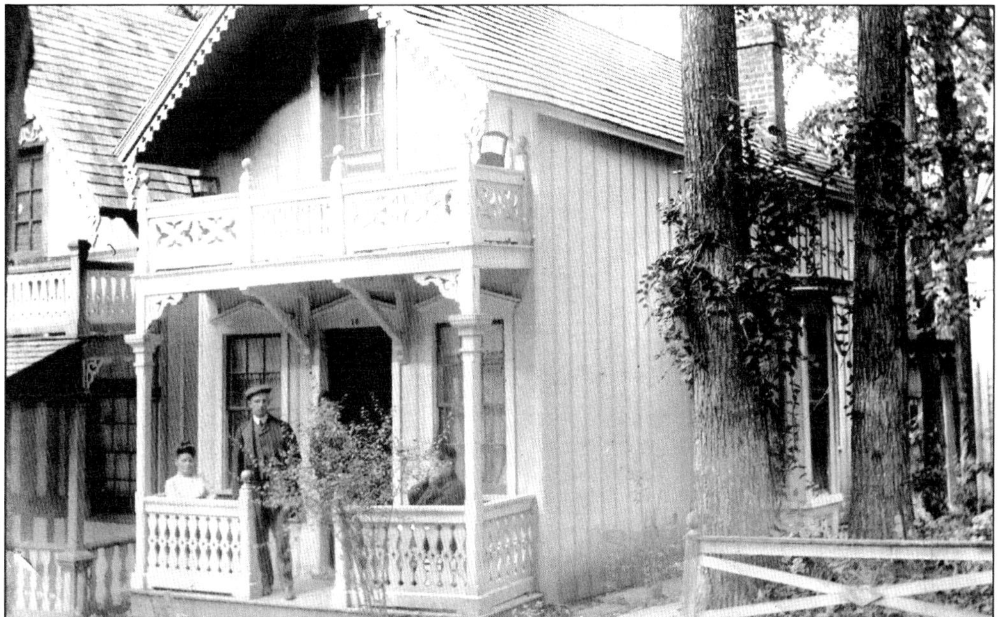

A classic example of camp-meeting architecture, this cottage was built within the confines of a 16-foot-by-25-foot tent site. The distance between cottages often was little more than a foot apart, causing the roofs to overlap. This cottage, once located at 14 Sommerfield Avenue and then owned by Anna and Horace Barrett, no longer exists. (Jeanne Apgar.)

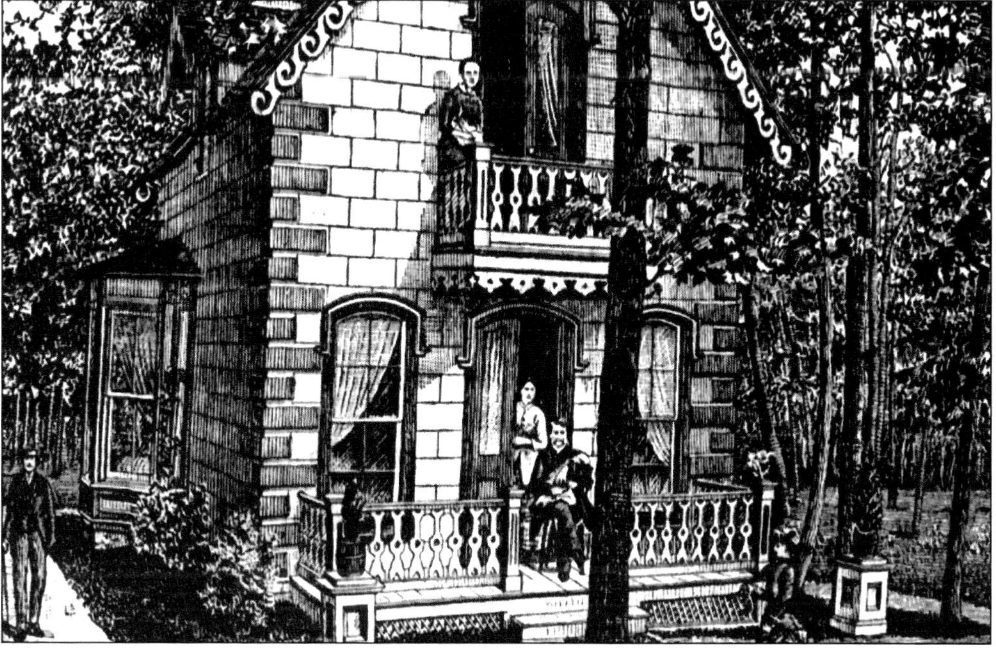

This charming etching depicts the cottage owned by Rev. Thos. S. Smith of Hackensack that is located on the corner of Sommerfield Avenue and Wesley Place. It sits near the summit of Mount Tabor, offering "superb views opening up in all directions." An article in the *Mount Tabor Record* asked, "Do you wonder that the pastor, worn by cares and responsibilities of a year's labor, should 'flee to the mountains' for a season of rest?" (Mount Tabor Record, 1880s.)

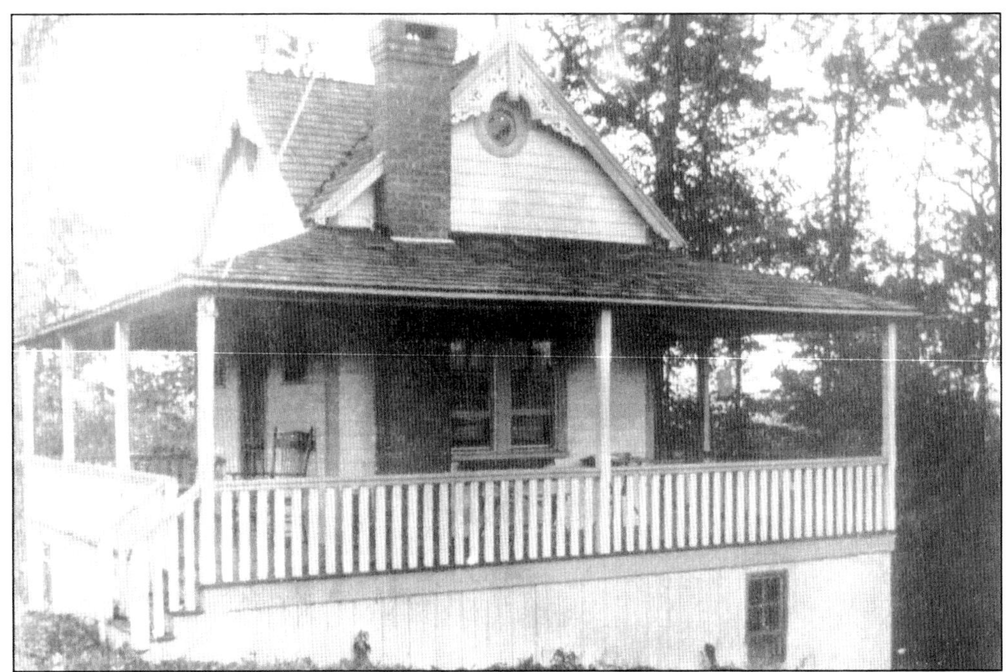

Halfway up the hill, at 14 St. Peters Road, the cottage shown in these two photographs offers an example of the conversion many of the cottages underwent to accommodate year-round living and expansion for much-needed living space. The wraparound porch extending on all four sides, which in an earlier time offered welcome, cool mountain breezes, was eventually enclosed, and the subsequent additions drastically altered the original facade. Only the gingerbread under the upper roof is recognizable. At one time, William Stephenson, pictured here, was clerk for the Town of Parsippany. He performed his duties as clerk in this very house. (John Sulpy Jr.)

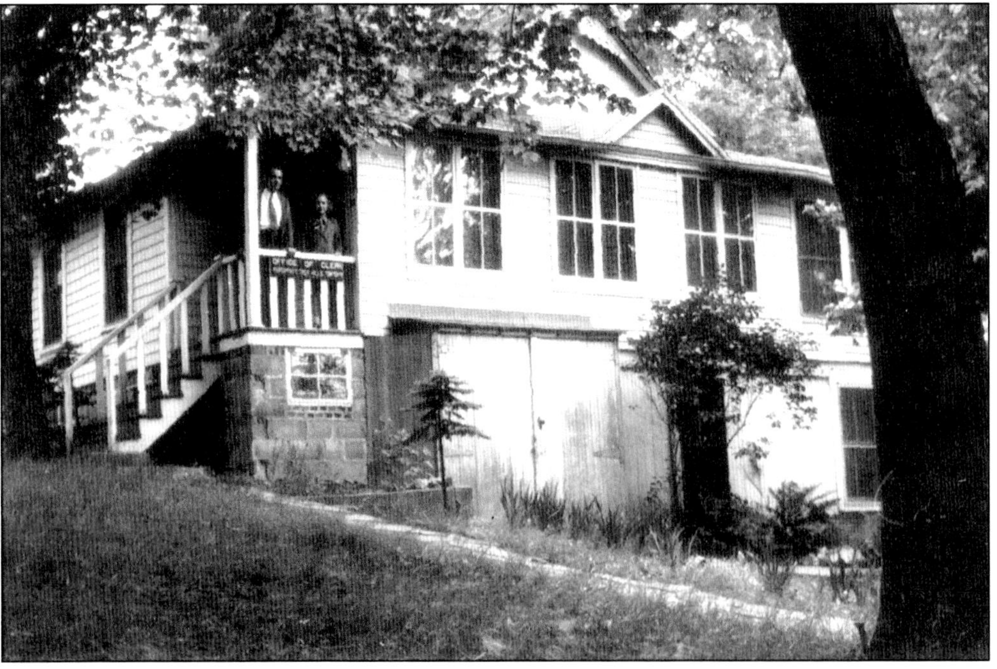

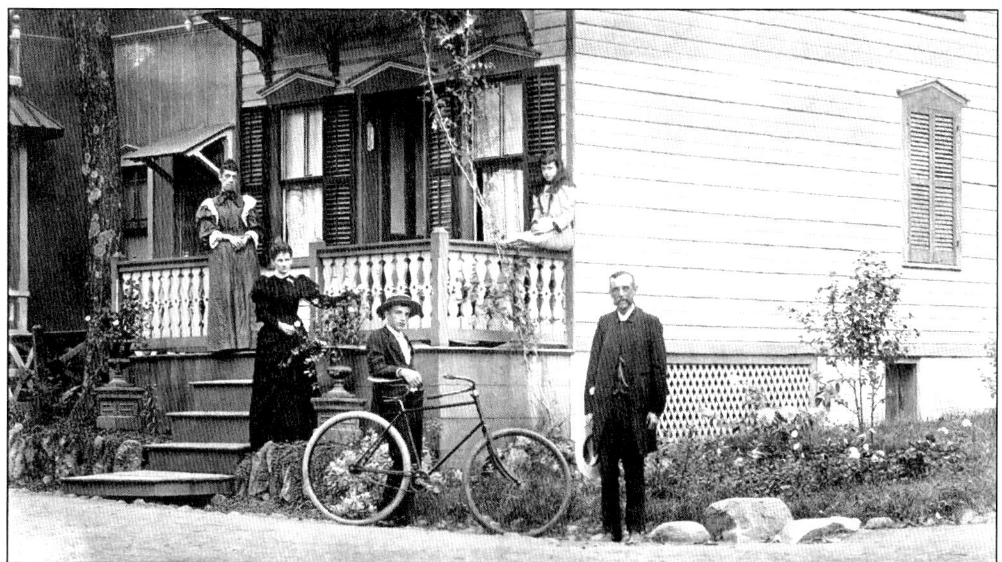

This family, dressed in its best finery, poses in front of its cottage on the corner of Morris and Strowbridge Avenues. The front porch is on the Children's Day parade route, and no doubt the boy will have his bicycle decorated for a chance to win a prize. Because the house is located on the corner, the family can take advantage of a small area for a garden. (Tom Nestor.)

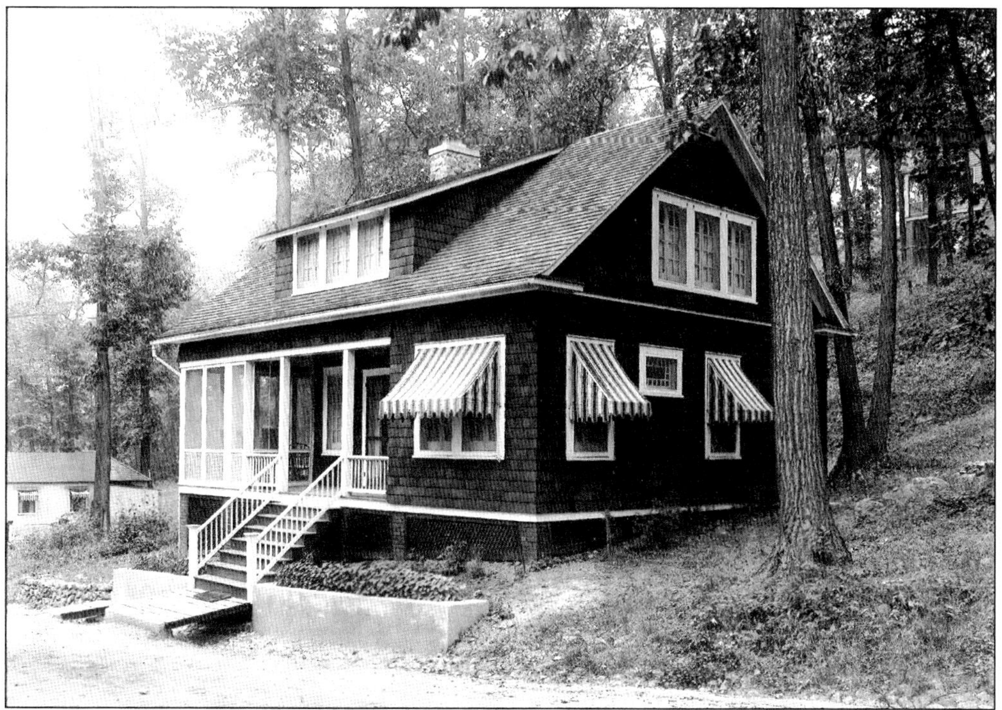

The house at 60 Morris Avenue dates to around 1920. The side gable roof and shed dormer are reminiscent of those found on many craftsman-style houses built in the decade leading up to its construction. Prominent furniture designer Gustav Stickley's own house, located nearby in Parsippany, shares this quintessential American roofline. Also of note are the divided-light casement windows. (Huetz family.)

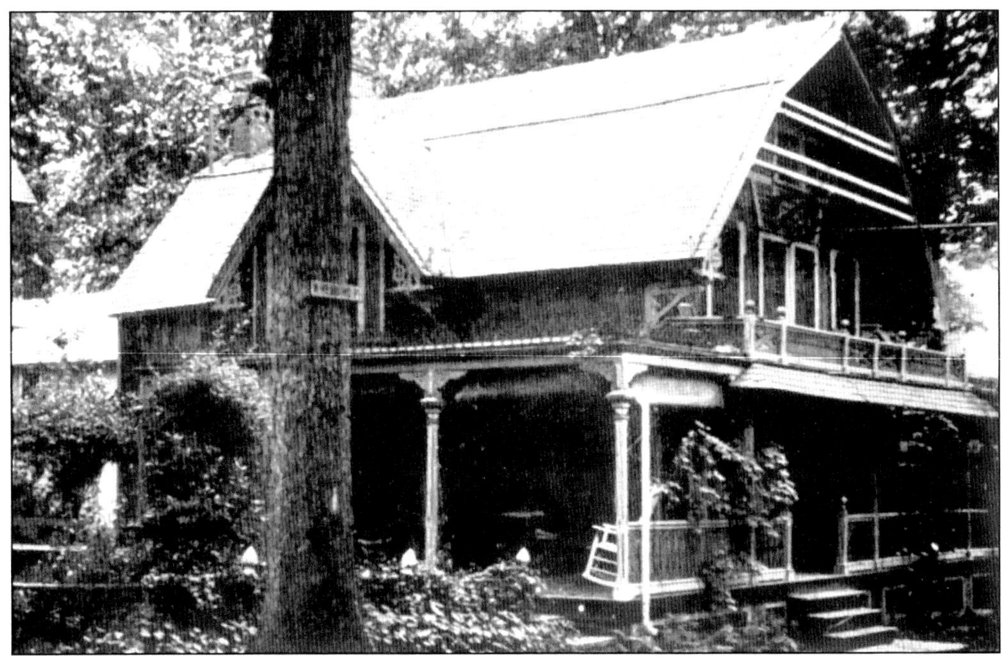

This house was originally two cottages fronting on West Hedding Place. They were constructed in 1875 by builder S. M. Mattox of Rockaway for Frank Wilkinson of Newark, who was a trustee of the Camp Meeting Association. Franklin N. Barrett of Bayonne purchased the leaseholds in 1886, and in 1888, the two cottages were joined, as seen above, with an addition across the back to accommodate a kitchen. (Michelle LaConto Munn.)

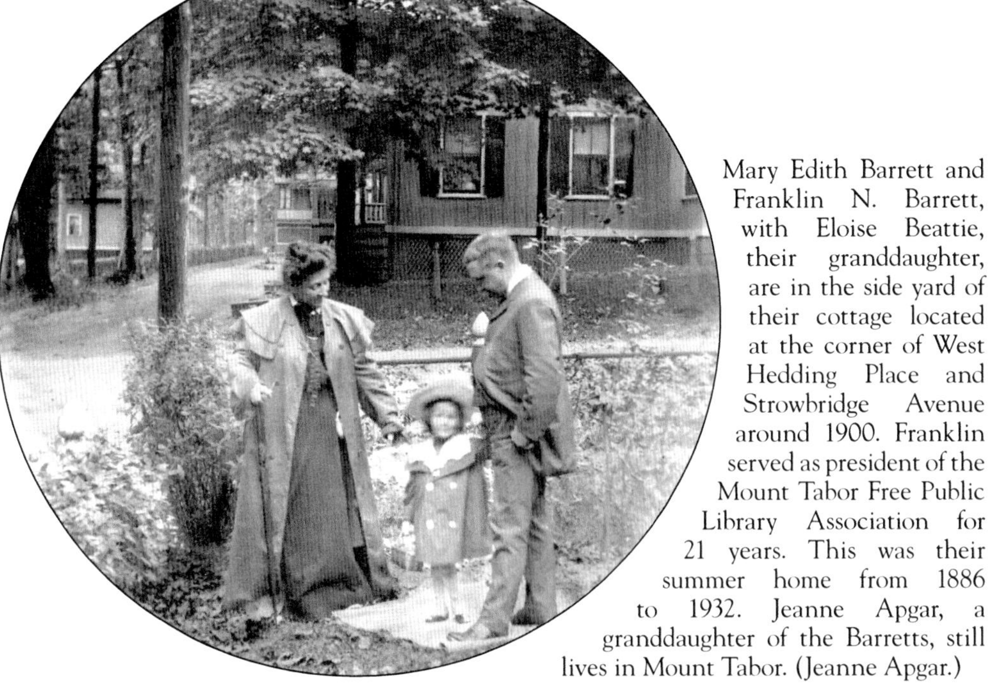

Mary Edith Barrett and Franklin N. Barrett, with Eloise Beattie, their granddaughter, are in the side yard of their cottage located at the corner of West Hedding Place and Strowbridge Avenue around 1900. Franklin served as president of the Mount Tabor Free Public Library Association for 21 years. This was their summer home from 1886 to 1932. Jeanne Apgar, a granddaughter of the Barretts, still lives in Mount Tabor. (Jeanne Apgar.)

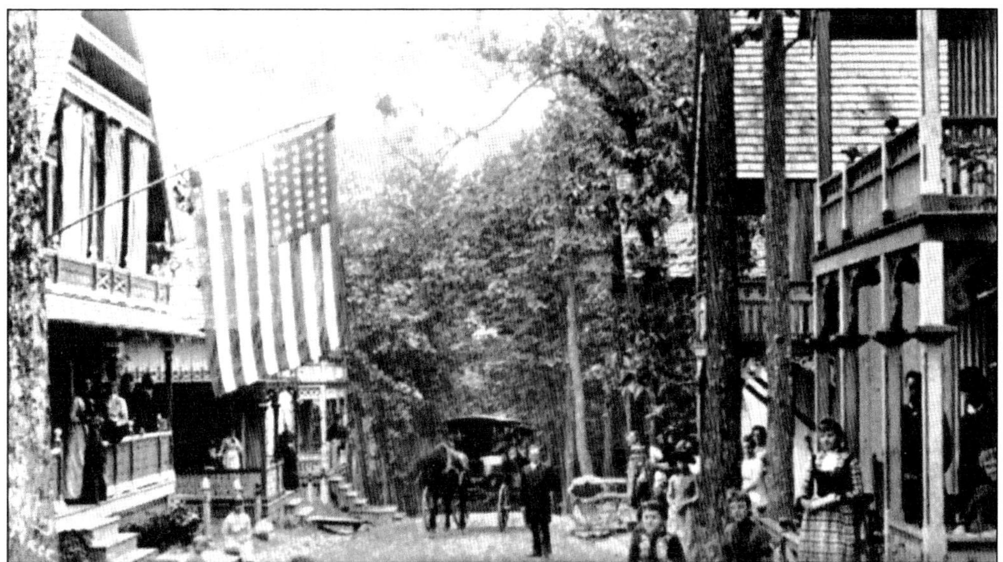

West Hedding Place was the "final frontier" of the original campgrounds. It was said, "The ladies can walk safely to the Tabernacle from the wilds of West Hedding." This image of a horse-pulled carriage reaching the crest of West Hedding on its way to Strowbridge Avenue shows a charming view of the street. Many of the houses remain today much as they are in the photograph. And the ladies can still walk safely to the tabernacle. (Mount Tabor Historical Society.)

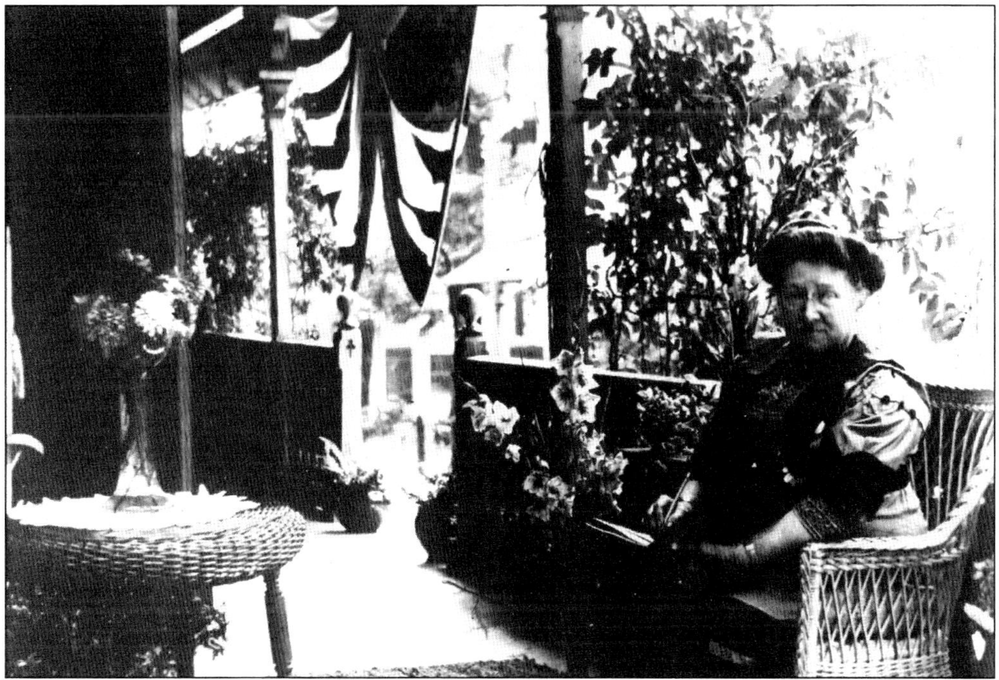

Mary Edith Barrett is seated on the well-appointed lower piazza of her cottage at 18 West Hedding Place (now 6 Strowbridge Avenue because the front entrance was moved). This house was described in the *Mount Tabor Record* of August 30, 1887, as "a neat little cottage with double piazzas, painted olive green and decorated inside and out with Chinese lanterns." (Jeanne Apgar.)

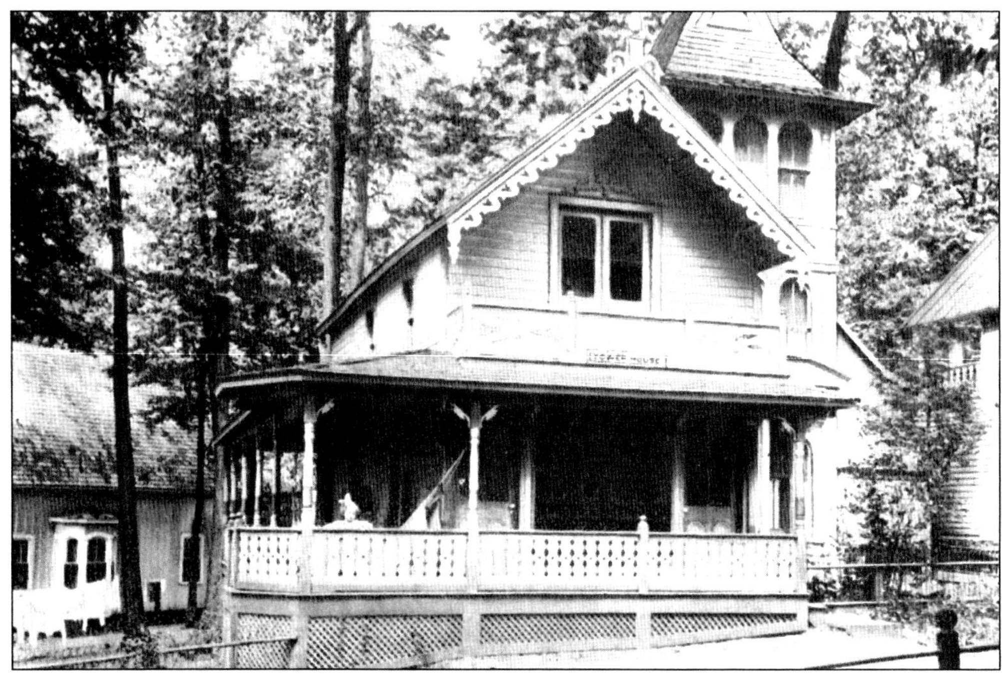

This cottage at 29 Asbury Place, known as the Tower House, was once the summer home of Jacob W. Stephens, Esq., of Newark. The *Mount Tabor Record* noted the "graceful proportions of the building in fine relief." Stephens also owned the lot to the left of the house and used the extra land to expand it beyond its original footprint. The square tower was a signature feature of cottages built by S. M. Mattox. (Mount Tabor Historical Society.)

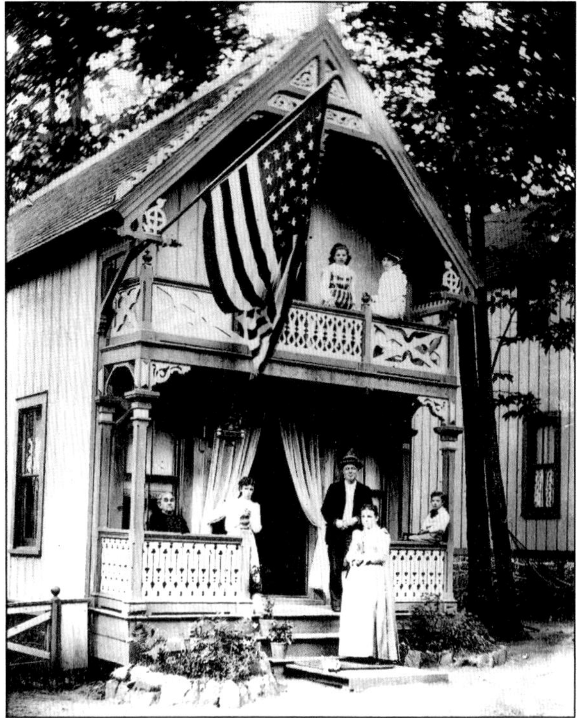

The family living at 35 Asbury Place is seen here enjoying the summer breezes from its double porches. The draped doorway is reminiscent of the tent flaps of an earlier time. This house was situated in an ideal location, just a short walk to Trinity Park via the west pass. The cottage still stands today. Both porches have been enclosed, but the original gingerbread pictured in the lower porch remains visible from the inside. (Camp Meeting Association.)

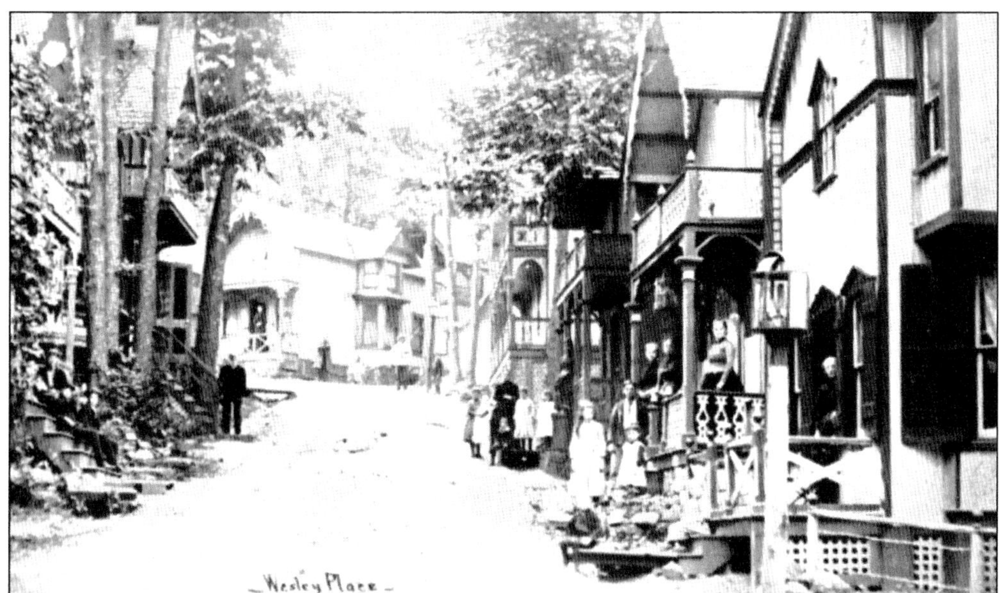

This postcard shows Wesley Place, named for John Wesley, the founder of Methodism. The street was developed very early because of its close proximity to Trinity Park. With few exceptions, the houses pictured still remain today. (Mount Tabor Historical Society.)

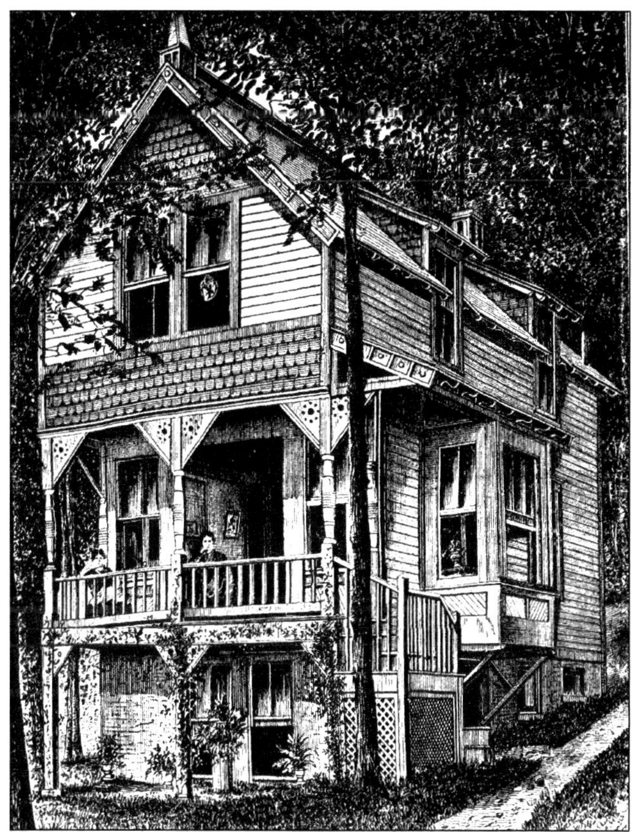

In 1881, architect George Bower of Chatham and Mount Tabor designed as well as supervised the construction of the cottage on the right for H. L. Bonsaline. The kitchen and dining room were located in the basement with a reception room, parlor, and front piazza on the first floor and sleeping arrangements on the second floor. The walls and ceilings of the first floor and basement were richly papered, while the exterior was painted dark green with India red trim. The cottage is located on Morris Avenue, adjacent to the Golden Stairs. (Mount Tabor Record, 1880s.)

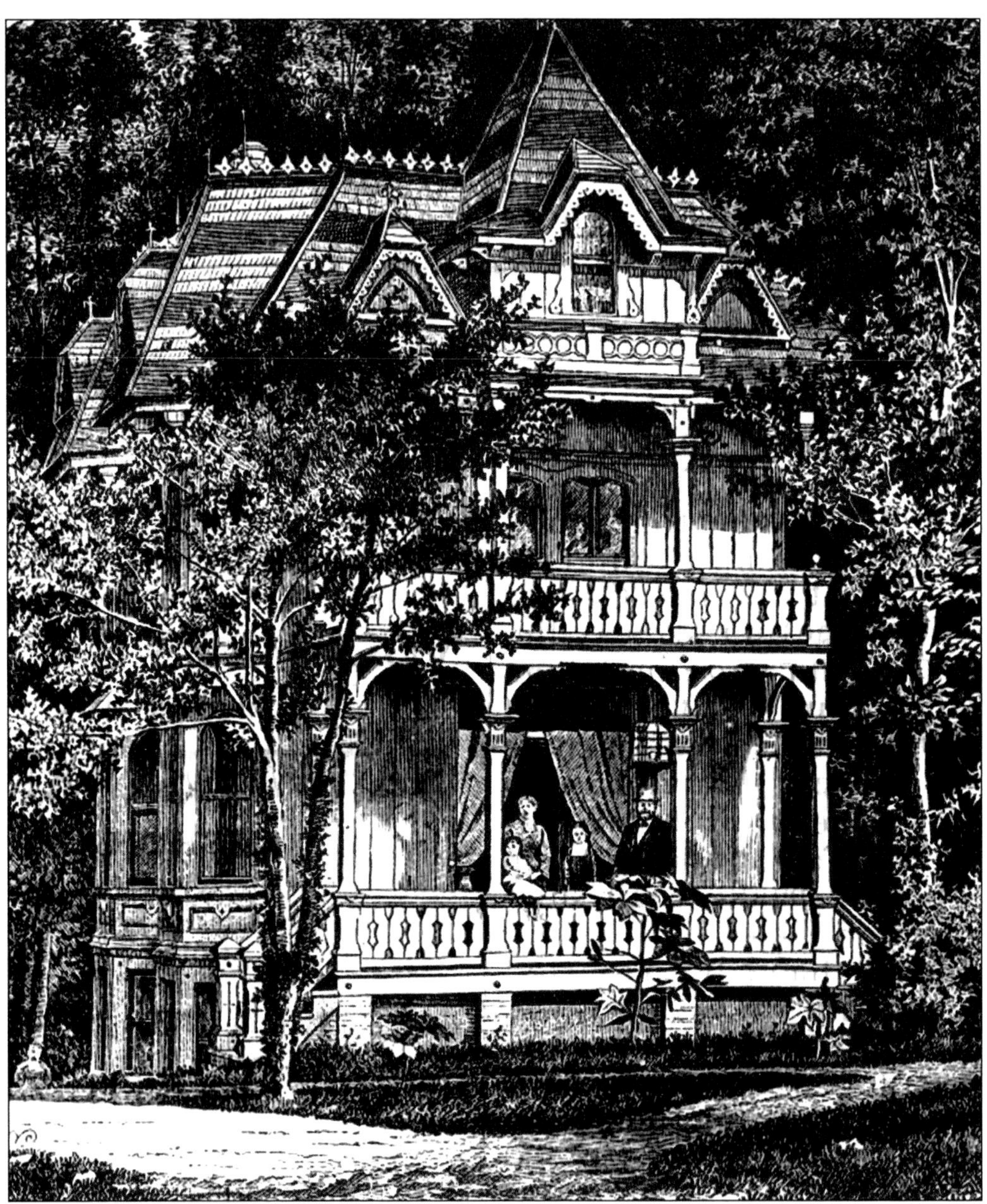

This cottage at 47 North Place was owned by Richard Grant, Esq., of Jersey City, shown with his wife and two girls. It sits on the highest point of Mount Tabor, located on the corner of North Place and Searing Place, facing St. James' Park. It was surrounded by a quarter acre of beautifully laid out flower beds and a lawn richly set with shrubbery. A wall was later added to the front of the property. It was formed of rich conglomerate stone, capped with sharp points and edges of the same flinty rock in what may be termed a cone or fish scale. It is centrally located between Trinity Park and the county club with easy access to both areas. Grant led the push to erect the Mount Tabor entrance sign and was also instrumental in starting the athletic fields near the county club. Many of the house's original elements have survived intact, including the fencing, stone walls, and fancy millwork. (Mount Tabor Record, 1880s.)

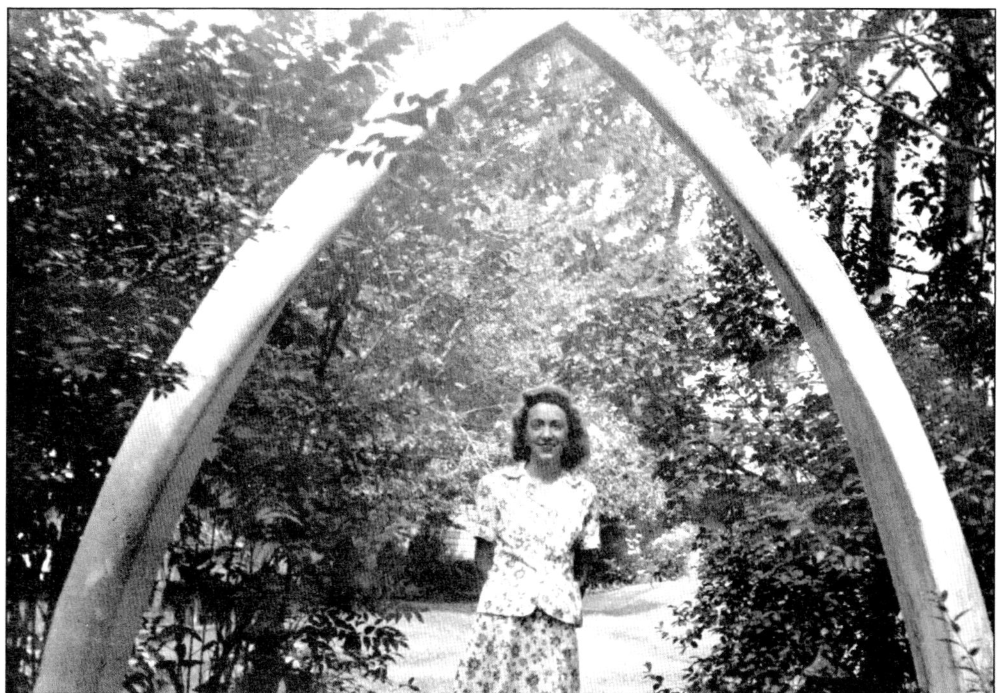

For many years, walkers ascending the Golden Stairs were amused to find an archway of whale jawbone set upright as an entrance to the backyard of the Grant family house. It was estimated to be just over 16 feet tall. The bones were secured from a whale captured on the coast of California. Only a small petrified piece remains today. This picture was taken around 1940. (Ruth Lynch Blazure.)

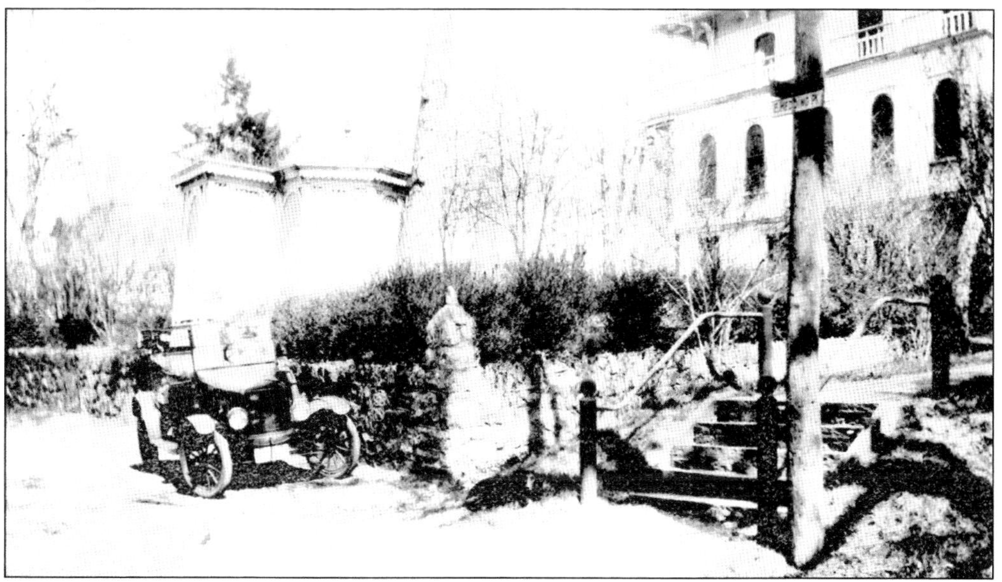

Pictured here is the back of the Grants' cottage with the boundaries surrounded by a pudding stone wall. The photograph just barely reveals a piece of the whalebone arch as one reaches the last landing of the Golden Stairs. The back of the property borders on East Hedding Place, allowing cars to access the house from the rear. (Tom Nestor.)

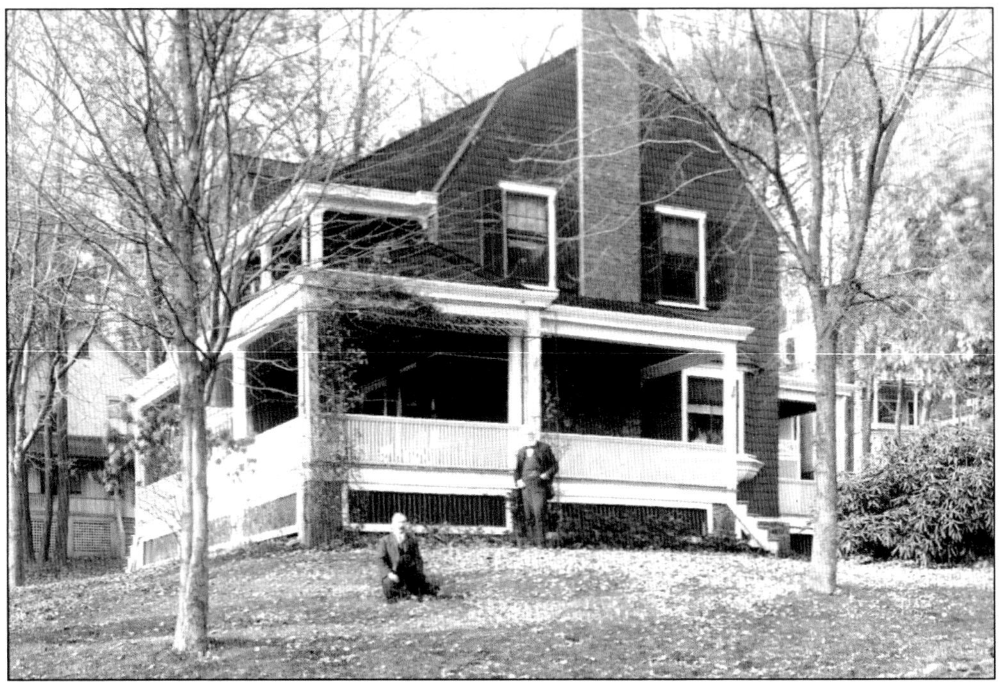

Above and below are two views of the house currently owned by Ron and Marie Dickerson located on the corner of Ridgewood and Strowbridge Avenues. Ron is a direct descendant of the family that sold its farmland to the Camp Meeting Association for the original Mount Tabor site. His family has lived in the area since 1745. The house was built for J. W. Cleveland, Esq., a merchant from Paterson, and was notable for having the first garage in Mount Tabor. The flag shown below had previously flown over the town hall in Paterson. (Ron Dickerson.)

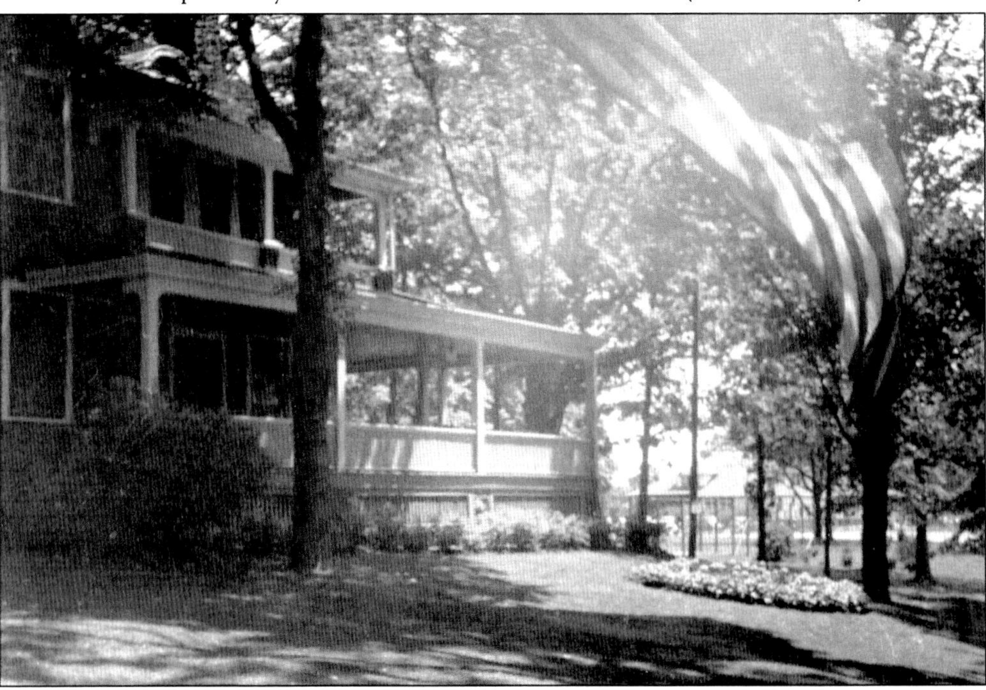

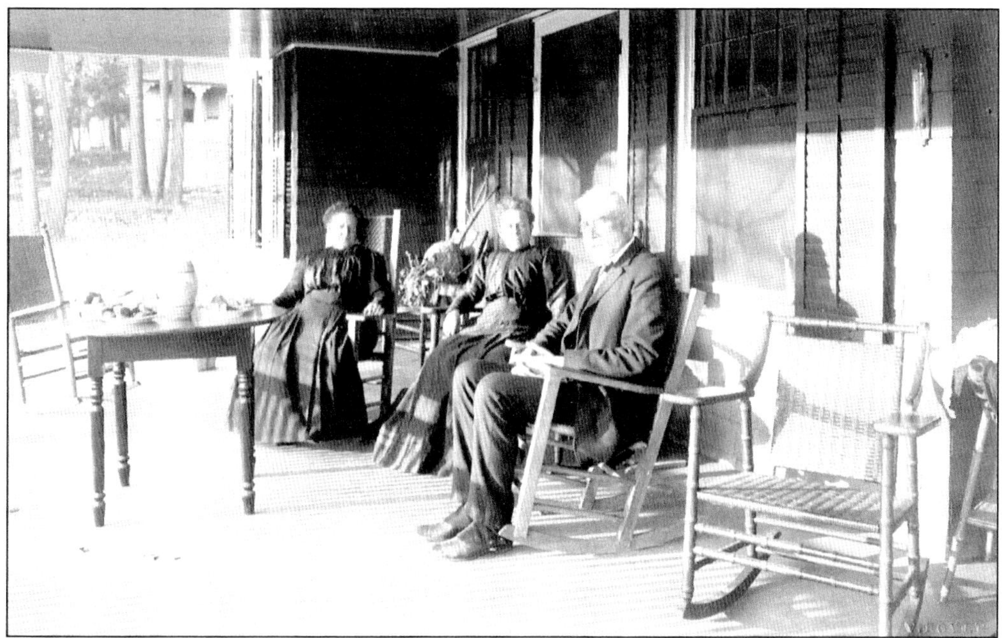

Verandas were the best form of air-conditioning in the summer months and were a welcome design feature. Summertime gossip on a porch filled with a cluster of rocking chairs has never lost its charm. As illustrated in both of these photographs, Cleveland and his family were obviously comfortable entertaining friends on the front porch. Carolyn Thornberry (the Clevelands' niece) inherited the house and ultimately sold it to the Dickersons in 1965. (Ron Dickerson.)

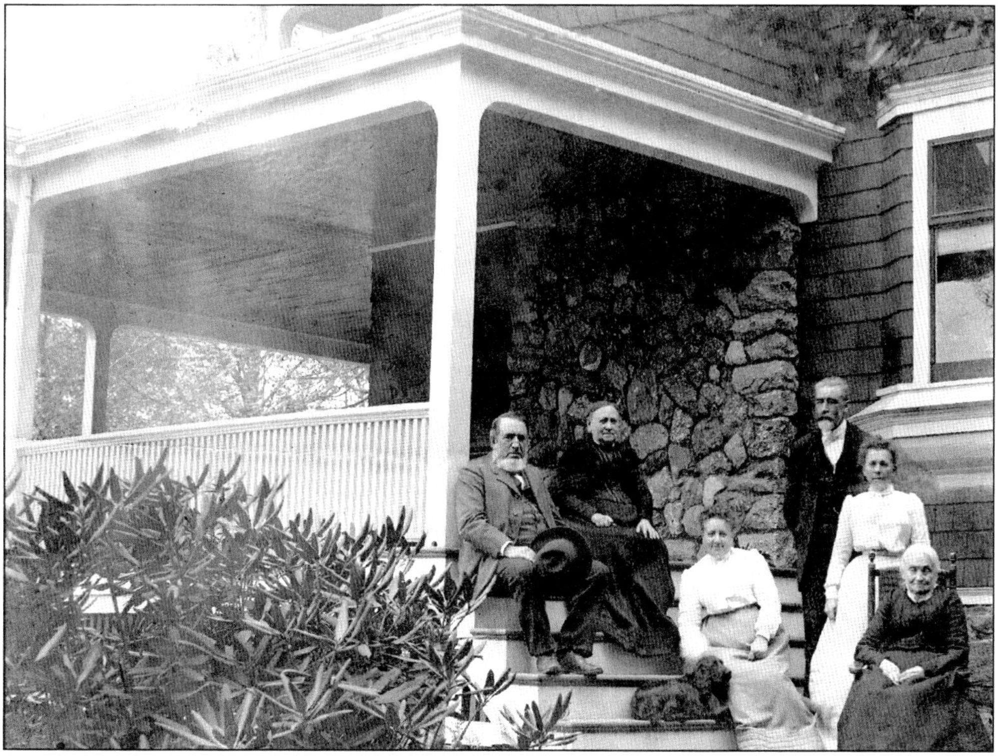

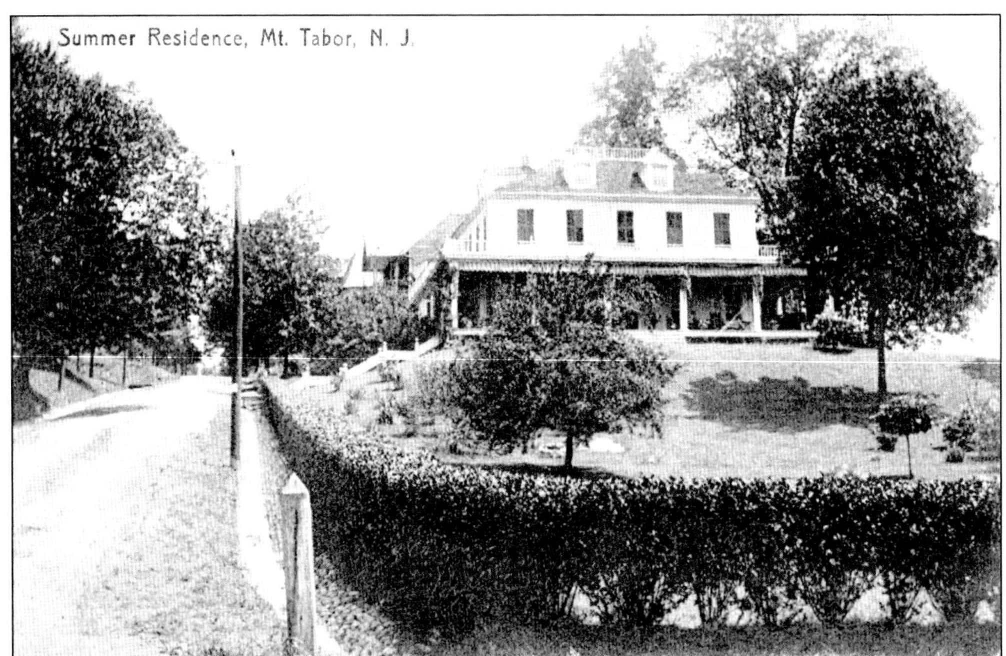

Although of the Victorian era, this house on Ridgewood Avenue, built in 1896 for Samuel Warren, adheres more closely to the design principles of the Colonial Revival period. The facade, which faces Route 53, has the symmetrical five-bay order of a classic Georgian house. The third-floor attic has eight gables and a traditional widow's walk. (Mount Tabor Historical Society.)

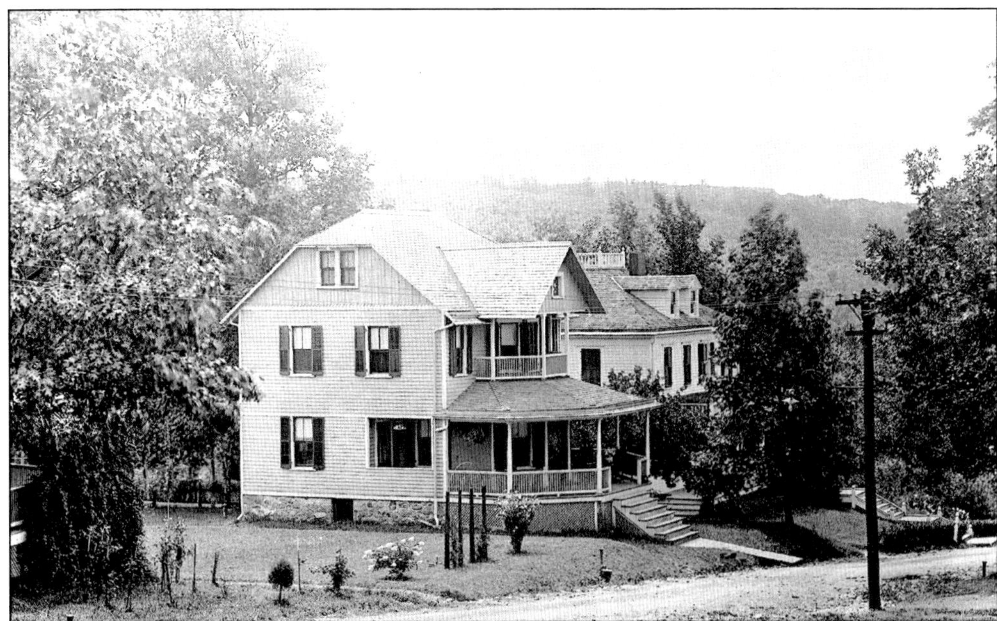

This Queen Anne–style house, located at 16 Ridgewood Avenue, was built around 1880. It was one of the new wave of larger houses built on more spacious lots on the newly purchased tract that expanded the original campgrounds. The house was seriously damaged in a 2002 fire and was painstakingly renovated with period sensitivity. The center portion of the house was preserved, and additions were made to the exterior. (Jennifer Roth.)

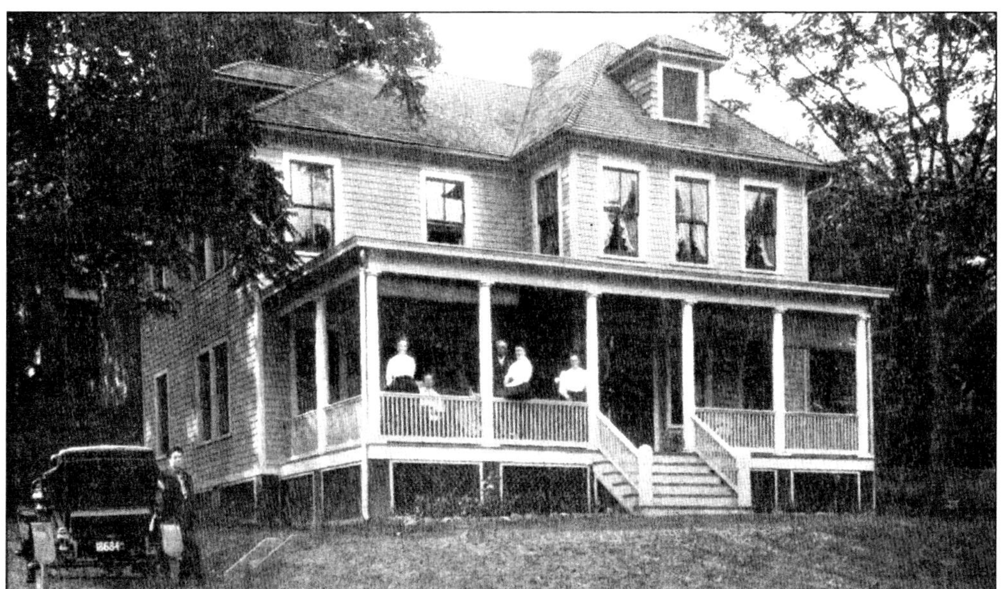

Above is the residence of John and Ida Higgins at 45 Ridgewood Avenue. Below is another view of the house, taken from a postcard. The Higginses were residents of Philadelphia who spent their summers in Mount Tabor. After John died, Ida turned the residence into a two-family house, spending her summers on one side and renting the other, resulting in the two front doors that the house displays today. The Higginses' descendents still live in the community. The view of Ridgewood Avenue looking southwest is very similar today to the one on the postcard below. The main difference is that the road has been paved. (Barbara Higgins Sulpy.)

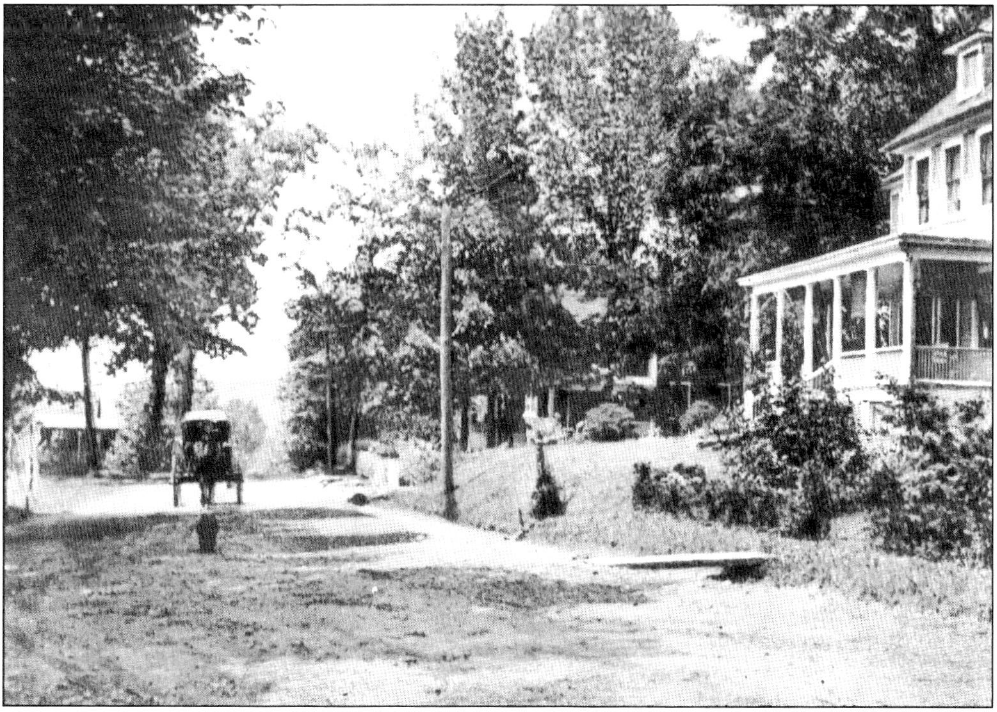

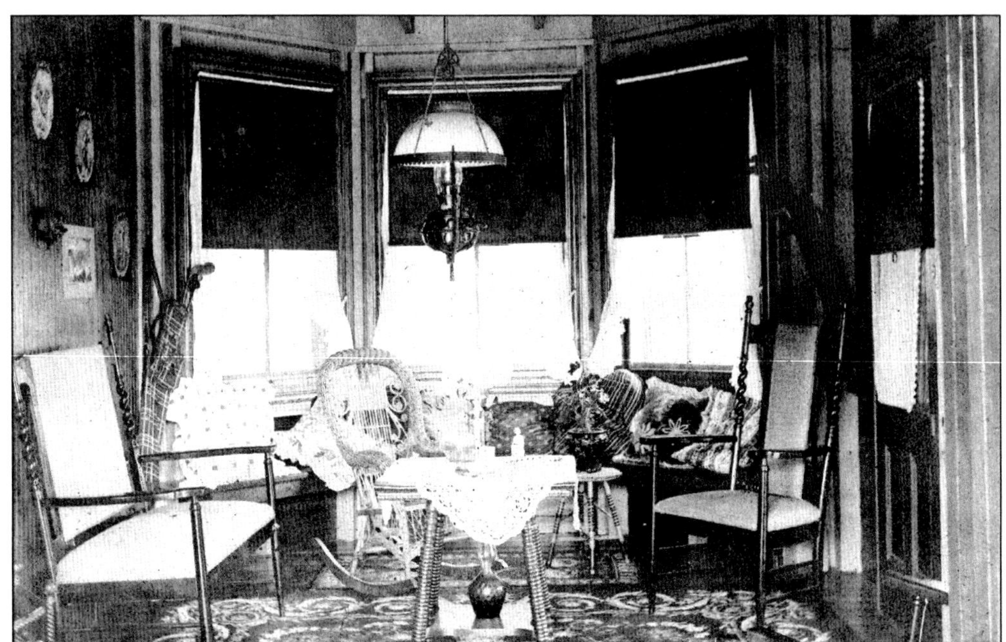

Edwin Franklin Britten built the houses at 1 and 5 St. Johns Avenue in 1880. His sons lived there during the summer, Edwin Franklin (Frank) Britten Jr. in number 1 and Clarence R. Britten in number 5. Both interiors shown here were photographed inside Clarence's cottage. The walls were finished with wainscoting, the ceiling beams were exposed, and wicker and wooden furniture filled the living space. They brought other furnishings from the city, such as lamps, lace table coverings, rugs, china, framed pictures, and wall decorations. Frank and Clarence both served as officers in the field club and were devoted to sports in Mount Tabor, as evidenced by the golf clubs hanging on both sides of the bay window. (Ann Britten Wilson.)

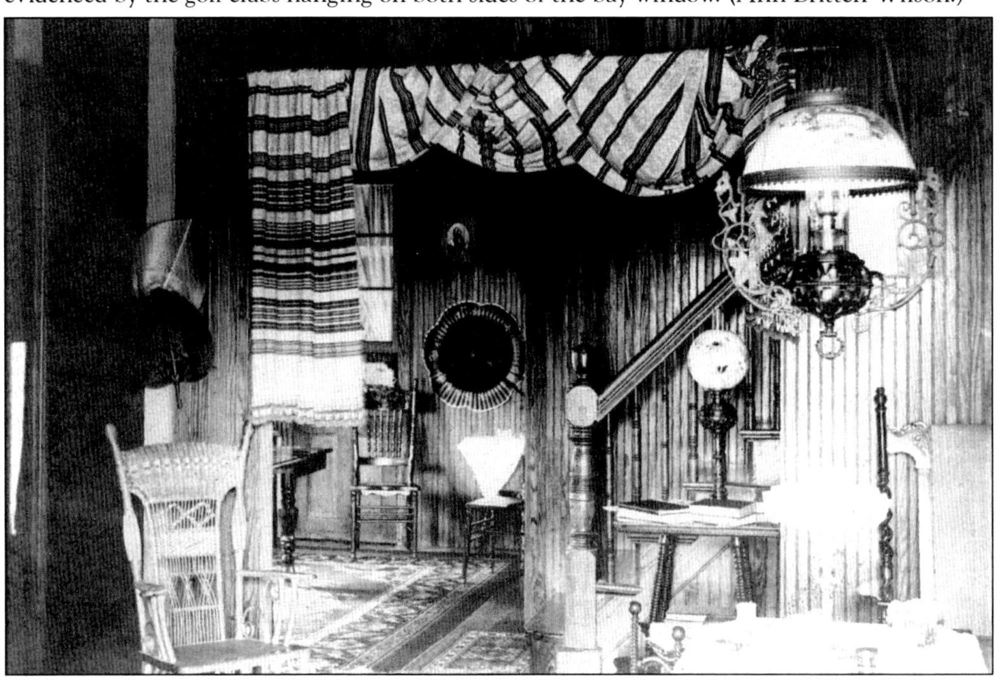

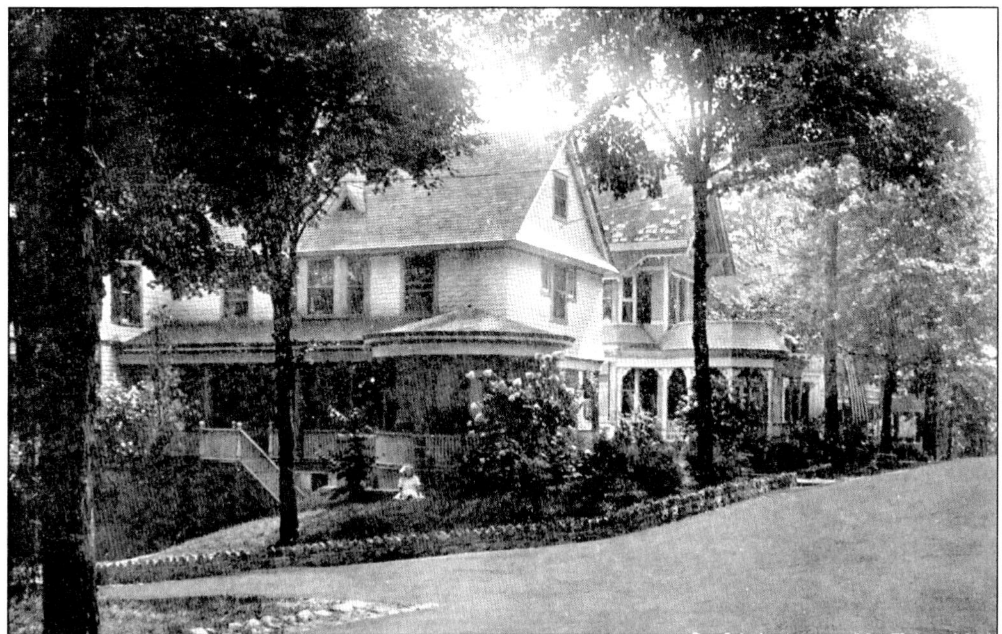

This postcard image shows a house on the corner of St. Johns Avenue and West Park Place (50 St Johns Avenue today). It has a beautiful circular porch, perfect for viewing parades and for entertaining. The property slopes gently down to Ridgewood Avenue. From the backyard one can observe the country club and all the activities. Note the young girl enjoying the summer day on the lawn in the side yard. (Mount Tabor Historical Society.)

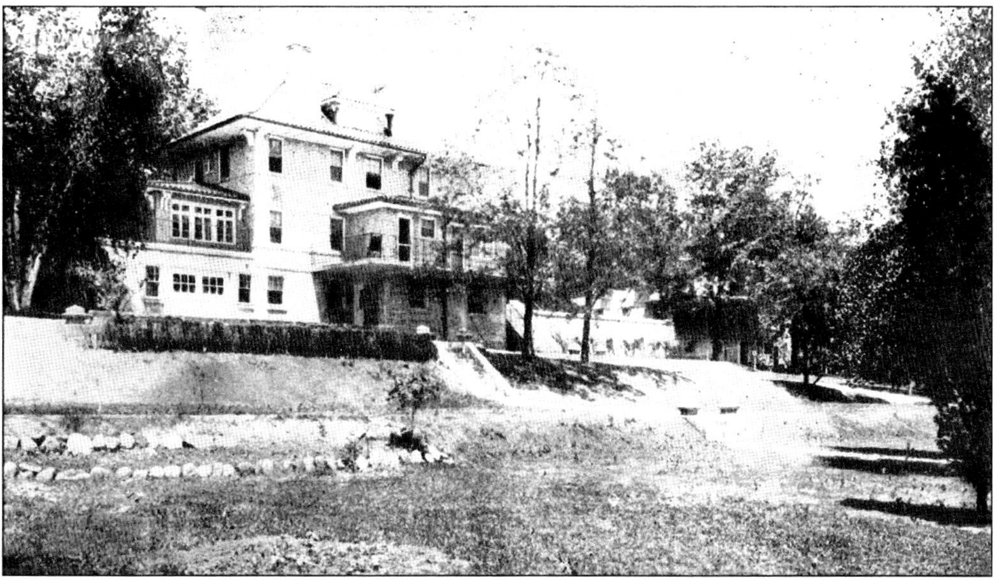

Although the postcard places this magnificent residence on Ridgewood Avenue, it did then and still does face St. Johns Avenue. The elaborate rear view with graceful steps to the rolling lawn and terraced gardens spilled onto Ridgewood Avenue and overlooked the wooded hills and green valleys beyond. It is no wonder that one would mistake the rear for the front. In the 1990s, a new house was built on a part of the property facing Ridgewood Avenue. (Mount Tabor Historical Society.)

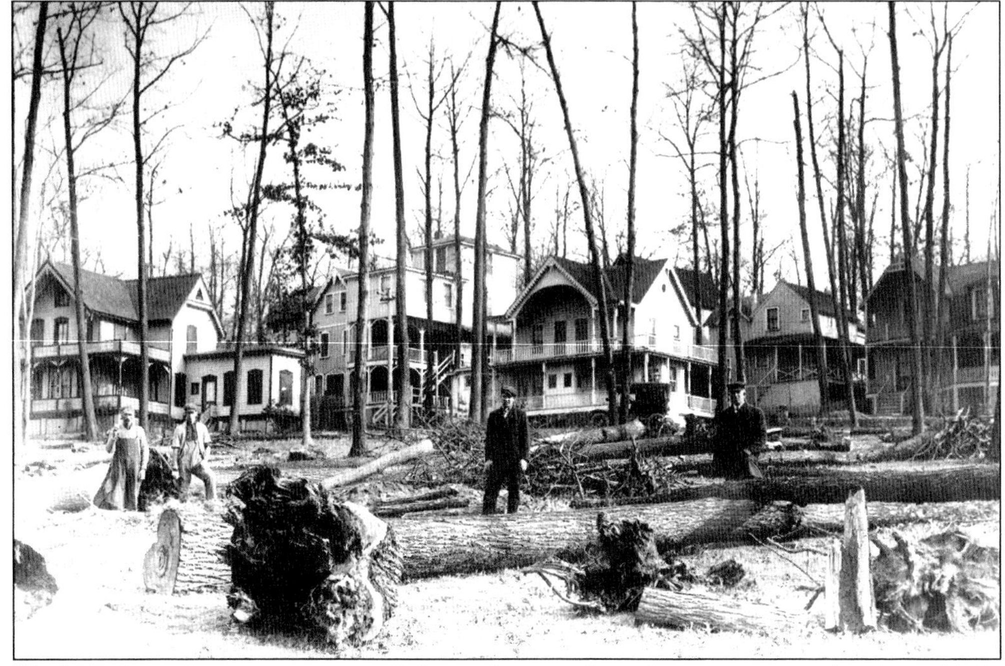

The branching chestnut trees provided a cool respite from the summer sun. An Asian blight in the late 19th century quickly spread to the American chestnut, and by 1950, it was all but extinct. In 1917, 1,200 trees in Mount Tabor were killed by the blight. The devastation is evident in this photograph from around 1920, showing workers felling the dying trees. The trees were sold to Western Electric. (Jo Campbell.)

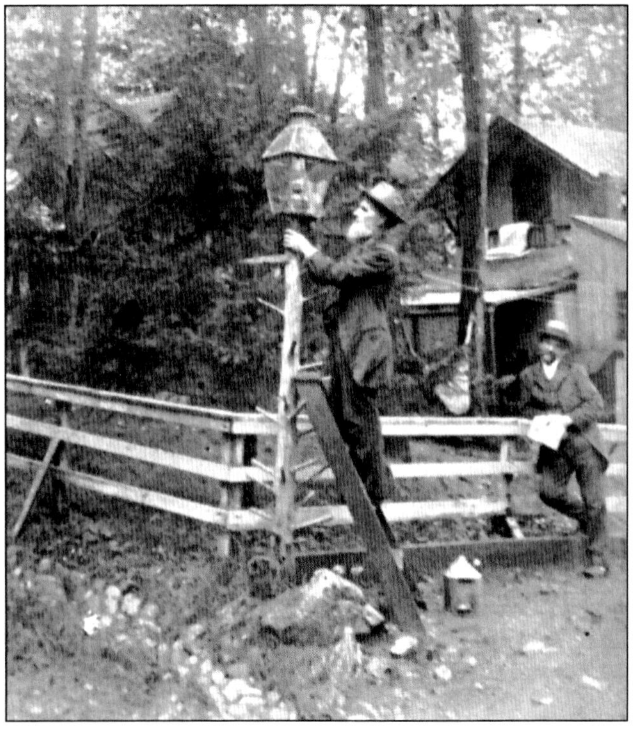

Joseph Ball of Boonton was the first recorded Mount Tabor lamplighter. He was replaced by a Mr. Aber, who also served as gatekeeper, charging a dime for buggies. Gas lighting was provided for the first camp meeting in 1869. In 1877, to economize, kerosene was substituted for gas. In 2004, with funds raised by the Camp Meeting Association and the Mount Tabor Historical Society, reproductions of the original lamps were installed in Trinity Park. (Mount Tabor Historical Society.)

Four

CHILDREN'S DAY

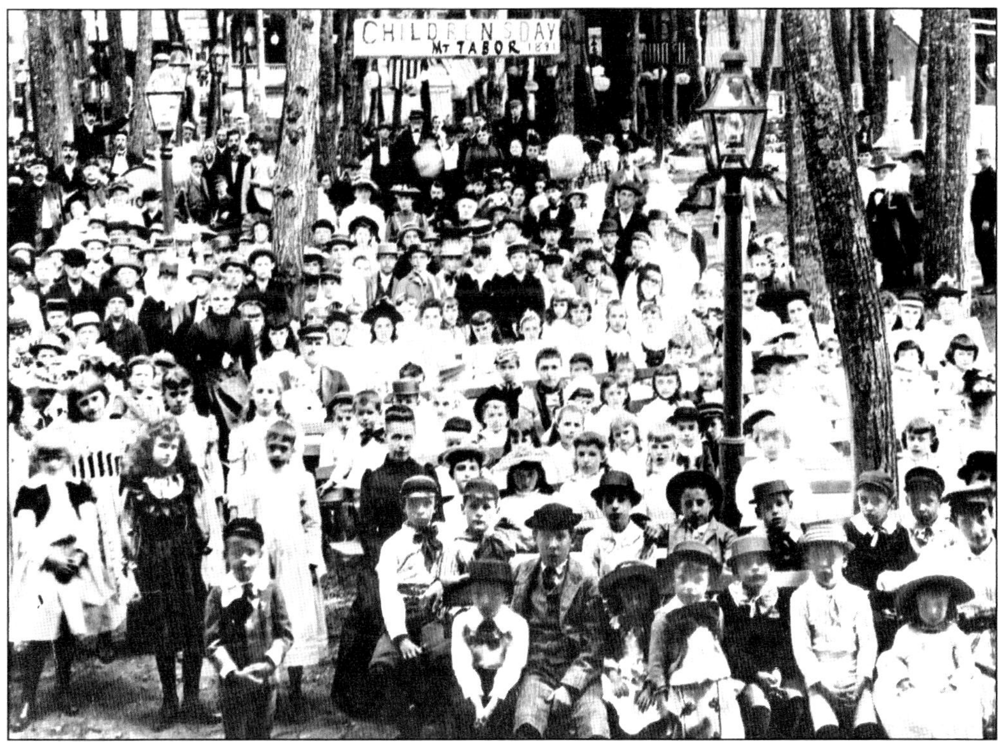

Hundreds of children dressed in their Sunday finery gather in Trinity Park for Children's Day in 1891. In *A Story of Camp Meeting*, Mary Harriott Norris describes the activities of the campers as the camp meeting draws to a close. People are packing their clothes, stacking their furniture, and saying their good-byes. When the tabernacle bell rings, the campers gather for the farewell meeting. Then they join in a line and go "marching around Jerusalem." Young and old march around the great inner circle, shaking hands with elders, ministers, and one another. "One after another they leave Camp Tabor, resolved to be more earnest in serving their Master." The children in the photograph are facing the tabernacle, perhaps waiting for their marching orders. (Mary Ellen Cheasty.)

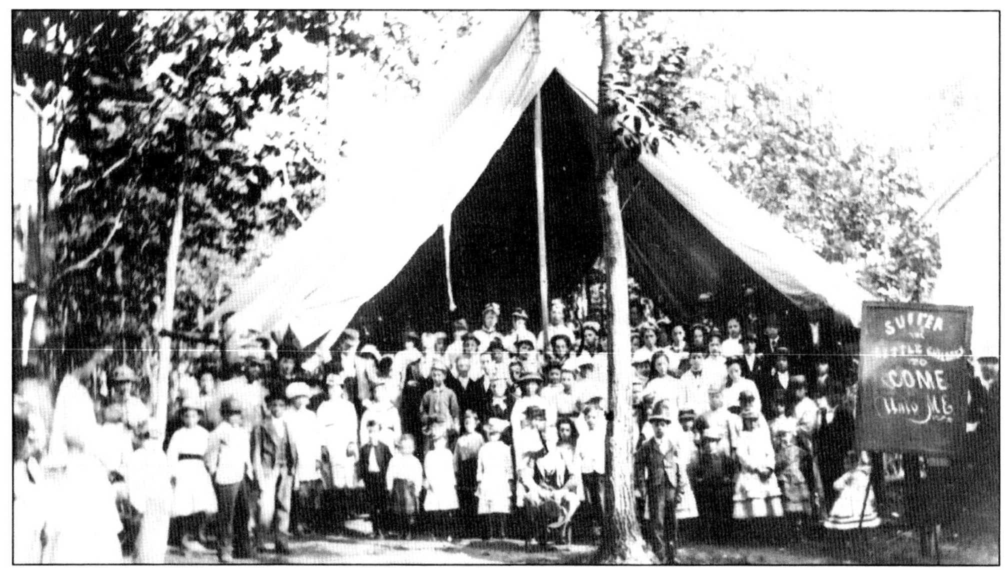

"Suffer the little children to come unto me," declares the sign in front of the children's tent on Sommerfield Avenue. Children attended special prayer meetings daily at 8:00 a.m. and 4:00 p.m. during camp meeting. The meetings combined both prayer and religious instruction. They were held in the children's tent from 1869 until 1886, when the Bethel pavilion was enclosed and renamed the Children's Temple. (Tom Nestor.)

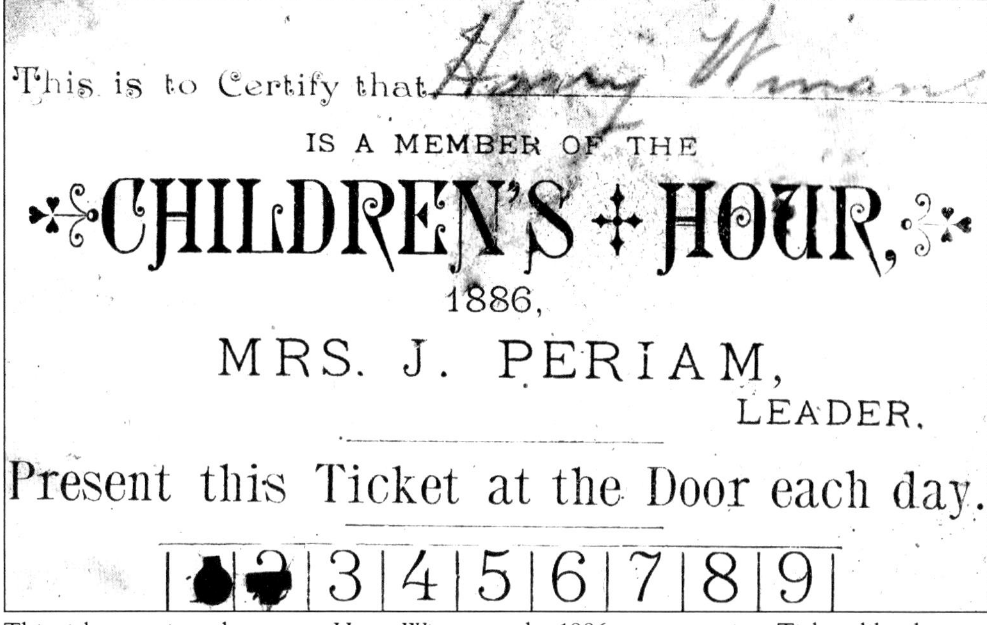

This is to Certify that _Harry Winant_

IS A MEMBER OF THE

CHILDREN'S HOUR,

1886,

MRS. J. PERIAM,

LEADER.

Present this Ticket at the Door each day.

1 2 3 4 5 6 7 8 9

This ticket was issued to young Harry Winant at the 1886 camp meeting. Tickets like this one were used to record attendance at the children's prayer meeting. A boy with a conductor's punch would stand by the door and punch the children's tickets as they arrived. Notice that Winant attended only two of the nine meetings. (Beth Shaw.)

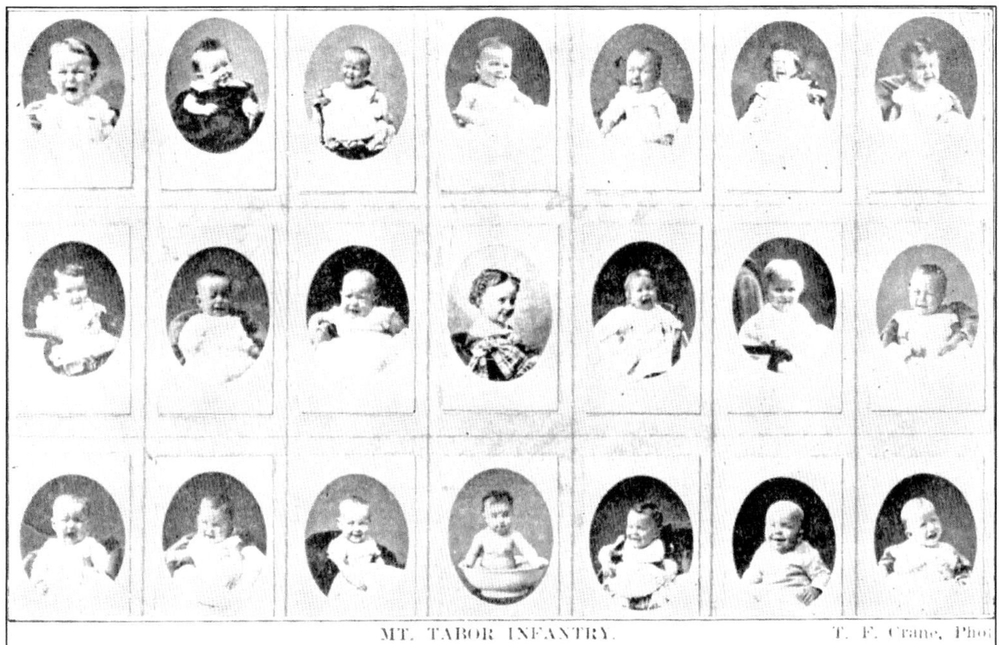

A World War I–era postcard, titled "Mount Tabor Infantry," fascinates viewers today with charming portraits of the newest generation of campers. This "infantry," no doubt, will win the hearts of all recipients, if not the war. (Mount Tabor Historical Society.)

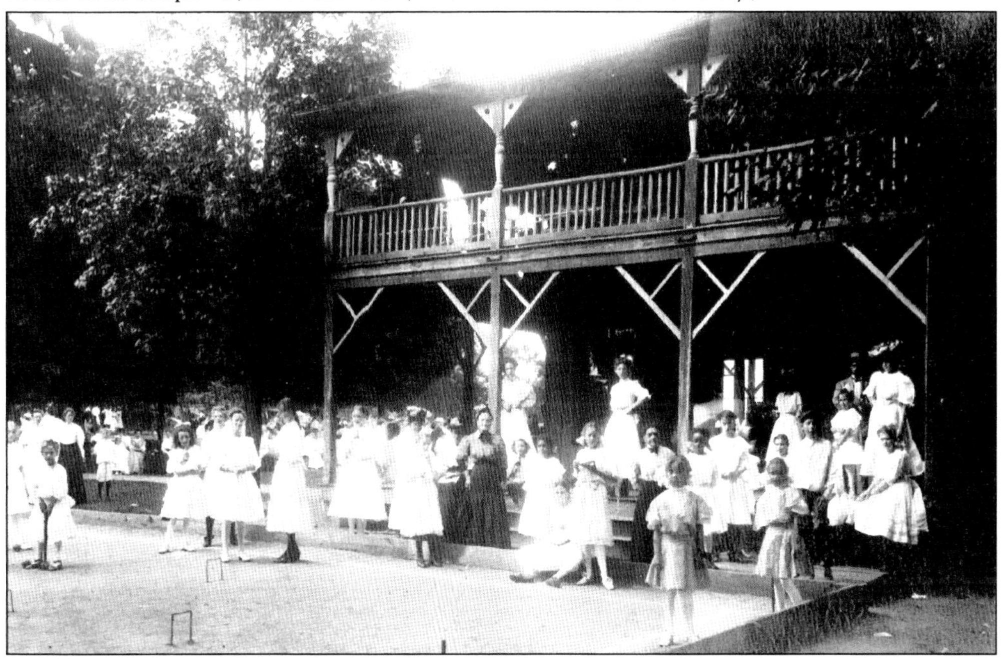

This picture is dated Children's Day, 1907. Playing a game of croquet are Margaret Lawless, Bessie Lahey, Grace Lahey, Martha Lahey, Madora Hegeman (Smethurst), Mrs. Vanderhoof, the two daughters of the caretaker Mr. Austen, Mariam Sellers, Madge Dorsy, and Mrs. Vanderhoof's twin granddaughters. The court was set up in front of the field house, and it was one of the scheduled events in a long list of activities planned for the day. (Tom Nestor.)

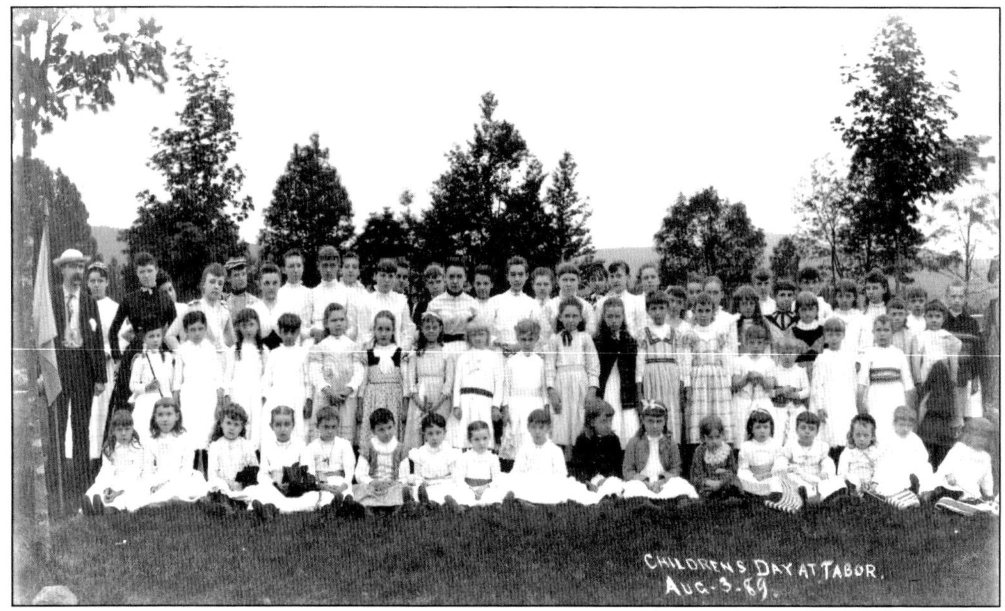

Children's Day in Mount Tabor was first celebrated in the early 1880s and was sponsored by the Mount Tabor Sunday school. It originally consisted of a parade of the Sunday school pupils through Trinity Park, followed by ice cream for all the children. The special festivities soon came to include games, singing, decorations, and a concert, along with religious instruction and the parade. By 1887, Children's Day was a three-day event, and, as such, it continues to be one of the highlights of a Mount Tabor summer. The photographs on this page are separate group portraits of boys and girls on Children's Day, August 3, 1889. It is interesting to note that the boys are all wearing hats, varying in style from caps to bowlers to broad brimmed. The girls pose for the photographer in their pretty Sunday finery. (Jo Campbell.)

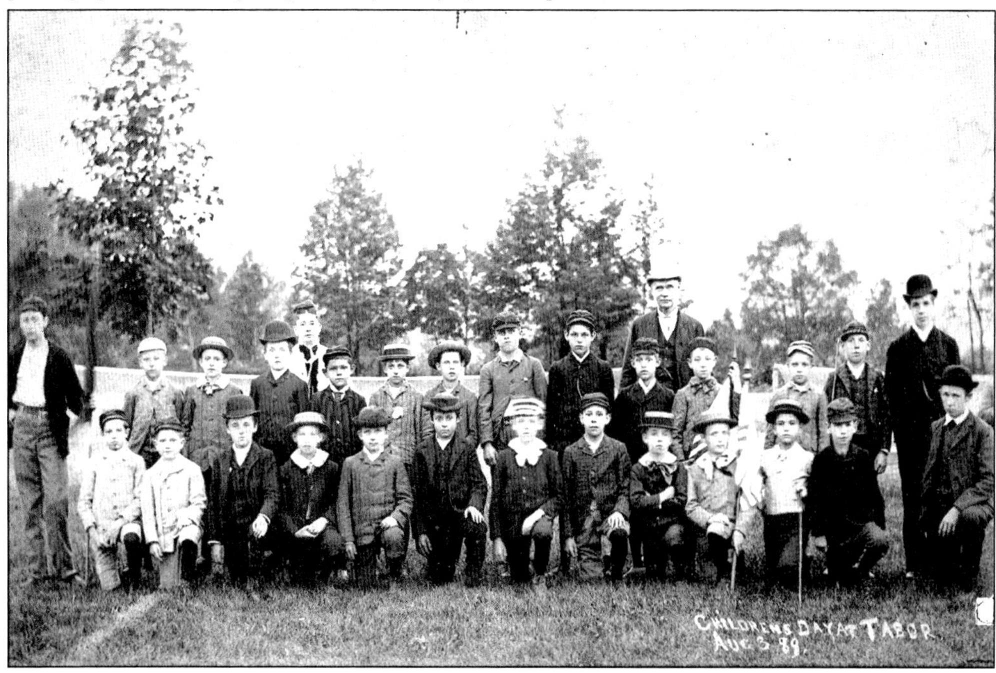

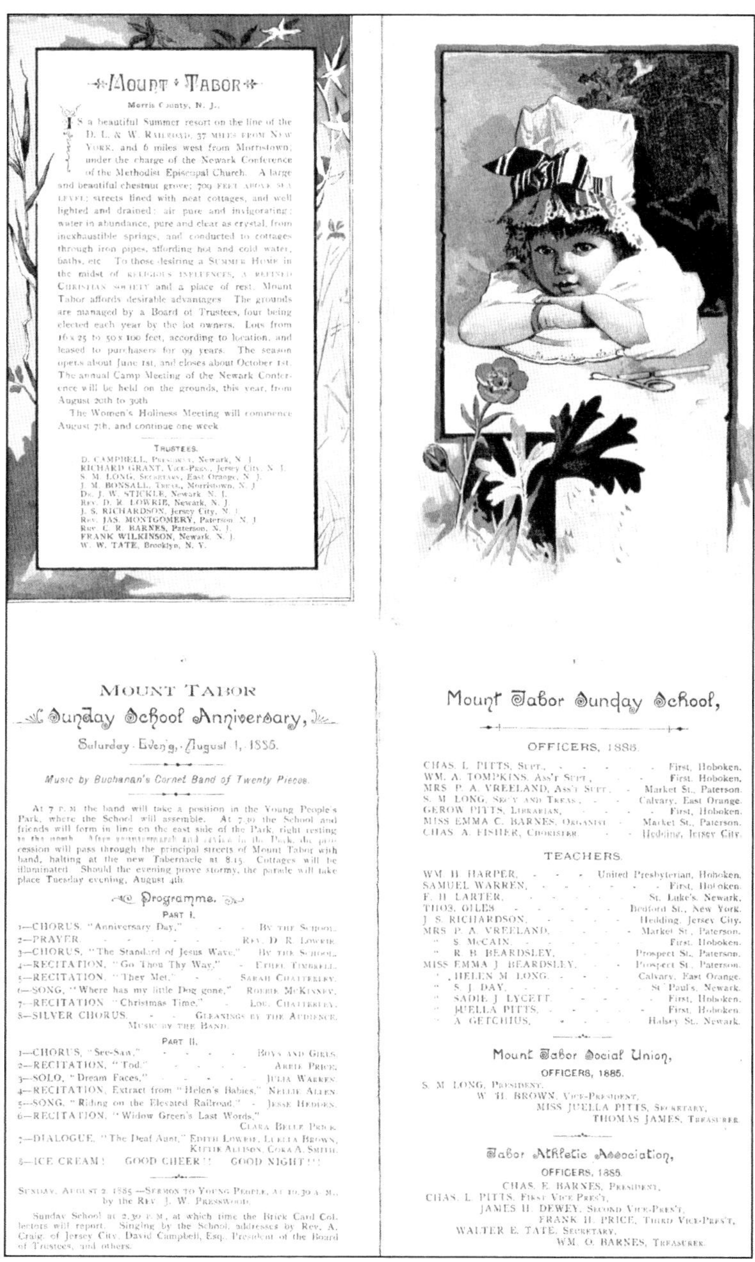

This Children's Day program titled "Sunday School Anniversary," dated August 1, 1885, lists the activities planned for the two-day event, beginning at 7:00 on Saturday evening. The band and school assembly formed a line at the Young People's Park. The procession passed through the streets with the band, halting at the new tabernacle. Cottages were illuminated. The two-part music program and recitation was followed by "Ice Cream! Good Cheer!! Good Night!!!" The next day, Sunday, a sermon was scheduled for young people at 10:30 a.m., followed by singing in the Sunday school at 2:30 p.m. Future Children's Day activities evolved into a three-day event that now encompasses a children's play, house decorations, adult and children races, other sporting events, two parades, midway food and entertainment, concerts, and ice cream, good cheer, and good nights. Sunday is still reserved for worship services. (Camp Meeting Association.)

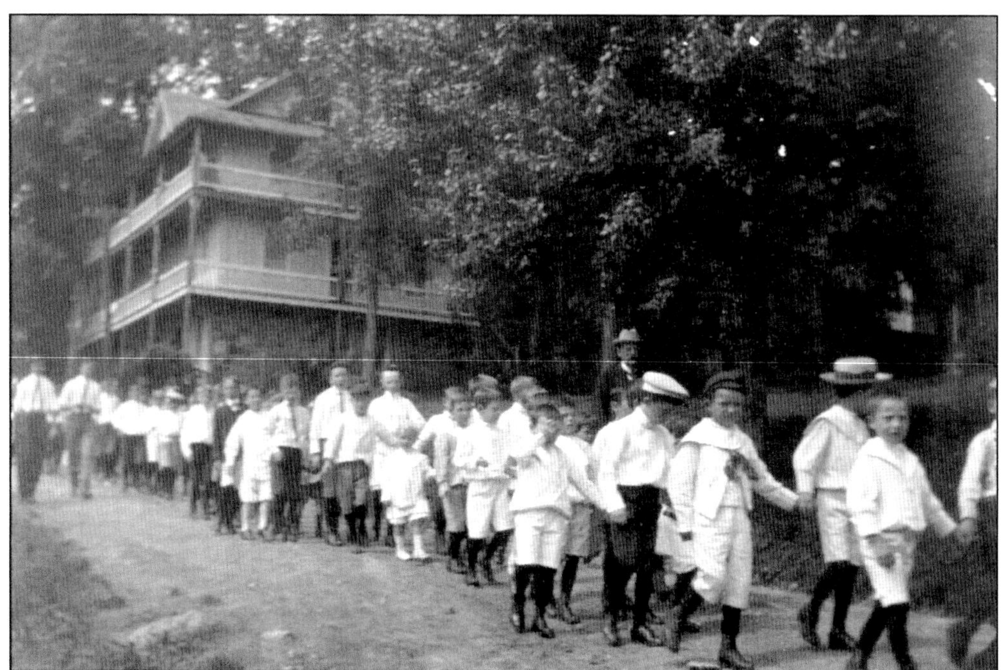

Children's Day was the name given to the one Sunday each summer set aside for a special church collection for the purpose of religious education. Special sermons and concerts were added later to make them, what one clergyman called, a "joy day" for children. The two parades of children captured in the photographs on this page are marching past the Mountain View House, located on the corner of Strowbridge Avenue and St. Johns Avenue. The parade route has not changed and continues to pass the house, a witness to over 100 years of annual celebrations. Although the children have changed, the excitement of participating in the festivities has not, preserving "joy day" for future generations to march past Mountain View House. (Ron Dickerson.)

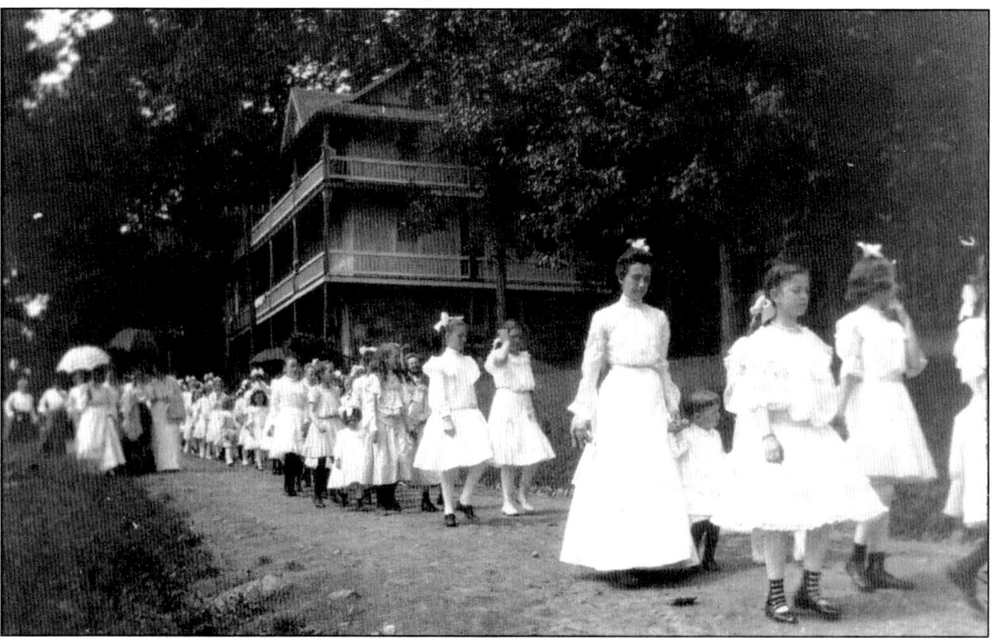

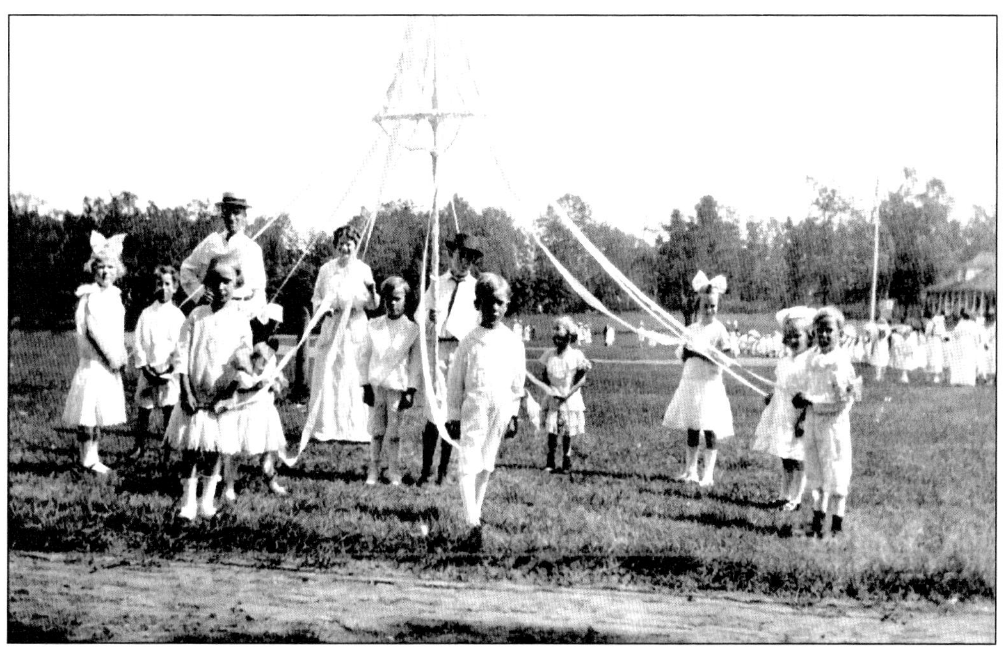

With Germanic roots, the maypole in America became a symbol of the celebration of youthfulness, community, and the beginning of summer. The long pole, festooned with flowers and streaming ribbons suspended from the top, was a favorite among children, who danced around the pole weaving the ribbons. The children dancing around the maypole in the 1911 photograph above are celebrating Children's Day with all the high spirits of youth and community in the fullness of a delightful summer day. The tents in the c. 1900 photograph below are gaily decorated with Chinese lanterns, a tradition that many Mount Tabor homeowners continue today. (Tom Nestor.)

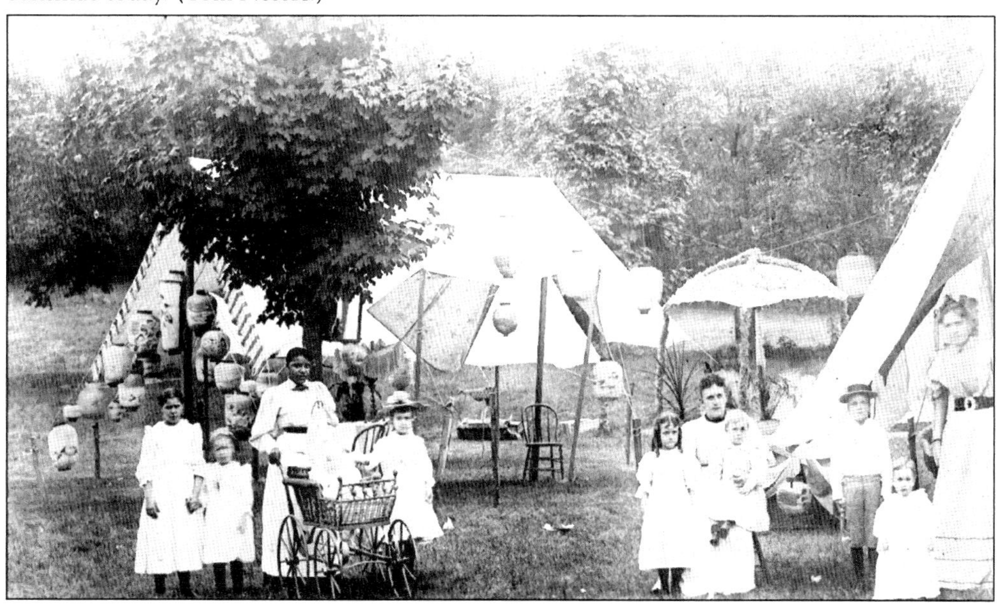

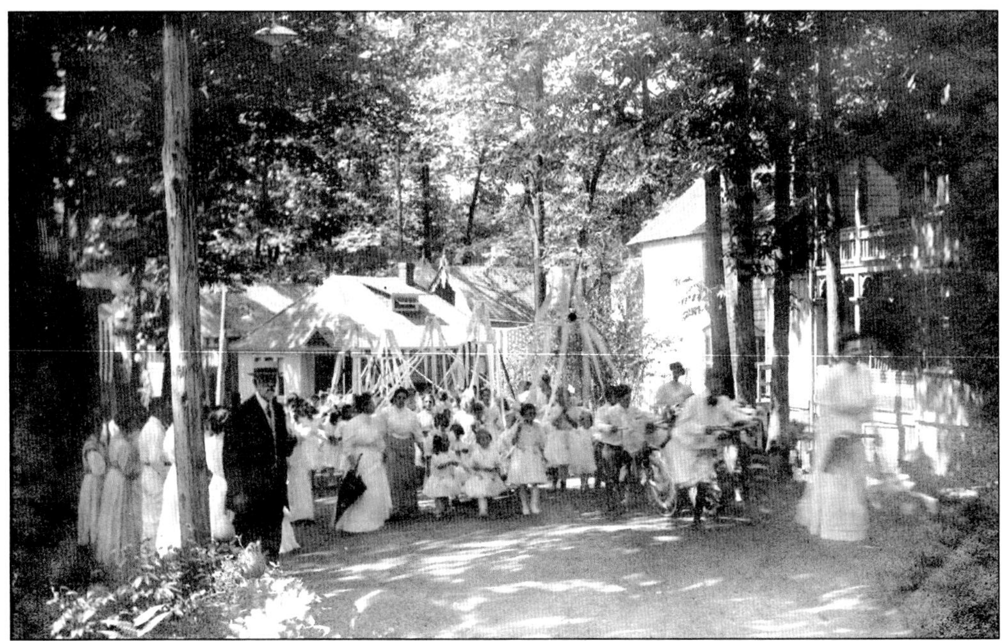

A lively group of spectators cheers on the Children's Day parade participants as the procession passes through a sun-speckled Mount Tabor street in this delightful 1906 photograph, a scene happily repeated every August to the present day. (Ron Dickerson.)

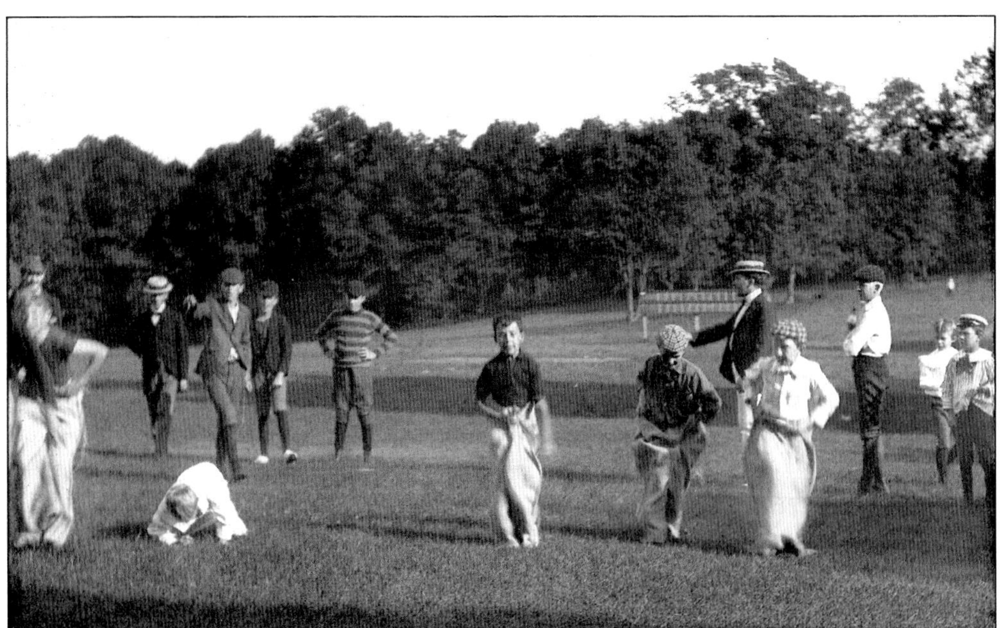

A favorite Children's Day event, the sack race shown in this early photograph provides a sweeping view of the golf course fairgrounds and the lush woods beyond. The sack race was part of the earliest Children's Day celebrations. (Mount Tabor Historical Society.)

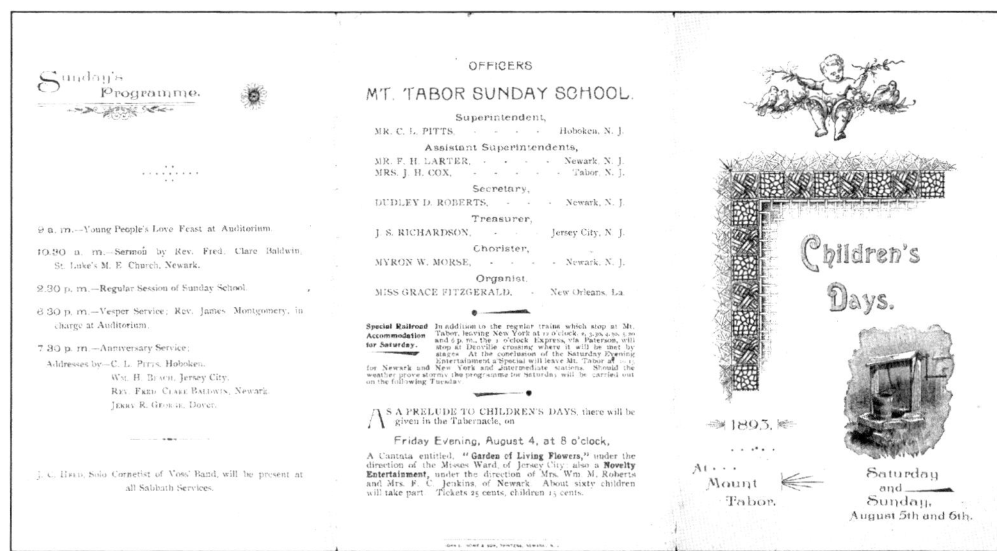

This is a copy of the Children's Day program from August 4–6, 1893. The celebration is always scheduled for the first full weekend of the month. To start this weekend off, on Friday evening at eight o'clock a cantata titled "Garden of Living Flowers" was presented. Sixty children took part in the program. Tickets were 25¢ for adults and 15¢ for children. Saturday morning started with a tennis tournament at 9:00. The afternoon brought music, a children's carousel, and balloon "ascensions," followed by various field games, including a sack race, three-legged race, ball throwing, and a bicycle race. The evening brought more music and a parade, and at 8:00 p.m. was a promenade concert in Trinity Park featuring Voss' Band from Newark. Sunday offered several religious services during the day. (Evelyn Clark.)

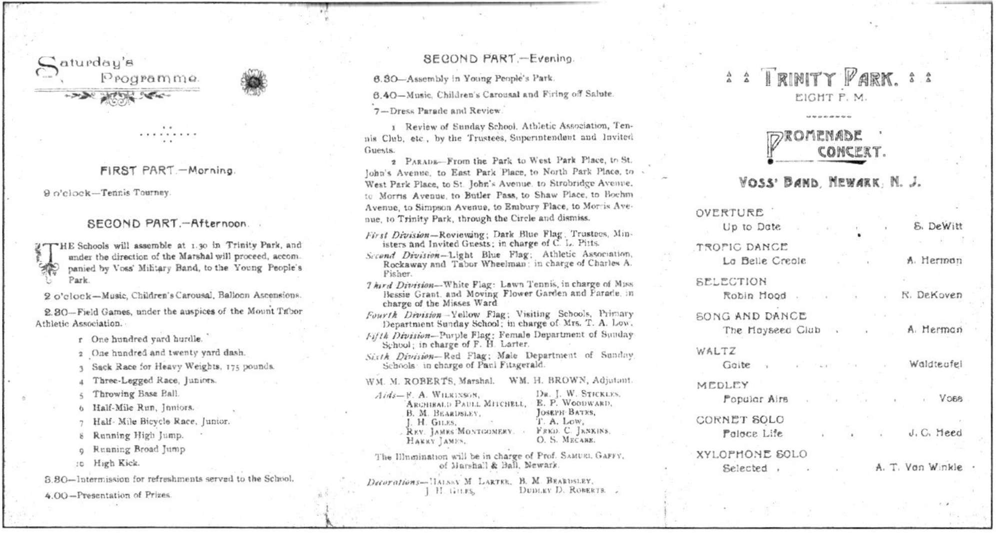

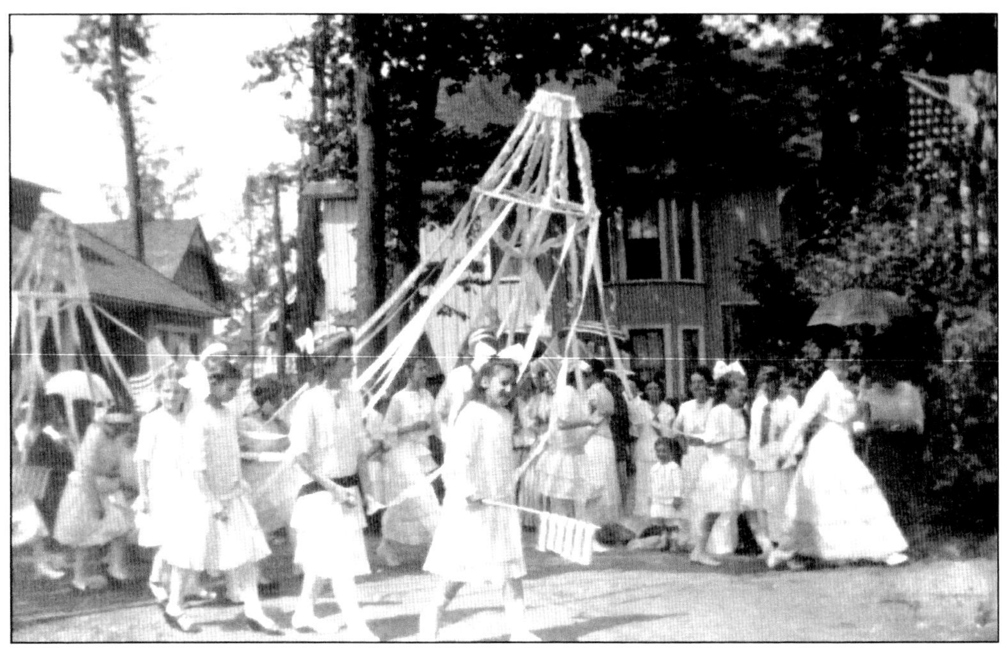

Children's Day as it is known today evolved by 1887 into a three-day celebration that included religious services, the dedication of a new playground, and a grand parade illuminated by torches and silk lanterns, with music courtesy of the Dover brass band. "It was a sight never to be forgotten, the long procession of gaily dressed children, with martial music adding life to the scene," noted the *Mount Tabor Record*, a chronicle of camp-meeting life. The two photographs on this page capture the pageantry of the event. The gaily dressed girls in the 1915 photograph above make a lovely procession. One can almost hear the brass band as it winds its way along the parade route. The photograph below, taken in 1913, includes a pony-pulled cart with young passengers, perhaps a forerunner of the elaborate floats constructed by residents today. (Tom Nestor.)

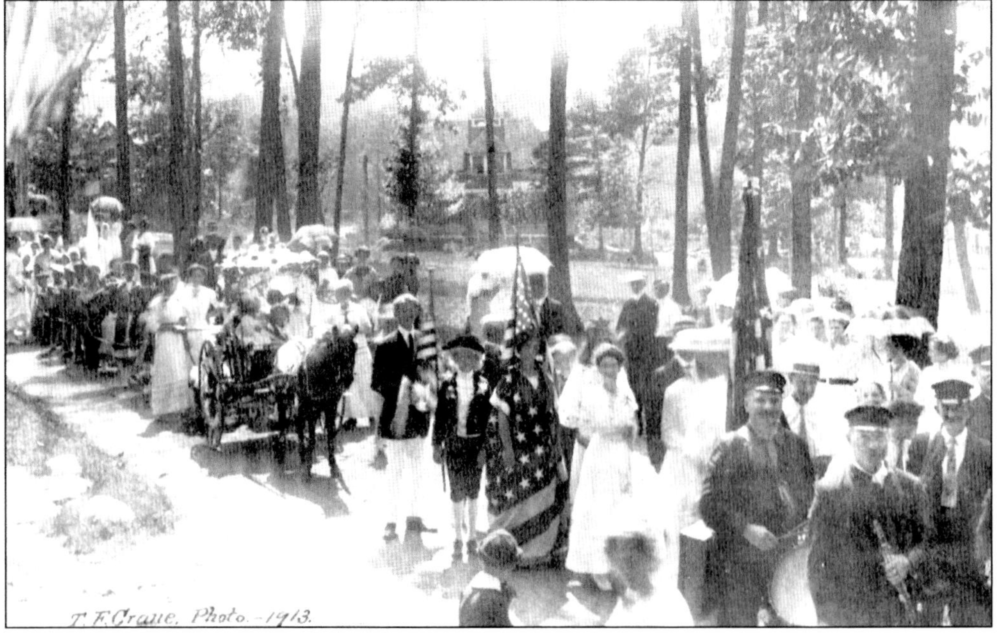

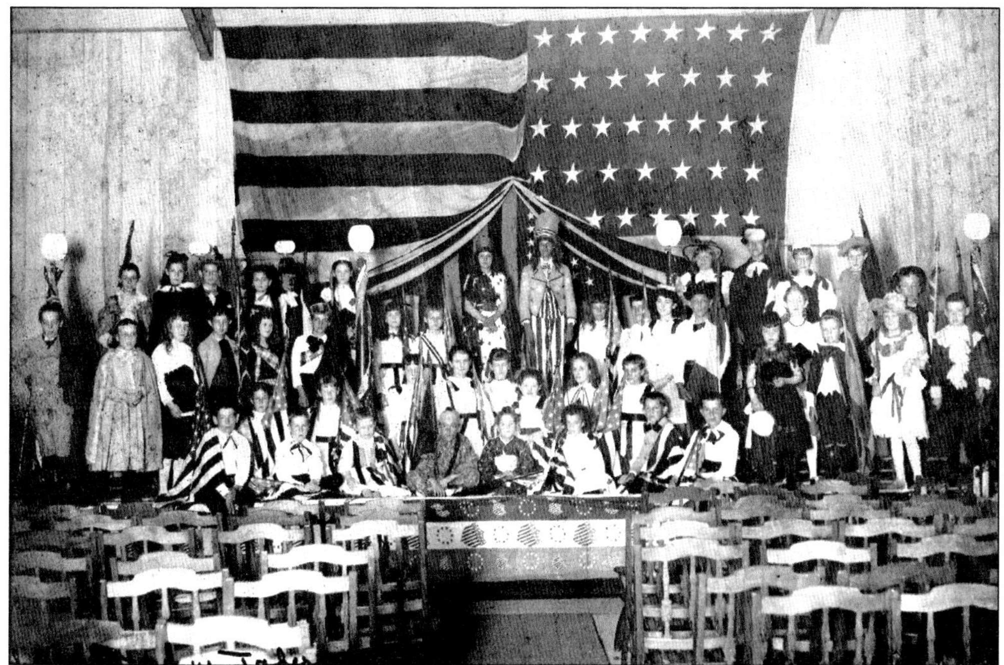

These children are preparing a show in the tabernacle for Children's Day weekend. The patriotic theme is evident, although the flag is hung backward. It must be a dress rehearsal, because there is no audience. The Children's Day play is always a standing-room-only event and the start of the three-day festivities. (Jo Campbell.)

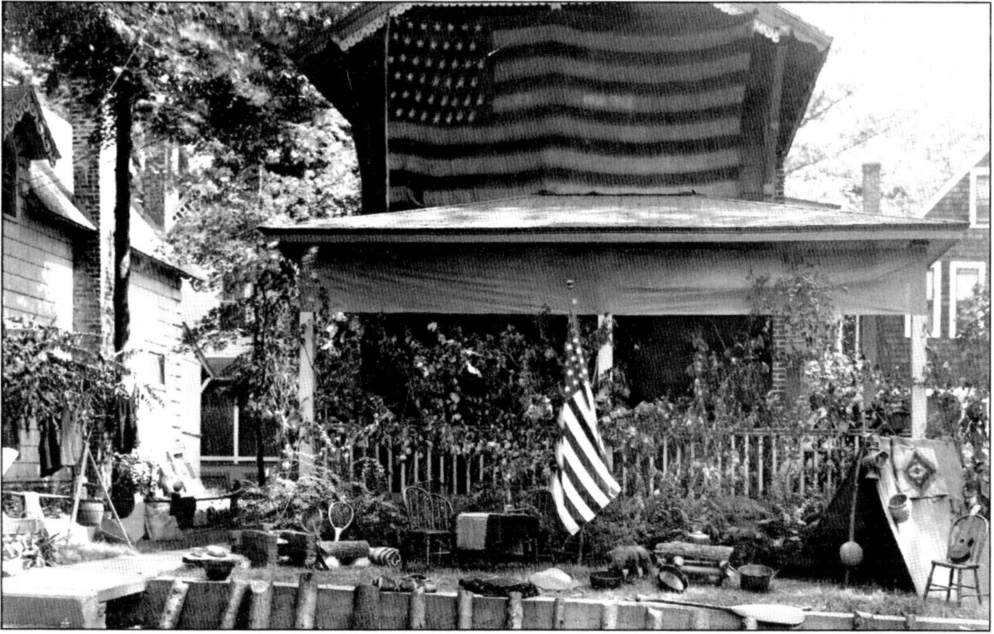

This house at 40 Sommerfield Avenue was decorated by the Girl Scouts on August 4, 1934, for Children's Day. It was a prize-winning display showing memories of past camp meetings. It shows a pitched tent, outdoor cooking pots and pans, flags, firewood, old trunks, and a tennis racquet and a canoe oar to highlight the importance of sports. (Mount Tabor Historical Society.)

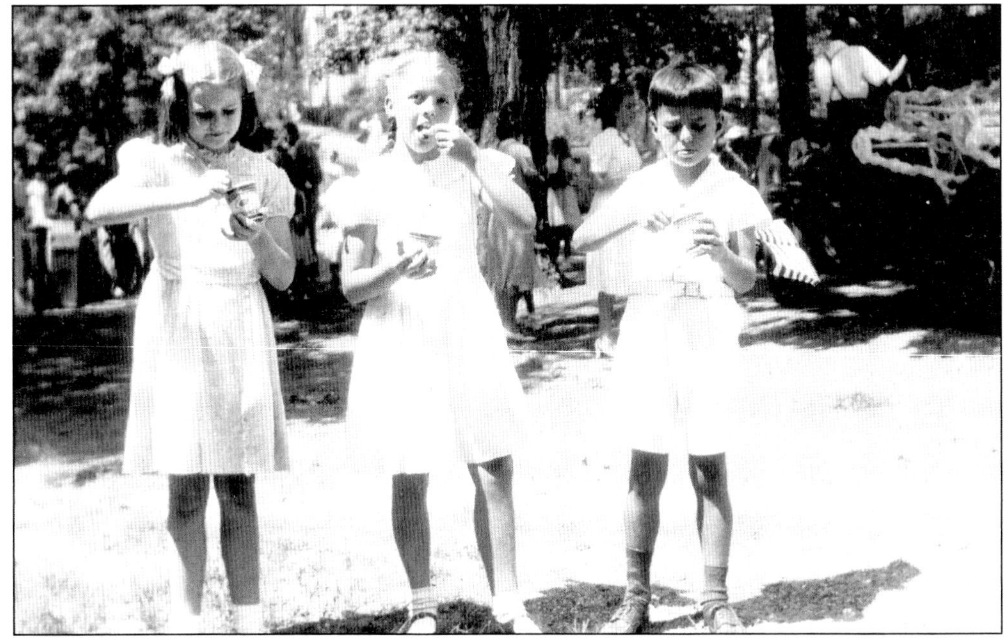

Traditionally on the last day of Sunday school the children would march around Trinity Park. When they had completed the circuit, they were treated to ice cream. Pictured here from left to right in 1940 are Ann Britten Wilson, Vallie Picking, and Bobby Roberts enjoying their well-deserved treat. Today each child who participates in the parade receives a ticket that can be redeemed for a free ice cream at the midway. (Ann Britten Wilson.)

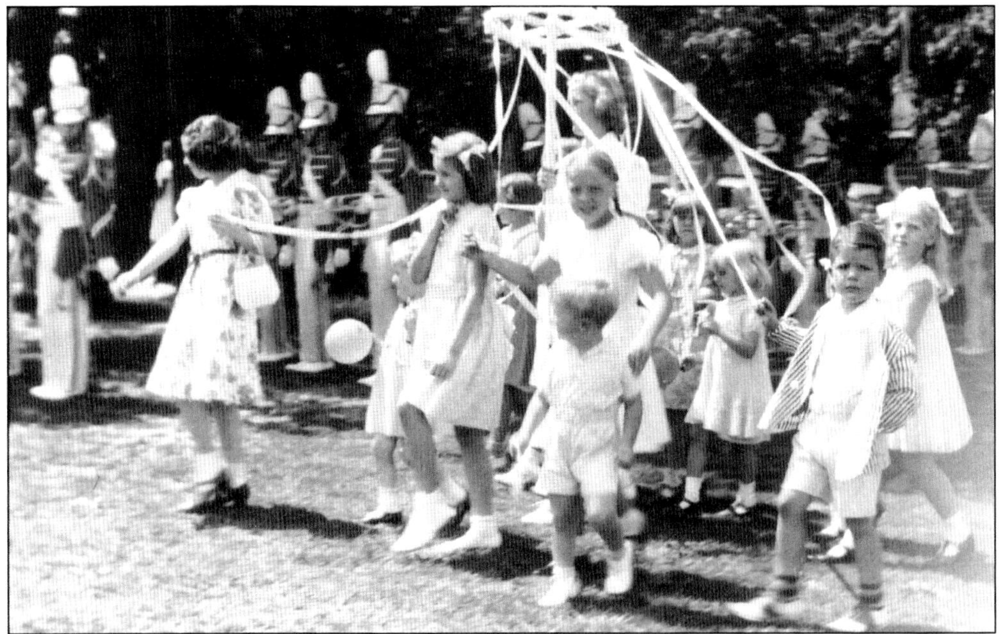

Louis R. Menagh Sr. recollected in his memoirs that James Darby, a Civil War veteran and uncle of Maude Britten of Morris Avenue, "originated" the maypoles used by the children in the Children's Day parade. In the 1940 photograph above, Ann Wilson is in front of the maypole, and Vallie Picking is next to her, looking at the camera. (Ann Britten Wilson.)

CHILDREN AT SCHOOL AND PLAY

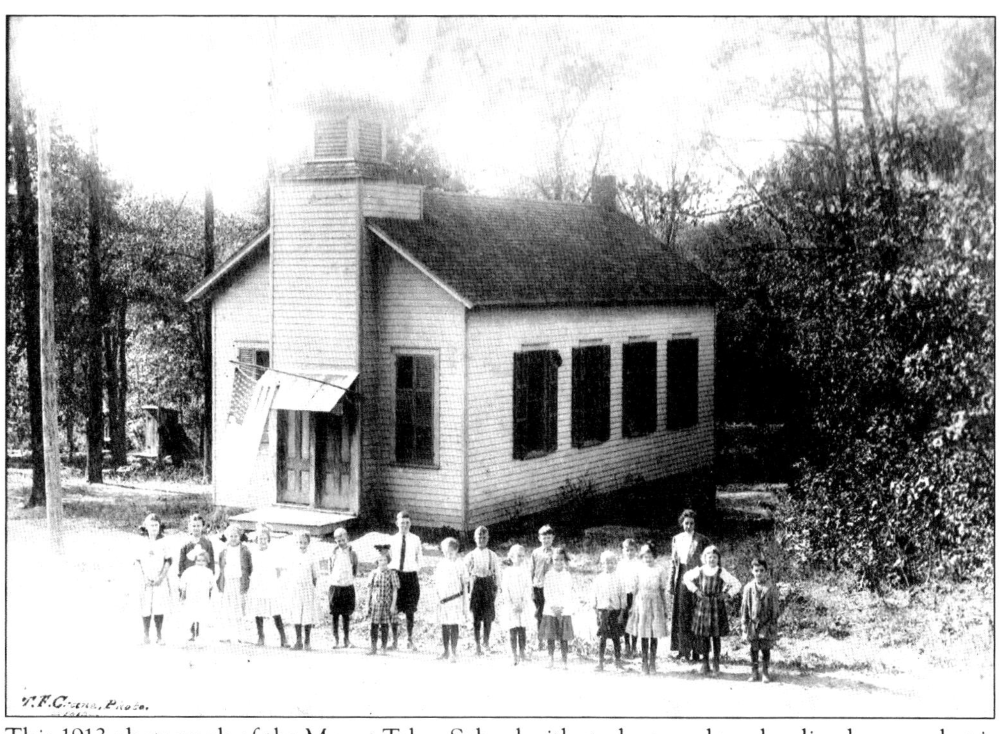

This 1913 photograph of the Mount Tabor School with students and teacher lined up on what is now Route 53 provides a splendid view of the rural surroundings opposite the campgrounds at the time. The little girl in the plaid jumper with arms akimbo may have been expressing her impatience with the photographer. The one-room building served as a schoolhouse for the community for many generations and continues to stand today, now serving as a chapel. The wooden outhouse to the left of the building made for a long walk on a cold day. (Ron Dickerson.)

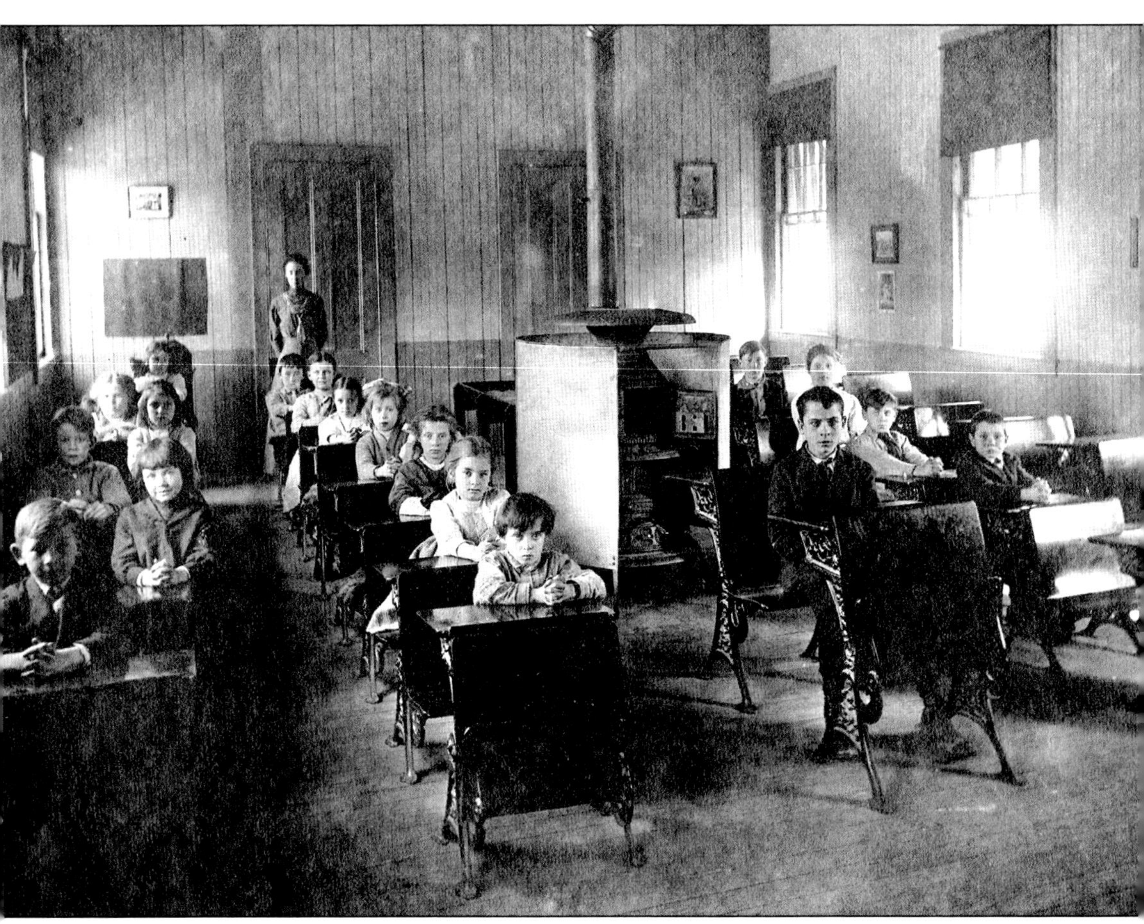

In the early 1900s, a small one-room schoolhouse was built on Route 53 to replace Mount Tabor's first school. This 1914 photograph provides a wonderful interior view of the classroom. The stove that dominates the classroom provided much-needed heat. Lucky were the children who were assigned desks close to the stove. The sunlight streaming through the windows highlights the lovely detailing on the cast-iron sides of the desks, called "knee knockers." William T. Leighton served as a longtime teacher in Mount Tabor. He also served as a clerk and was a member of the board of education in Hanover and Parsippany–Troy Hills Townships. (Ron Dickerson.)

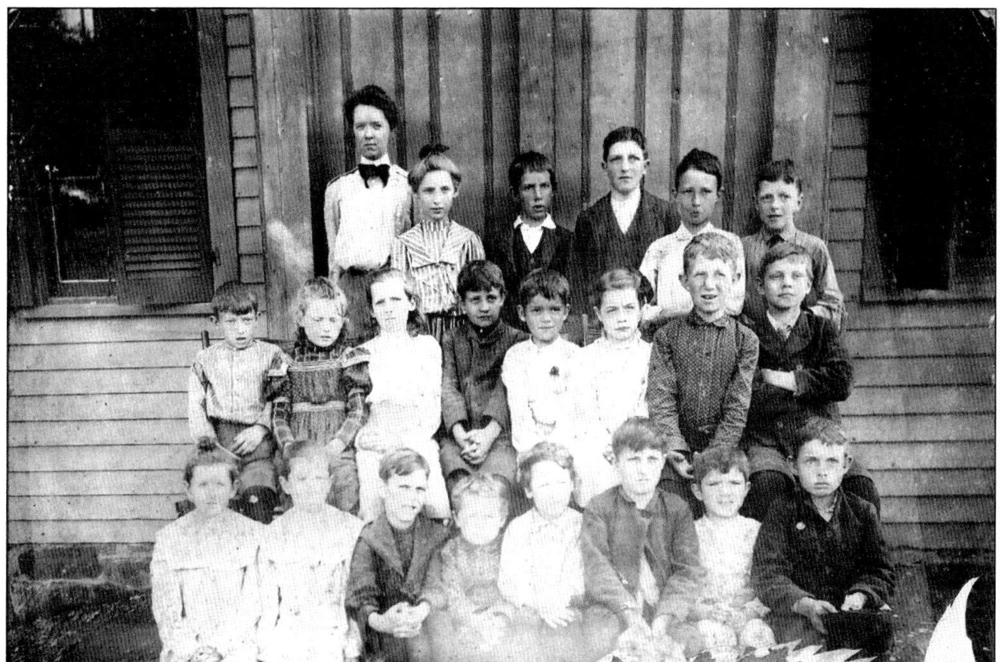

A young teacher poses with her students on the front steps of the old Mount Tabor School. Teaching children of differing ages in the same classroom must have presented its own set of challenges. The young fellow on the right side of the second row, with folded arms, boldly faces the camera. (Mount Tabor Historical Society.)

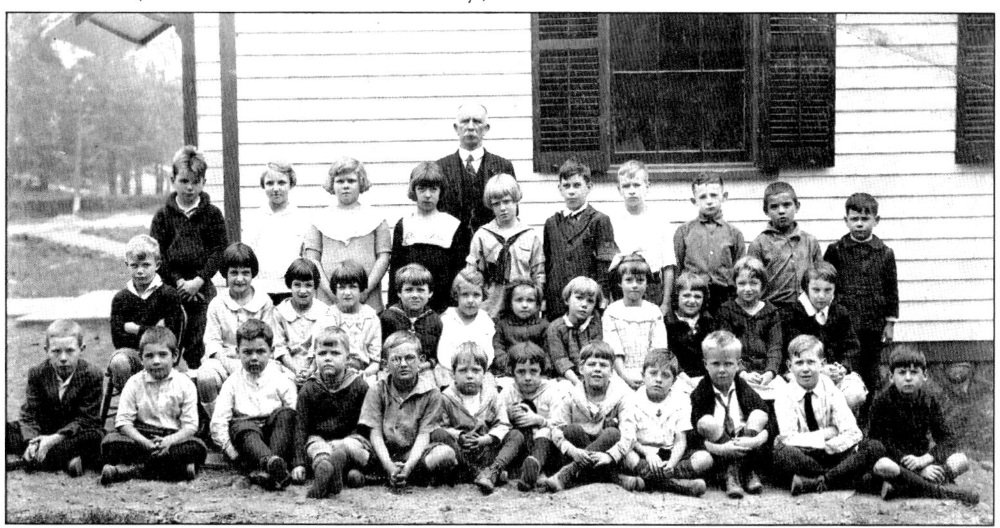

Leighton stands behind his class at the old Mount Tabor School around 1926. Pictured from left to right are (first row) unidentified, Andrew Van Heusen, Thomas Mitchell, ? Stephenson, Harry W. Goble, Loy Harmon, Walter Ehrenberg, Charles Harmon, Francis Hoover, unidentified, Arthur McCurdy, and James Thomas; (second row) unidentified, Grace Bonnaviat, two unidentified students, Adele Glysencamp, Beverly Vanderhoff, Nora Tonking, Dorothy Heavey, Ruth Ehrenberg, unidentified, Annabelle Lynch, and Dorothy Hickerson; (third row) William Kuhmichel, Ruth Eichorn, unidentified, Alice Payne, Thelma Gould, Frank McCurdy, unidentified, Herbert Simonson, Luther Van Heusen, and Richard McCurdy. (Reda Moore.)

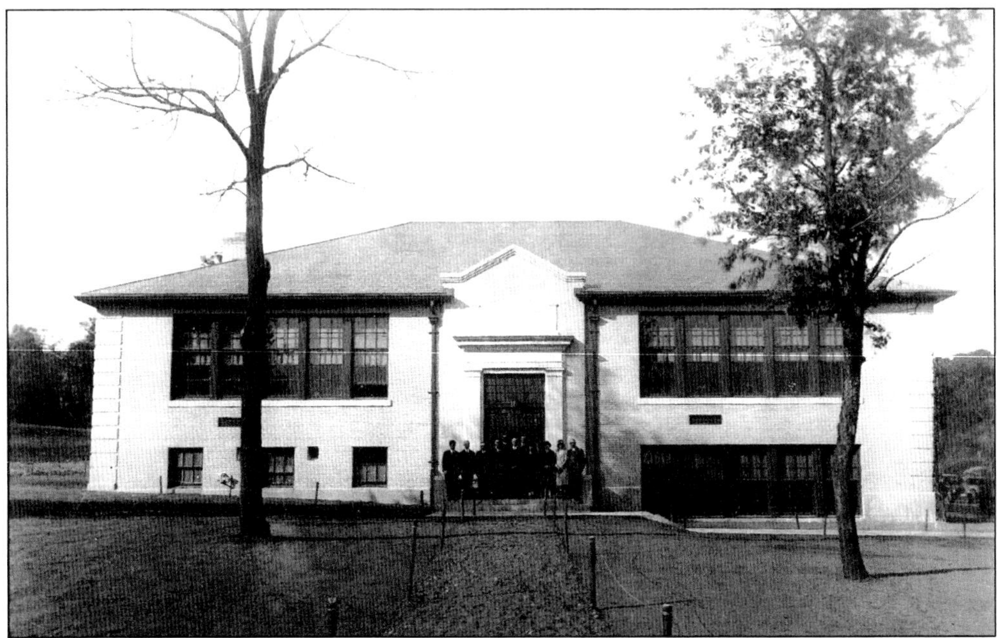

The Mount Tabor one-room school became overcrowded as more families took up permanent residence, and for a time, students moved into the Morris Plains School from the sixth to the eighth grades. In response to the continued growth of the school-age population, this four-room brick building on Park Road was erected in 1932. The photograph below shows township school officials as they attended the opening day of the new school. Pictured from left to right are (first row) contractor Patsy Bucco, county school superintendent Walter B. Davis, supervising principal George Clark, board of education member Dudley B. Kimball, district clerk William T. Leighton, board member Mrs. Herbert D. Tunis, and teachers Gladys McCartney, F. Fern Scheer, and Charles Williamson; (second row) board members LeRoy Wilson and William O. Farrand. (Mount Tabor School.)

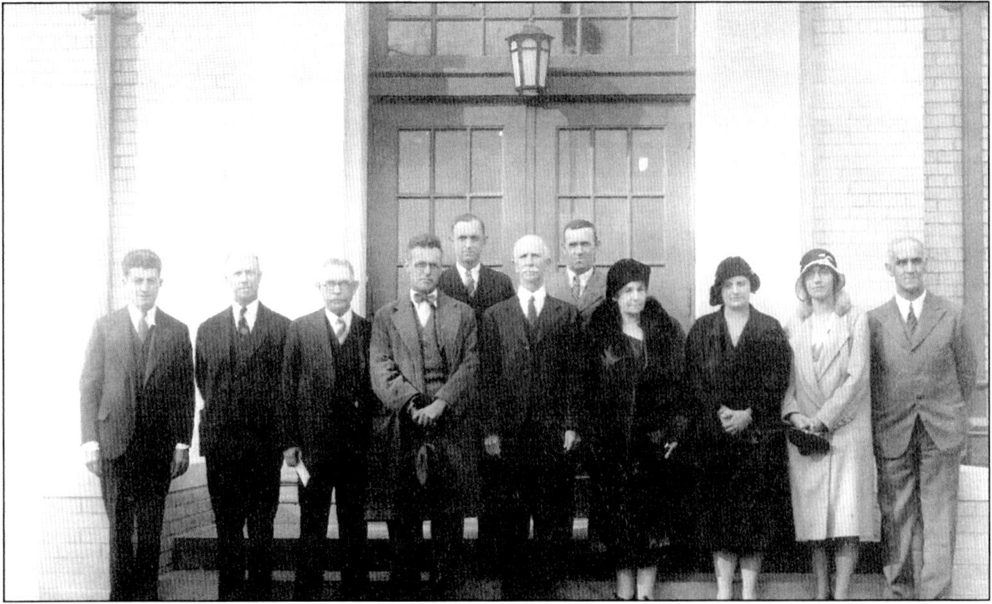

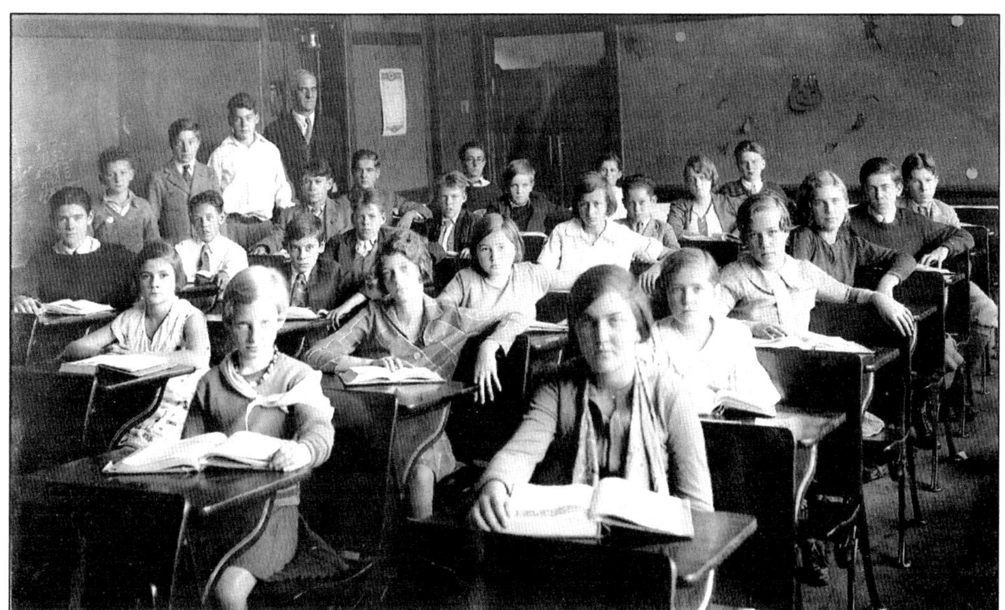

The photograph above is of the Mount Tabor School sixth-, seventh-, and eighth-grade classes in November 1930. Pictured from front to back are (first row) Mary Benbrook, Leonora Tonking Harrison, Dorothy Heavey Luscheur, Edith Stephen, Albert Eisel, and John Bardit; (second row) Frances Kuhmichel Quackenbush, Doris Conover, Eleanor Glysencamp, Reda Lynch Moore, James Bonnaviat, unidentified, and Cornelius Beers; (third row) Regina Allman, Edward Eisel, Fred Harman, Loy Harman, Richard Stephen, and Harry Allman; (fourth row) Luther Van Huesen, Woodrow Eisel, Richard McCurdy, Clarence Theil, and Norman Heller. Standing are Herbert Simonson, Clarence Hoover, Thomas Mitchell, and Charles Williamson (principal and teacher). Annabel Parson's 1950 fifth-grade class is shown below. When the Mount Tabor School was first constructed, most of the ground floor was an auditorium. In 1954, the space was converted into additional classrooms and a library to accommodate the increased enrollment. (Above, Kevin Simonson; below, Mount Tabor School.)

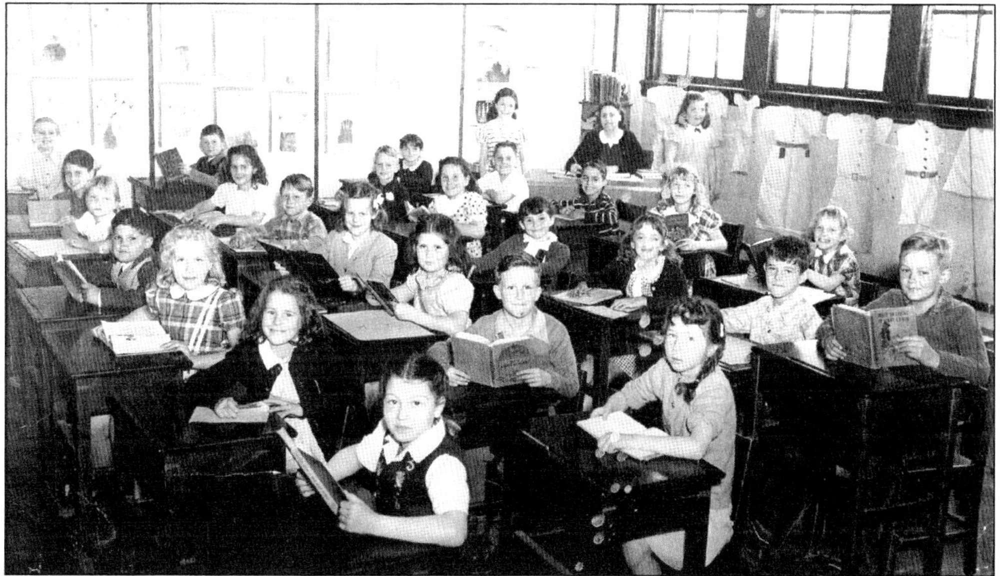

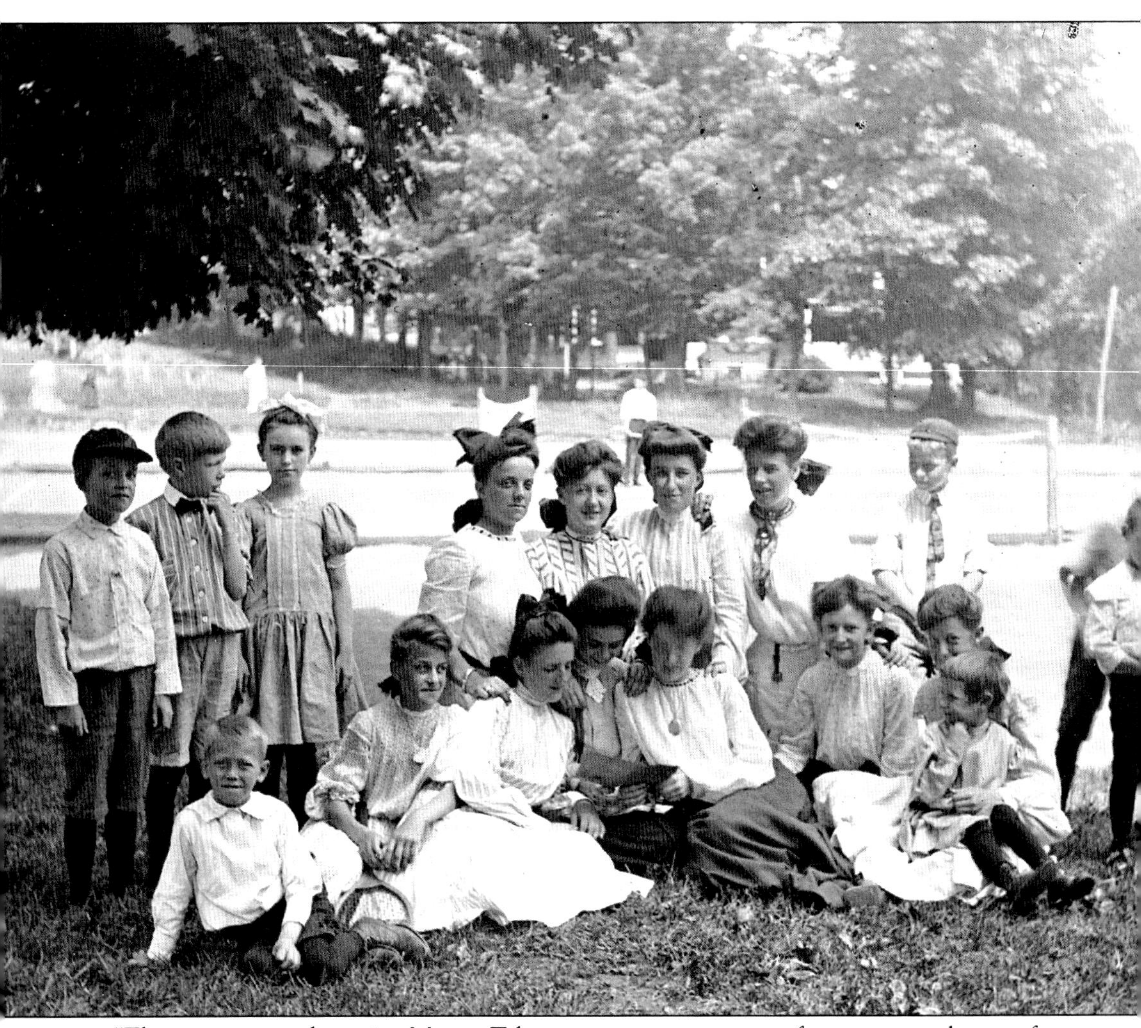

"There are none who enjoy Mount Tabor to a greater extent or form a more pleasant feature than the children who daily revel among the trees," stated the *Mount Tabor Record* on August 24, 1877. The young people pictured above near the tennis courts are focused on the center trio, who are happily oblivious of the photographer. (Mount Tabor Historical Society.)

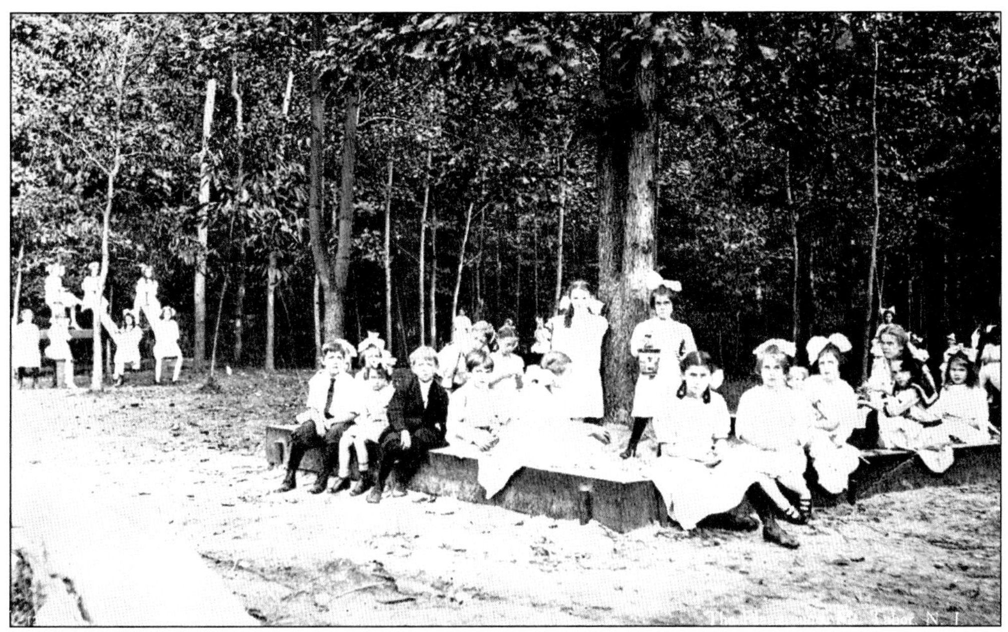

In this photograph from 1915, a group of young people relax in Pleasure Park. The park was created in the 1880s and boasted facilities for lawn tennis, croquet, archery, quoits, and other sports. The association had the park landscaped with 200 shade and ornamental trees. It was a favorite gathering place for young and old, particularly before and after camp meetings. (Mount Tabor Historical Society.)

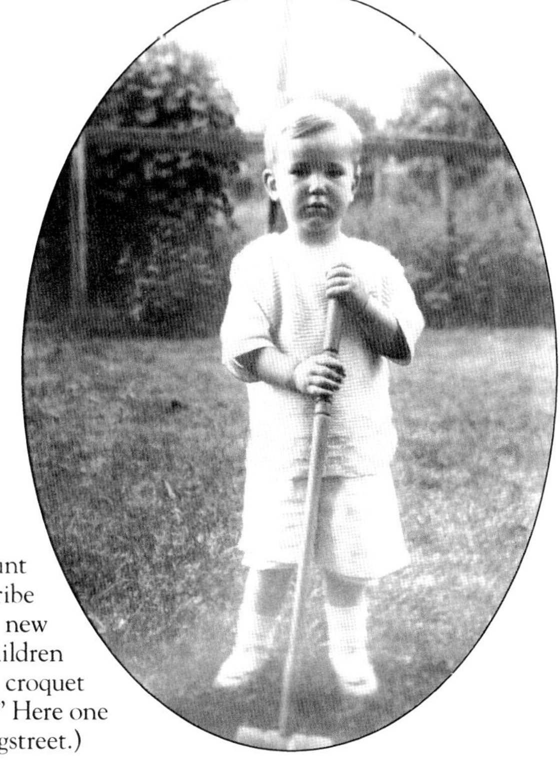

The August 20, 1887, minutes of the Mount Tabor Camp Meeting Association describe the recently opened Pleasure Park: "A new plot devoted to the use of the younger children and equipped with safe swings, sea-saw, croquet and other games suited for the little folks." Here one of the children plays croquet. (Bobbi Longstreet.)

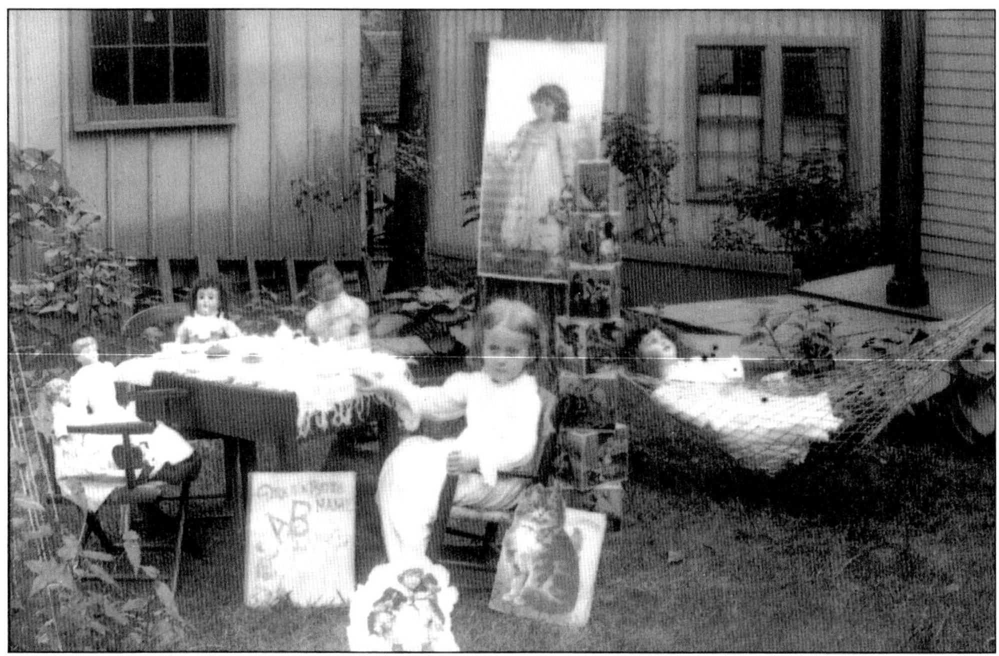

Pictured here is Edith Lydia Jones (1888–1967), having a tea party with her dolls in the backyard of a Trinity Park house. She was the granddaughter of J. Smith Richardson (1842–1911), the resident and builder of 18 Trinity Park (now 32 Trinity Park) and the treasurer of the Camp Meeting Association for 22 years. He married Lydia Ann Auton, and they had one child, Lizzie, who married James H. Jones. Edith Lydia was their only child. (Evelyn Clark.)

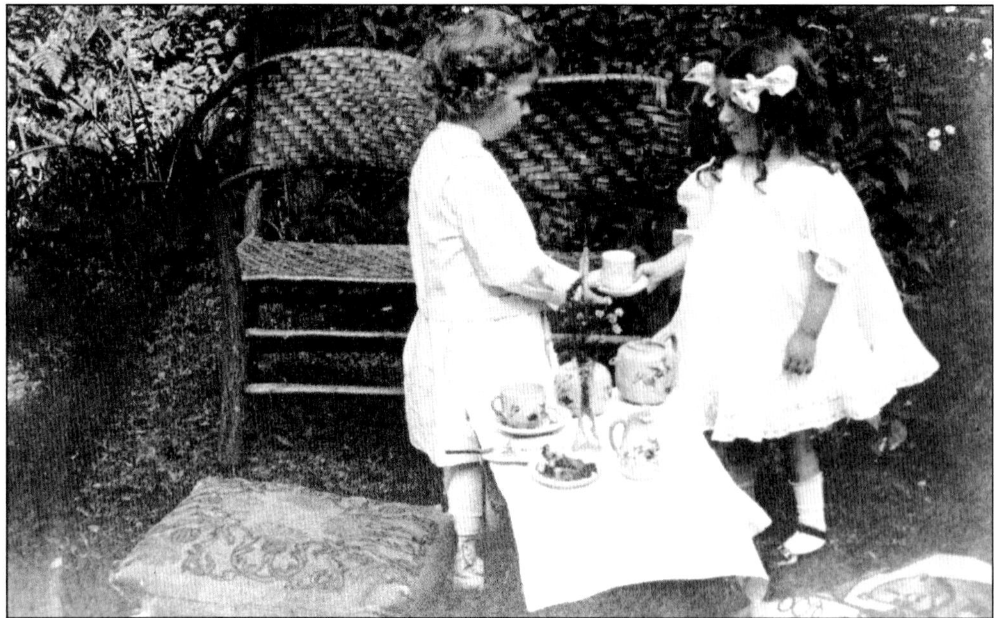

Tom and Helen Beattie enjoy a tea party on a summer afternoon in 1902 in the garden of the cottage owned by their grandparents Frank and Mary Barrett (now 6 Strowbridge Avenue). The Beatties owned a cottage on Trinity Park (35 Trinity Place). Tom and Helen's mother, Nell Barrett, and her tennis partner were the Mount Tabor mixed doubles champions in 1889. (Jeanne Apgar.)

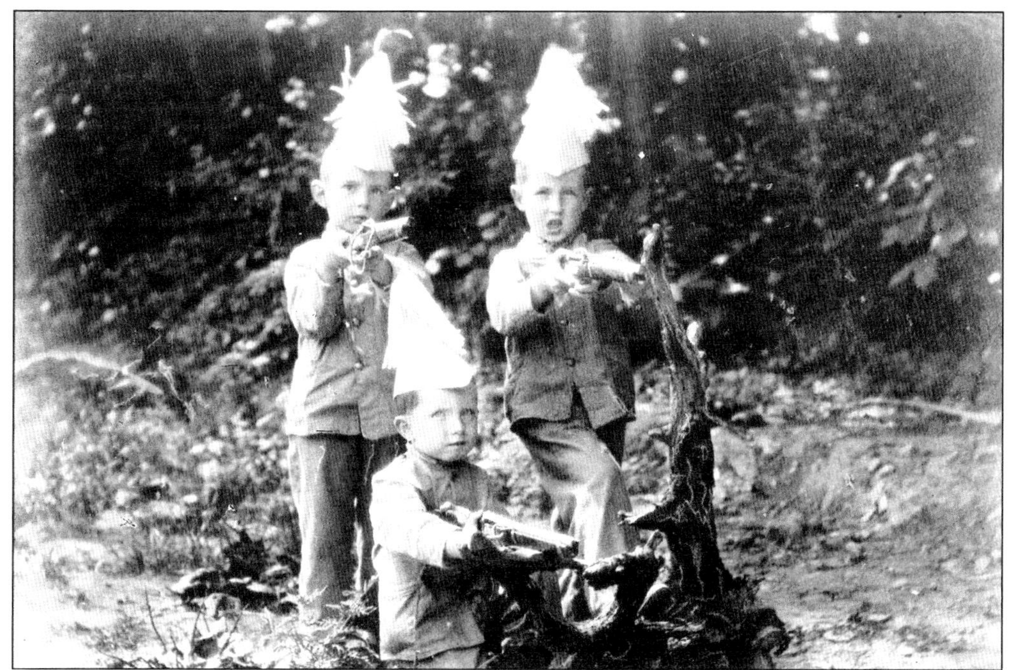

Three young soldiers at their battle stations are a contrast to the young children on the previous page and below, playing with their dolls, throwing a tea party, and blowing bubbles. The boys' tasseled helmets are a fine counterpoint to the large hair bow almost dwarfing the girl blowing bubbles. (Mount Tabor Historical Society.)

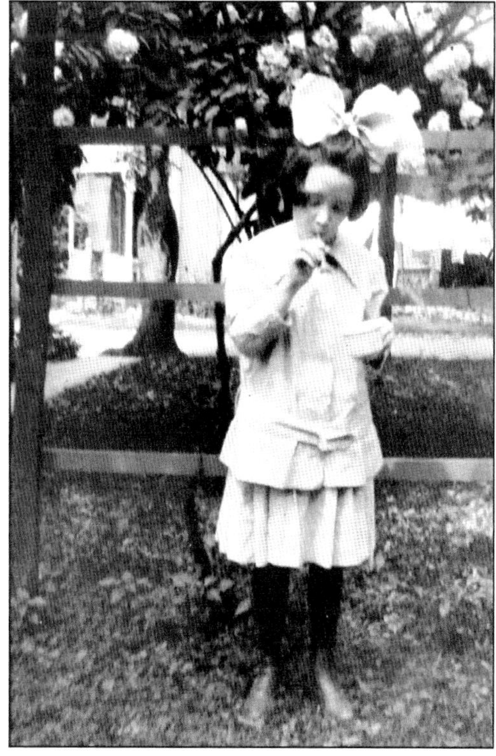

Mary Shelley, blowing bubbles, stands in the yard just east of 28 West Morris Avenue. The house at 31 West Morris Avenue appears in the background. The photograph was taken in August 1914 by Shelley's cousin Anna Menagh. Shelley later married Frank Waterman, of the Waterman Pen family. (Ann Britten Wilson.)

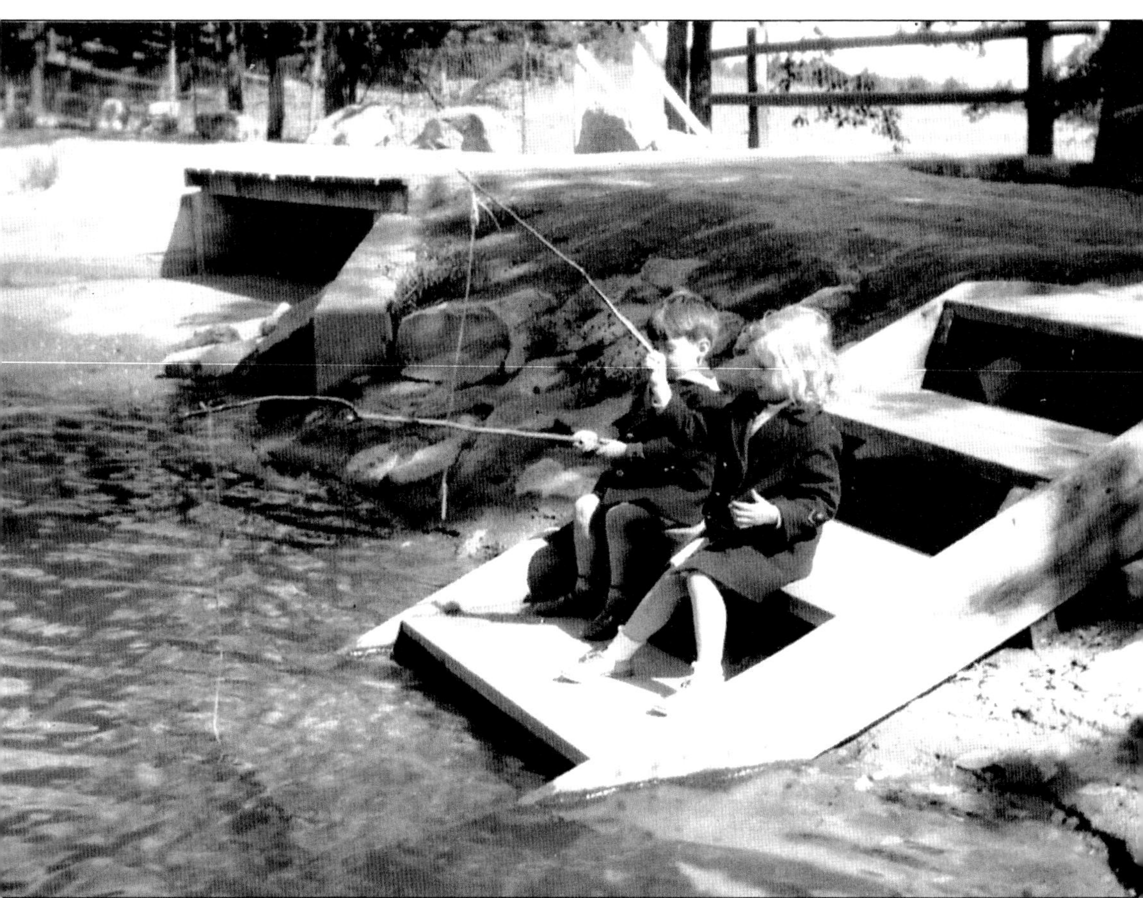

Ann Britten Wilson and Bobby Roberts try their luck at a nearby stream. The trout in the lakes and streams in the Tabor area were abundant, and fishing as well as small game hunting would have been attractive to the campers. A sunny day, a stick for a fishing pole, and a hungry fish or two were all that these children needed. (Ann Britten Wilson.)

Six

SPORTS AND LEISURE

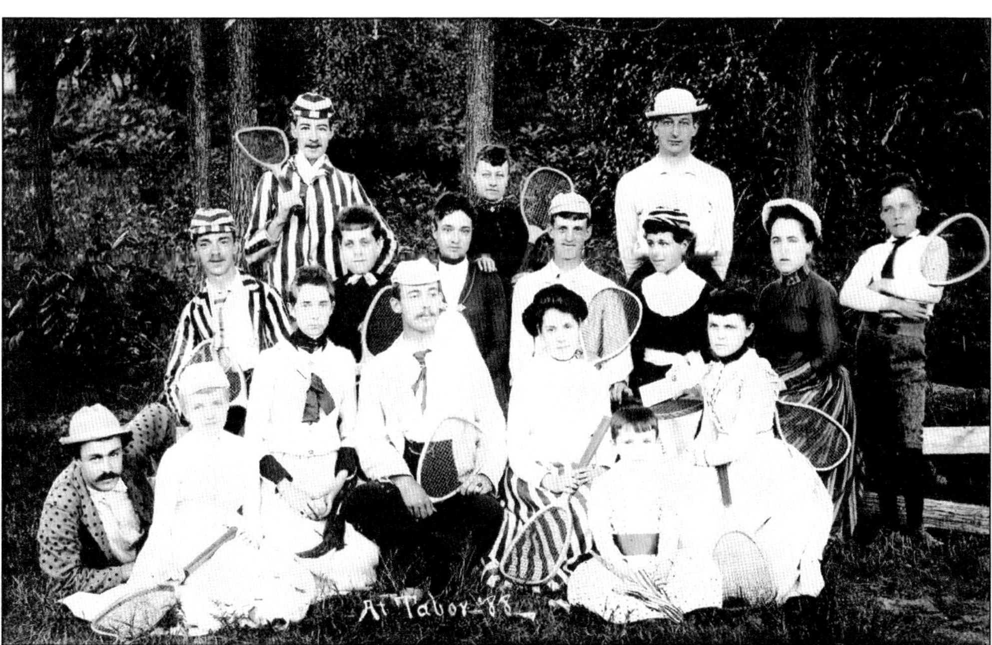

The annual Tabor Tennis Tournament was a hotly contested event. Rivalries, although friendly, were intense and long-standing. Accounts of matches were published in the local newspaper. The board of trustees had donated land for a Young People's Park in 1881, including provision for croquet, archery, baseball, and lawn tennis. By 1887, it was felt necessary to caution young people against practicing on the tennis courts while services were underway in the tabernacle, although in that same year the board donated additional land for the construction of a field house for the Tabor Athletic Association. In 1887, a company of young ladies, led by a cornet band, dressed in white and carrying tennis racquets paraded through the village in two platoons, extending the width of the widest avenues. The newspaper account mentioned that "their exhibition of skill in the manual of arms created much admiration and something of a 'racket.'" The parade initiated the fund-raising campaign for the new Tabor Field House. (Mount Tabor Historical Society.)

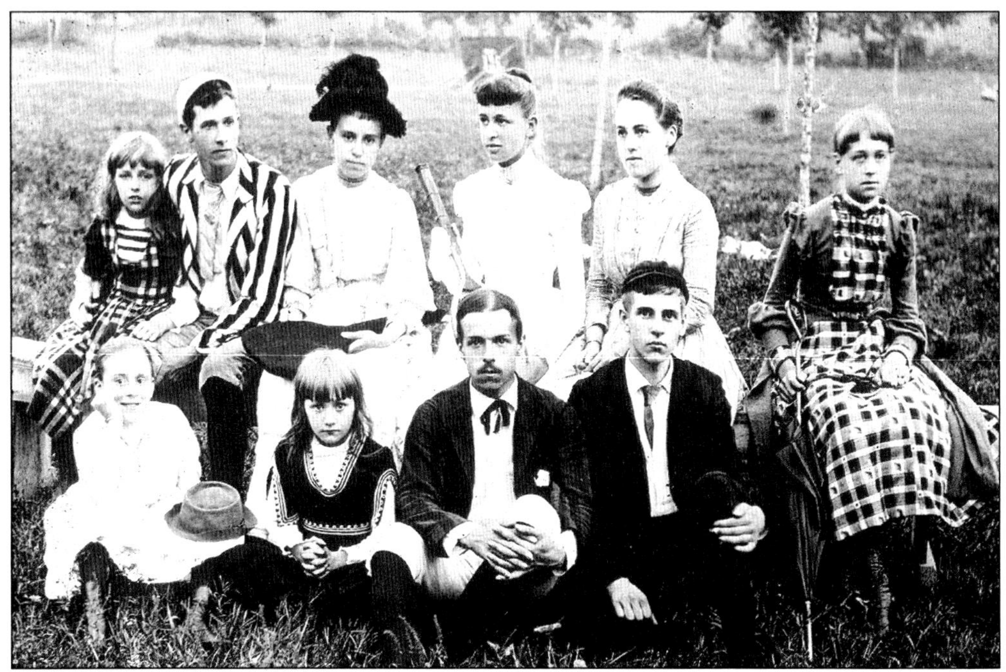

Bright plaid dresses and jaunty caps offset the gloomy faces on the young athletes in this photograph. With the exception of the smiling young girl in the front row on the left, one can only believe that they lost their game or lost their patience with the photographer. (Mary Ellen Cheasty.)

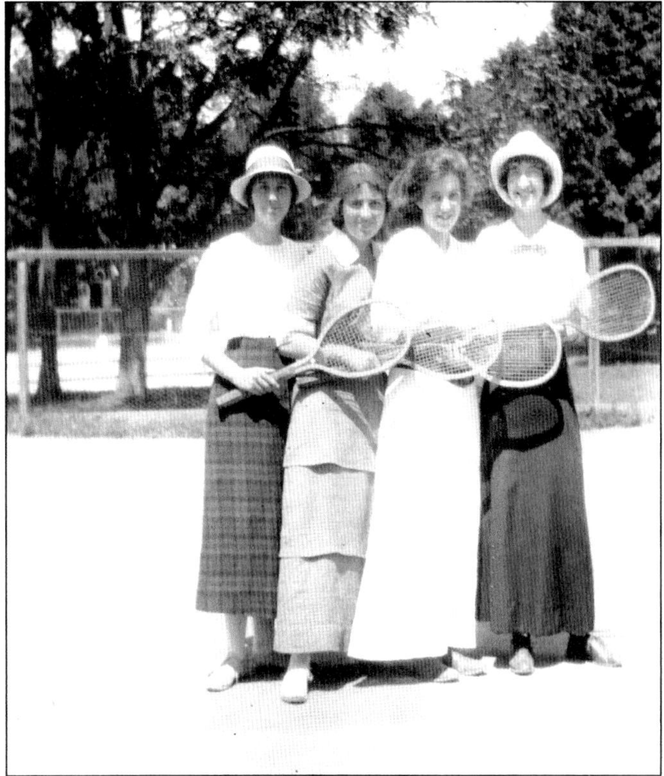

Tennis players, pictured from left to right, Bessie Baldwin, Dorothy ?, Anna Okie, and Mildred Husk pose for Anna Menagh, who took this picture and explained, "It was the last day we all played together in 1914." (Ann Britten Wilson.)

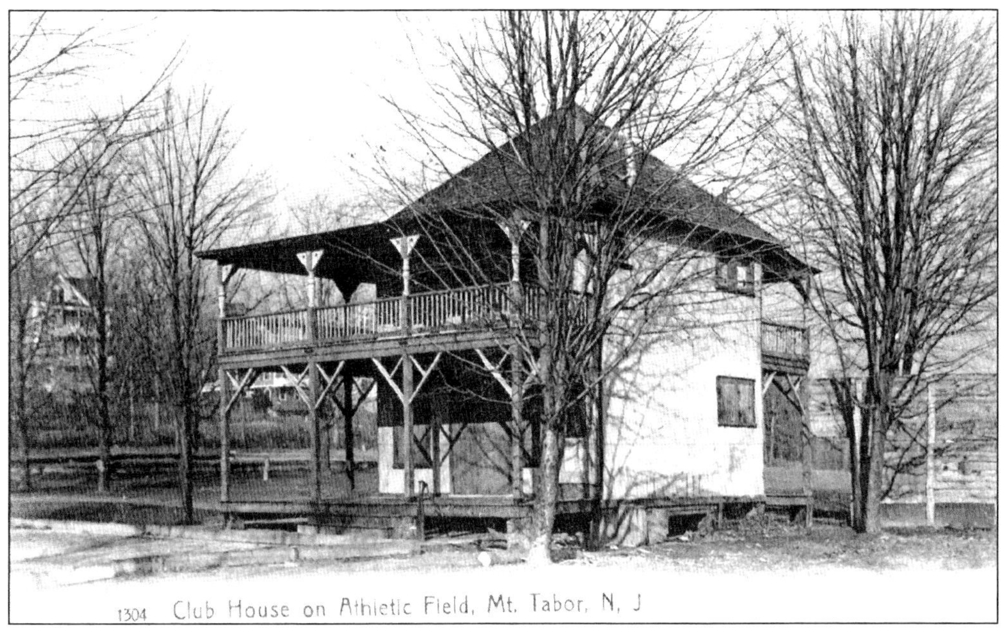

After two years of fund-raising parades through the streets of Mount Tabor, entertainments in the tabernacle featuring local talent, lawn parties, and passing the hat, the Tabor Athletic Association raised enough money for this field house. Built in 1889 near where the baseball diamond is now, it served as a gathering place for the Mount Tabor residents who looked to sports as their favored recreation. The Mount Tabor baseball team was the Alerts, pictured below. Through the 1880s and 1890s, it was a formidable team. The games were slugging matches rather than pitching battles. Scores in the 20s and 30s were not unusual, and endurance was important. The golf course was added in 1906, the new clubhouse was built in 1911, and the old field house was removed in 1931. (Mount Tabor Historical Society.)

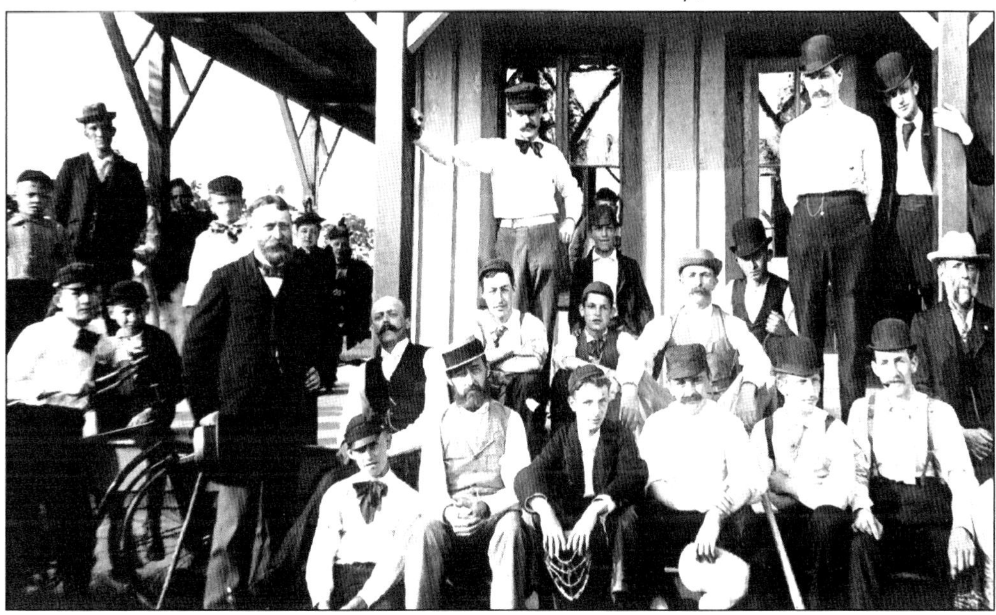

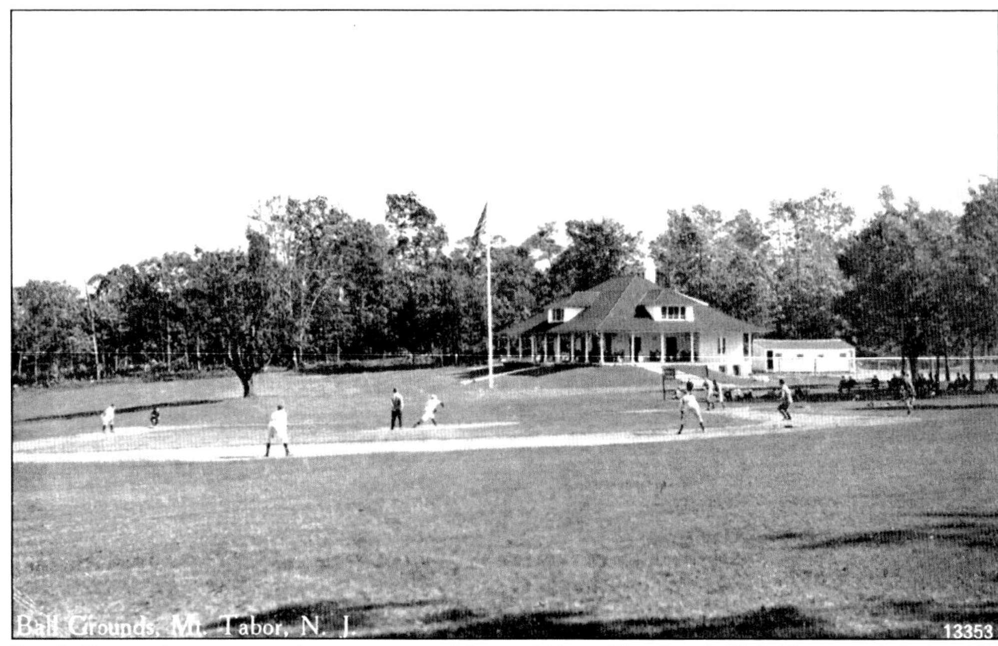

Baseball was always a popular pastime in Mount Tabor. The first ball field was set up in 1877 on land donated by Samuel Coss. During the camp meetings, almost every day except Sunday featured a game. In 1881, the board of trustees set aside land for the Young People's Park. In 1883, Mount Tabor formed its first baseball club, the Alerts, and in 1887, the field house was built next to the diamond. The photograph below shows a corner of the field house and a large crowd intent on the next pitch. Carriages are lined up in the background. Above is the new clubhouse, built in 1911. (Above, Mount Tabor Historical Society; below, Tom Nestor.)

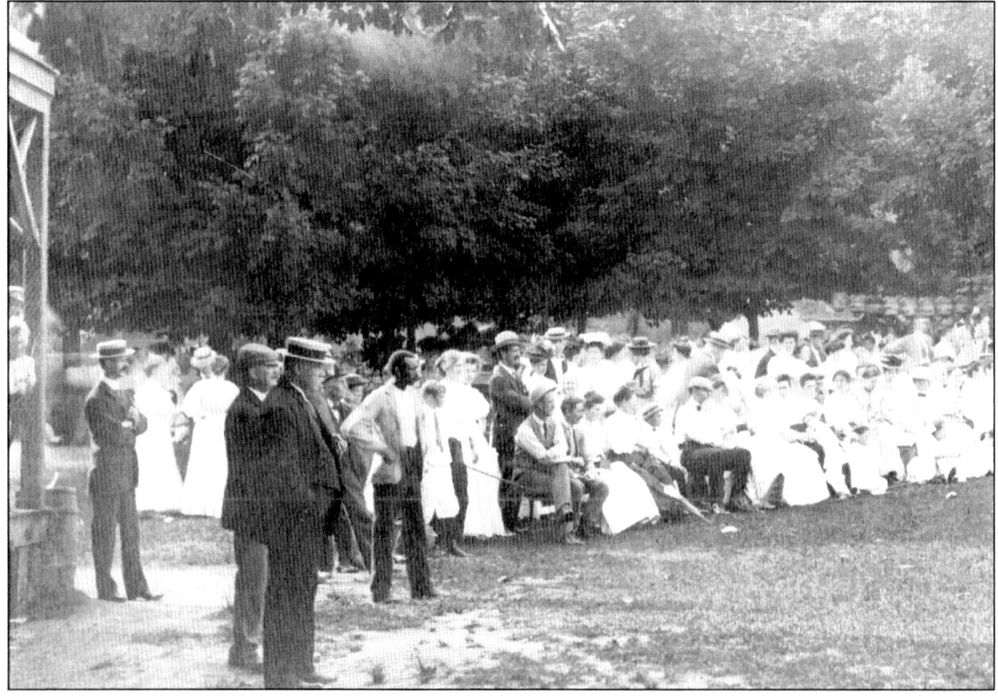

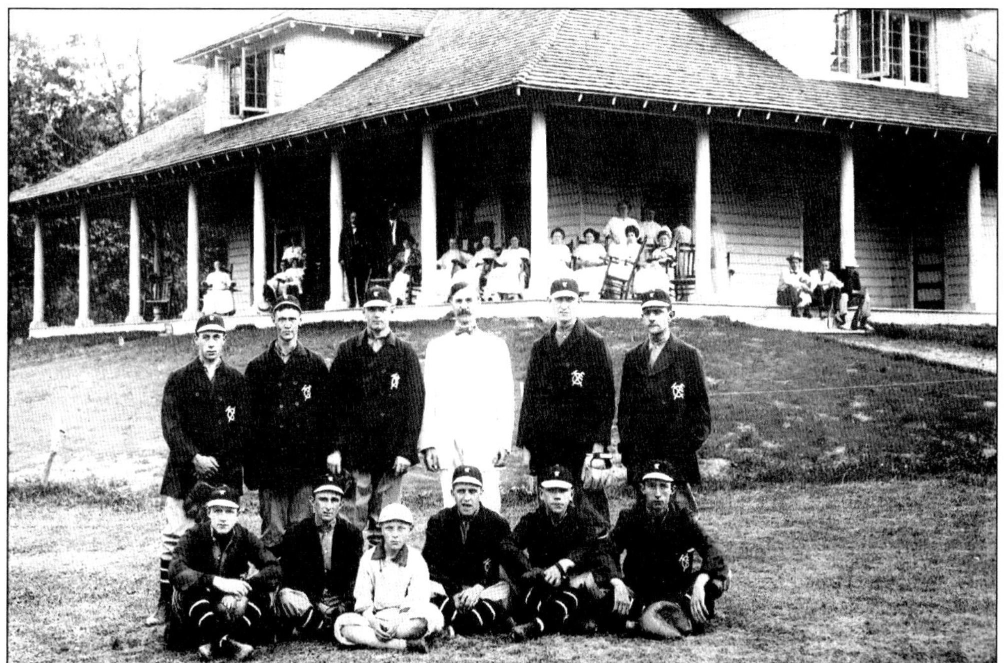

The Mount Tabor baseball team poses in front of the new clubhouse. Pictured are, from left to right, (first row) Al Collins, Fred Lynch, Harold Sofield, Chauncey Lungstroth, Al Cockshaw, and Bob Cantrell; (second row) Mike Simonson, Bill Hill, Cy Henderson, Mr. Rendall, Frank Bulger, and Mr. Singleton. (Kevin Simonson.)

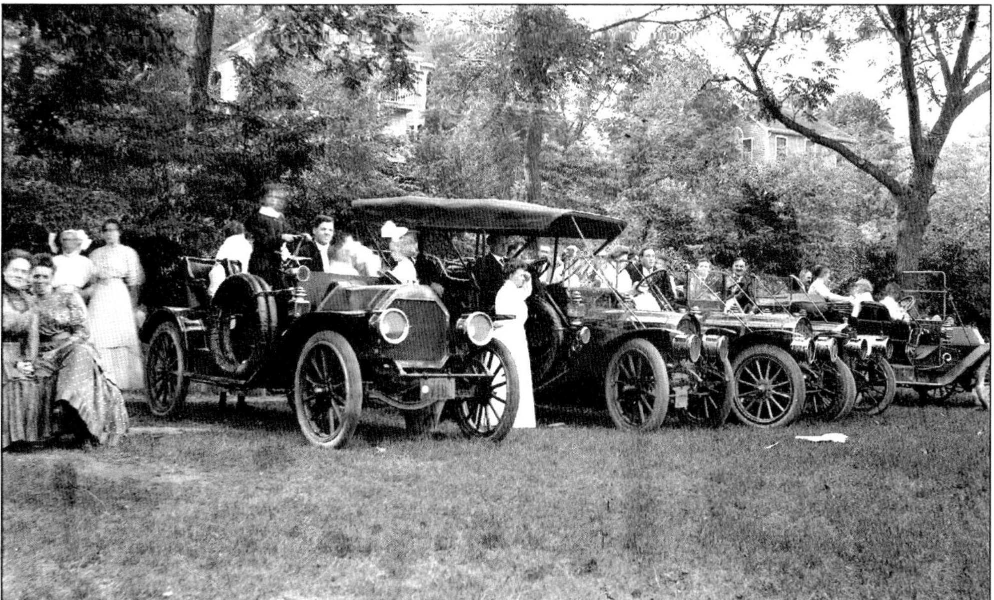

In the early days, automobiles had been forbidden on the grounds; fishing, swimming, and sunbathing had been forbidden during the camp meeting days. By 1909, the board of trustees had recognized that "the summer resort idea has modified the original character of our community." Here roadsters are lined up along the baseball field in the spot filled by carriages in the earlier photograph. (Mount Tabor Historical Society.)

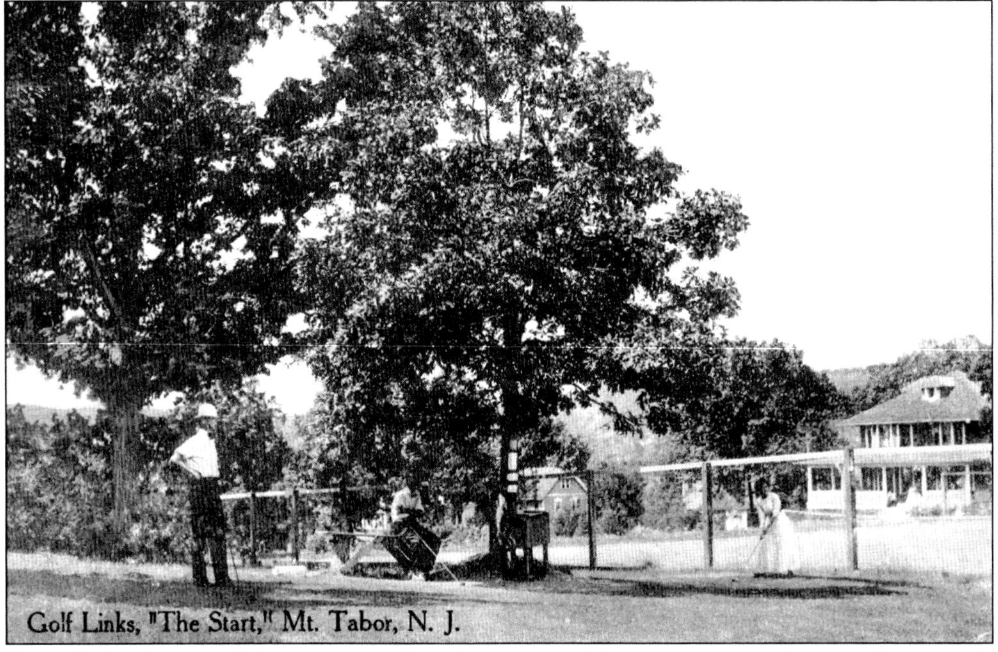

From the beginning of the camp meeting, it was essential to reserve certain spots for open-air recreation and enjoyment. At the end of the summer of 1900, the Mount Tabor Field Club was organized, later incorporated in 1904 and renamed the Mount Tabor Country Club in 1931. Early on, the club opened a six-hole golf course using tin cans as cups. It was set on a limited space of dry ground on the face of the hill on the southeastern slope. The lower meadow, a marsh, was reclaimed in 1908 to extend the golf course to nine holes. The entire cost of reclaiming the lower marsh was about $3,000. In 1911, the current clubhouse was erected. Croquet, tennis, and baseball were added to the facilities, popular pastimes at the beginning of the 20th century. Playgrounds dotted the community, providing welcome entertainment for the children. (Mount Tabor Historical Society.)

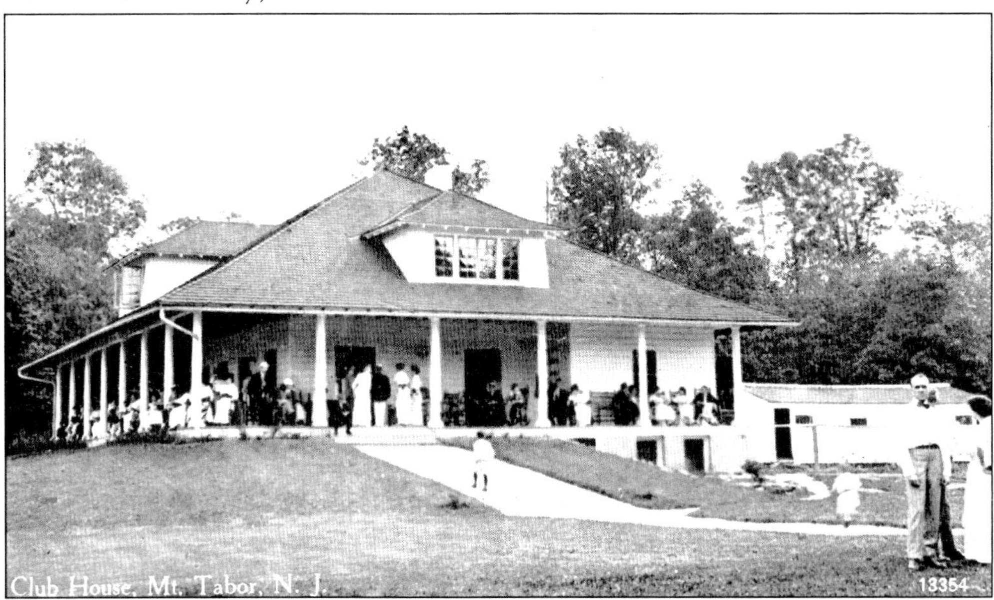

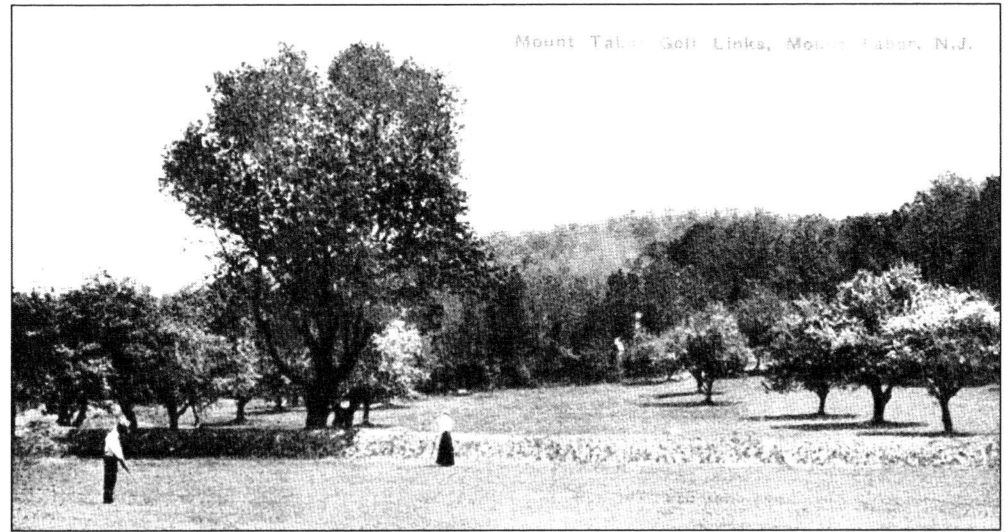

In 1928 and 1929, new additions and improvements were made to the clubhouse at a total cost of $10,000, providing it with a fine dining room, a kitchen, a reception room, a "special room for ladies," a new pro shop, a locker room, a shower room, and an upstairs apartment for occupancy by the professional. The open, rolling green fields of the golf course form a desirable breathing space to all those who live in Mount Tabor. The c. 1917 postcards on these pages provide wonderful views of the clubhouse and the lush fairway. The map, created by Antonio Petruccelli, shows the swath of land offset by the narrow streets of the old section of Mount Tabor. The fairway layout is included on the map. (Mount Tabor Historical Society.)

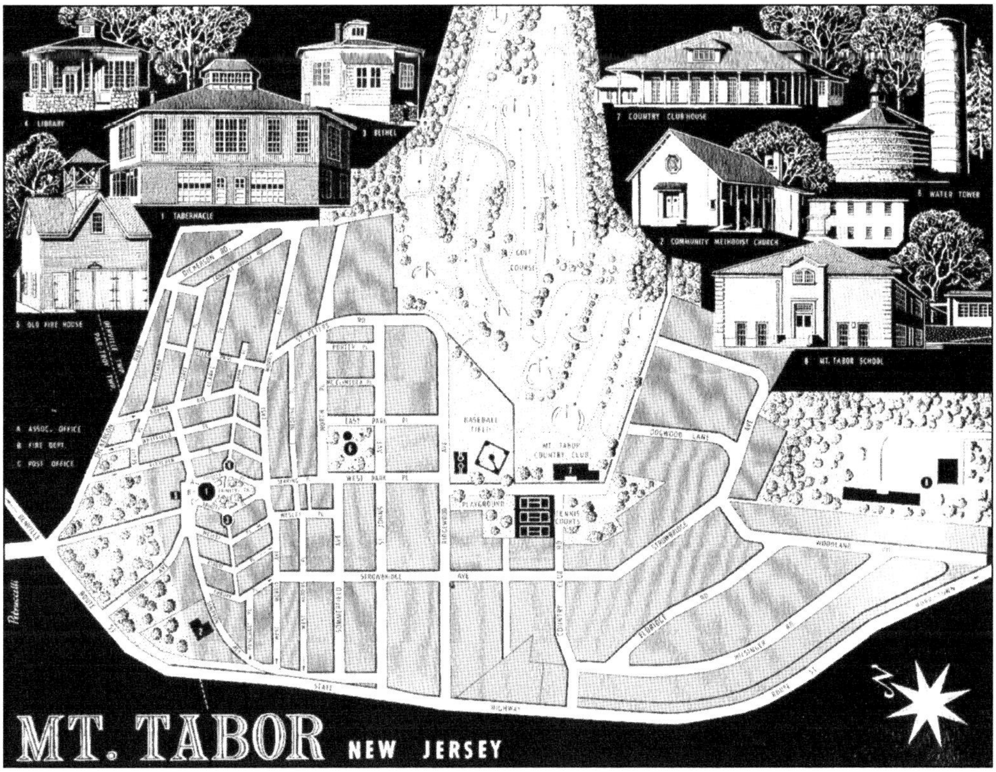

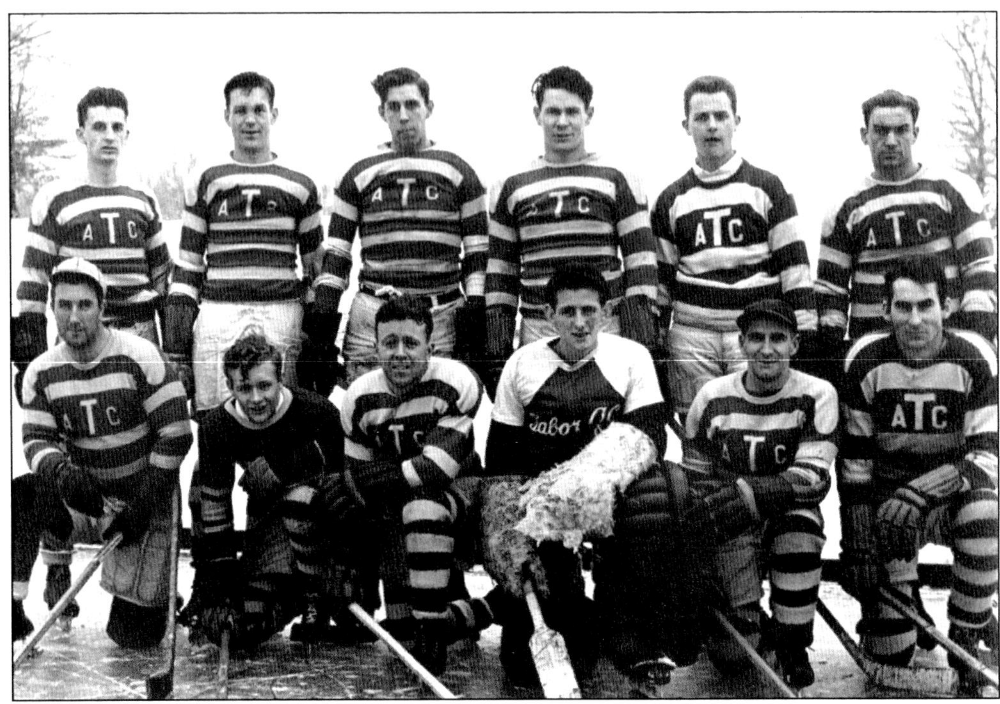

The Tabor Zebras were described in the newspapers as being the "best ice hockey team in North Jersey." The home rink, located along the railroad tracks where Dickerson's Foodtown is now, was the site for many league games. One of the most memorable games played was held on February 5, 1948, for the benefit of the Morris County Sports Polio Fund. On that Sunday afternoon, the attendance was the largest to witness a hockey game in Morris County. (Kevin Simonson.)

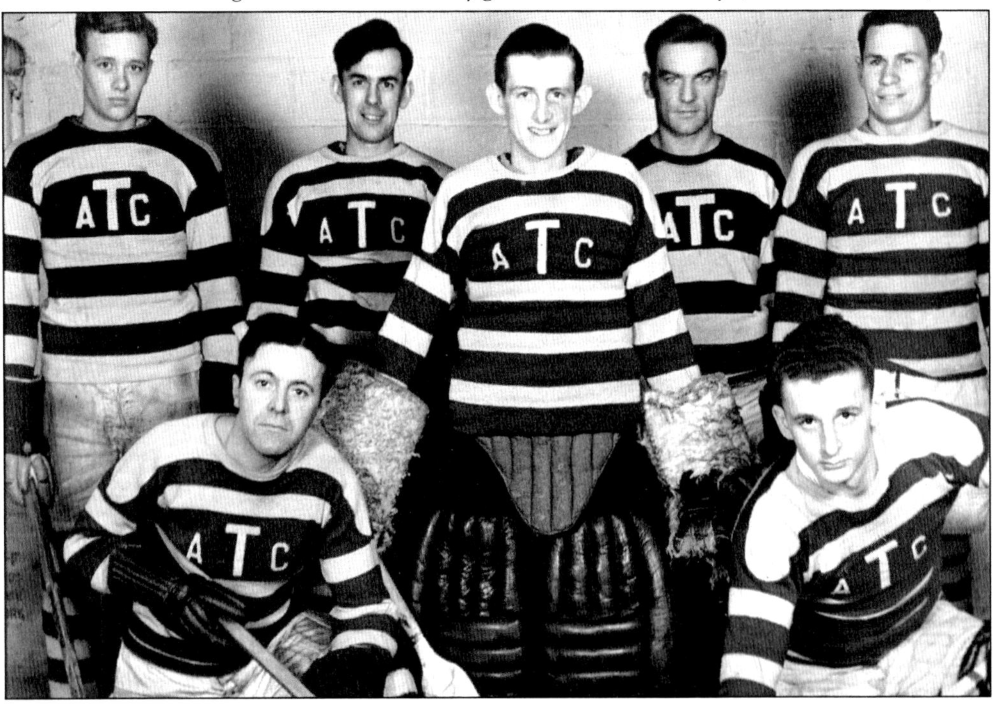

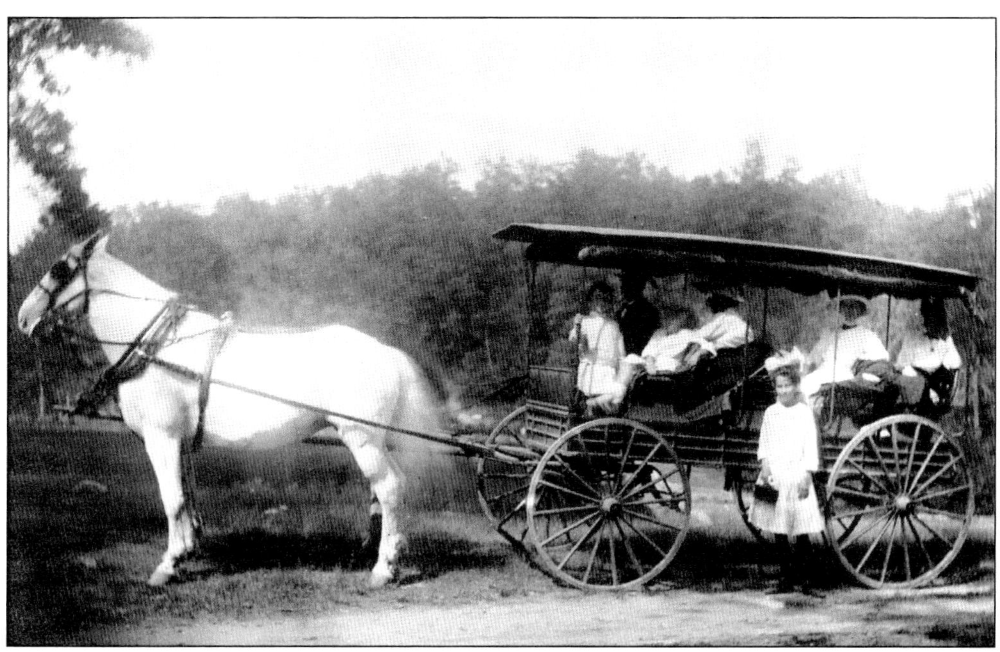

A favorite entertainment for young people at the camp was excursions by wagon to one of many destinations in the surrounding area. In 1885, a trip to Lake Hopatcong, including a boat ride up the canal and across the lake to a picnic area at Sharp's Rock, could be completed in a long day. Tabor Lake, a much smaller body of water located close to the campgrounds, offered boating, fishing, and bathing. The lake was previously owned by A. W. Cutler of Morristown. Parties of bicyclists from Morristown often made the run up to enjoy a dip in the pure cool waters. In the background is the Morris and Essex branch of the Delaware, Lackawanna and Western Railroad. (Above, Jeanne Apgar; below, Mount Tabor Historical Society.)

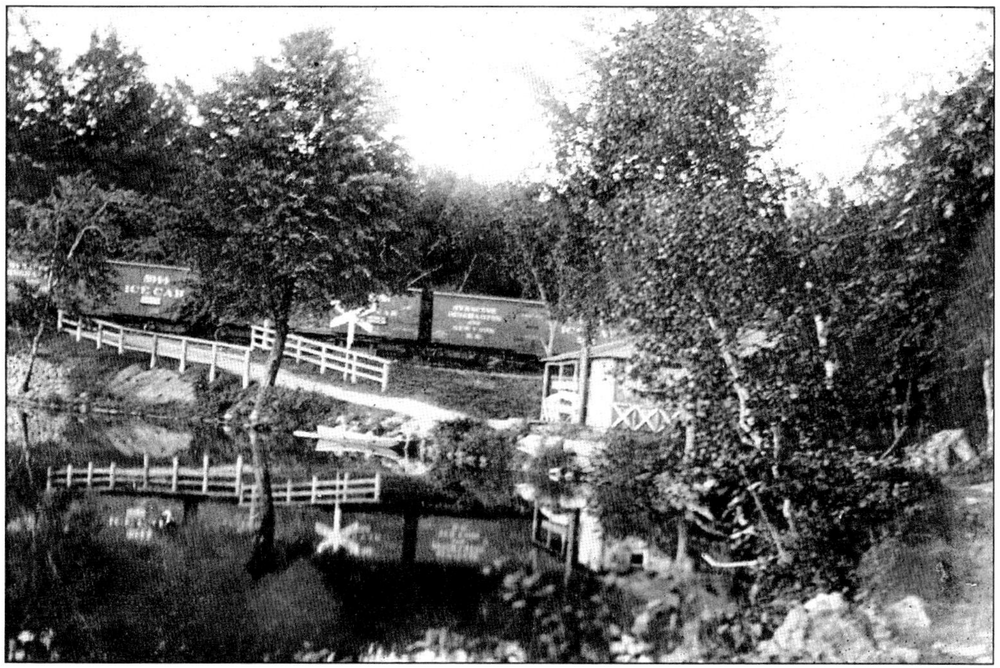

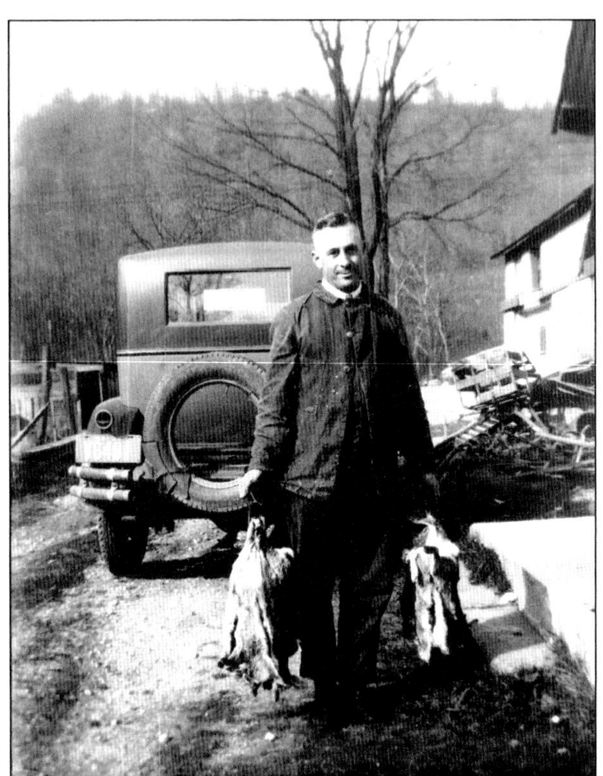

Clarence Simonson is shown here with small game in 1929. In addition to the excellent fishing, the area around Mount Tabor was a natural habitat for birds and small game. Even though most markets and butcher shops in the area offered game, hunting for market was not an important local industry. The trout in the lakes and streams and the game in the hills, particularly woodcock, were important selling points for those considering the area for either summer or full-time living. (Kevin Simonson.)

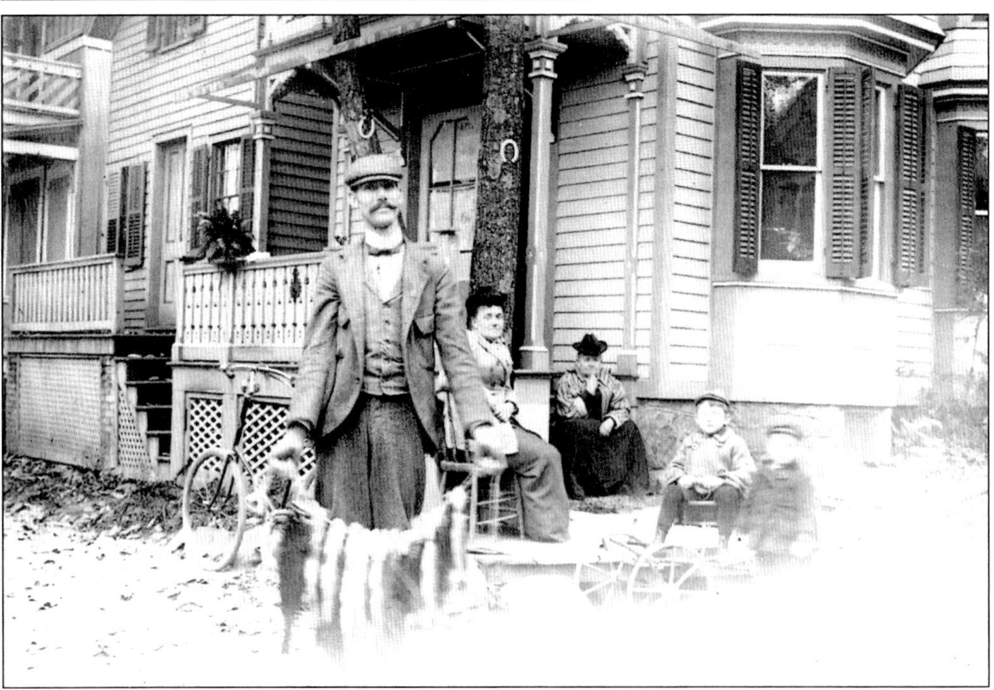

Dr. Jessie Hedden stands in front of his cottage at 36 Morris Avenue, showing off his catch. His wife, Isabelle, is seated in the chair and his sons, Harold (left) and Howard, are to the right. (Marc Miller.)

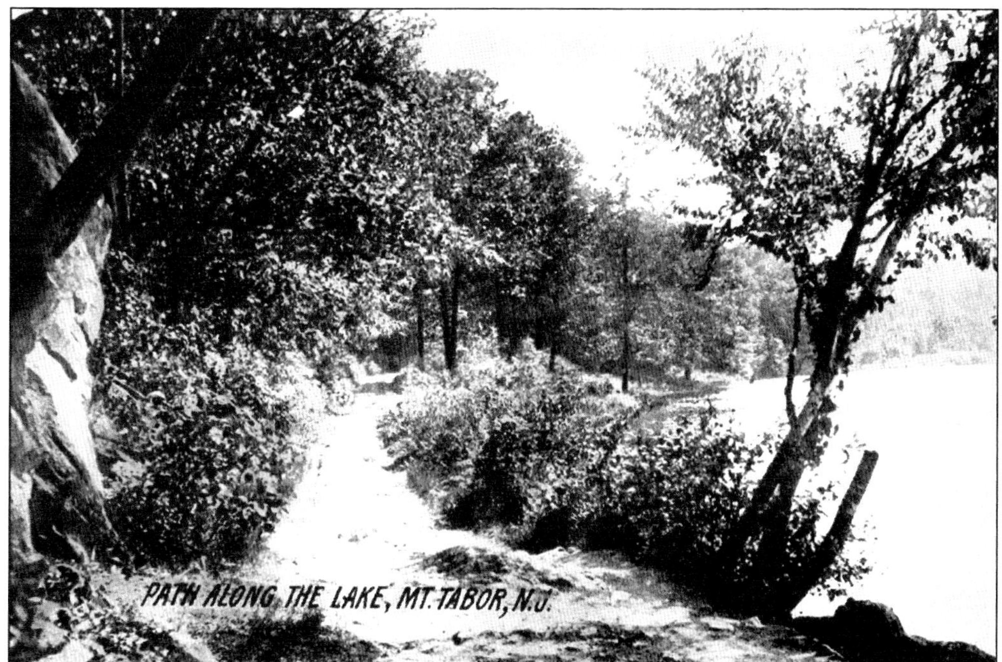

Whether for boating, fishing, swimming, or just strolling, Tabor Lake was a favorite destination of the campers. This view of the path along the lake was the most frequently produced image of Mount Tabor. The lake had an important part in the economic life of the community as well. During the winter, as much as 300 tons of ice were harvested and stored in an icehouse on the lake for use by the summer residents. (Mount Tabor Historical Society.)

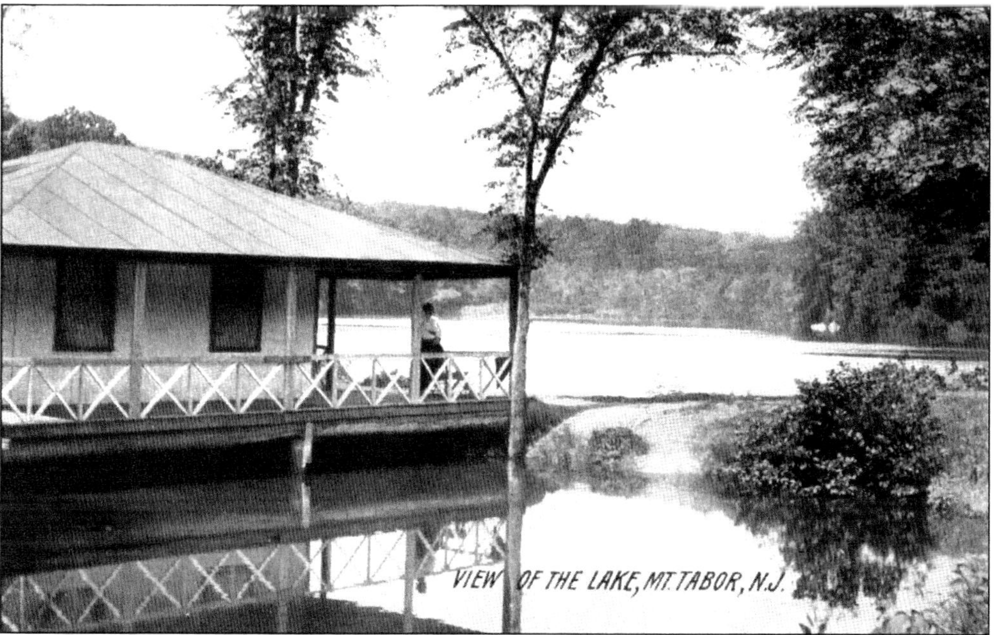

Both the boathouse, seen here, and the icehouse were demolished during the 1920s. Mechanical refrigeration had made the icehouse redundant, and maintenance on the boathouse, with its "wet" foundation, became prohibitively expensive. (Mount Tabor Historical Society.)

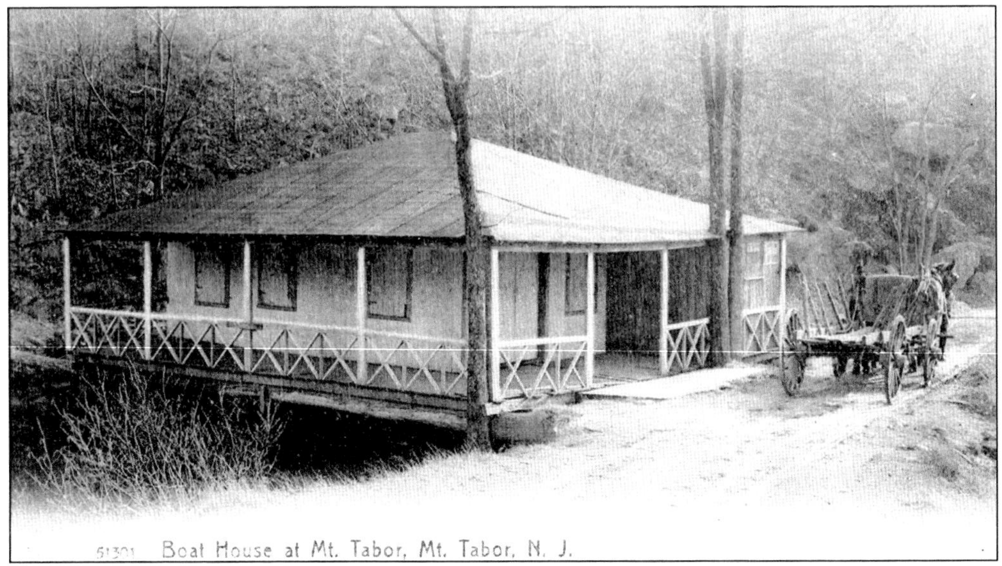

The boathouse on Tabor Lake is featured on this 1906 postcard. During the summer, boats were available for fishing or just for rowing on the lake. (Mount Tabor Historical Society.)

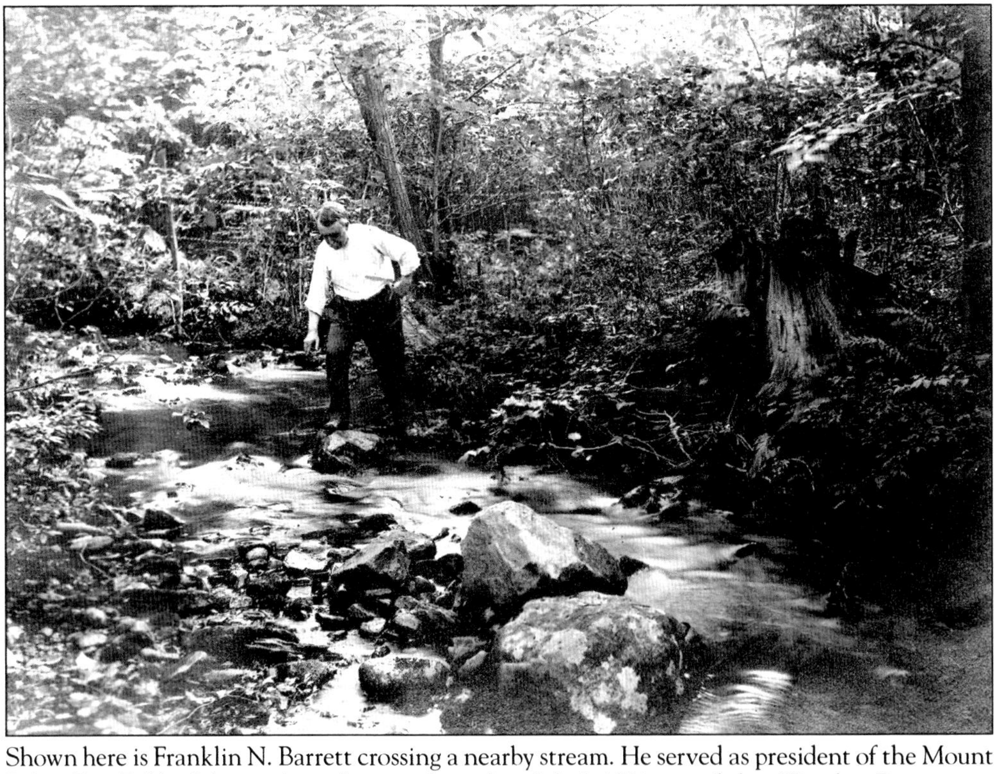

Shown here is Franklin N. Barrett crossing a nearby stream. He served as president of the Mount Tabor Free Public Library. A resolution adopted on July 1, 1921, stated that "Brother Barrett was not only a lover of good books, but always alert to the charms of nature as attested by the large collection of wild flowers gathered about him. He could read nature in all its glory and explore the rocks and rills of Mount Tabor and its vicinity in search of the golden treasure they contain." (Jeanne Apgar.)

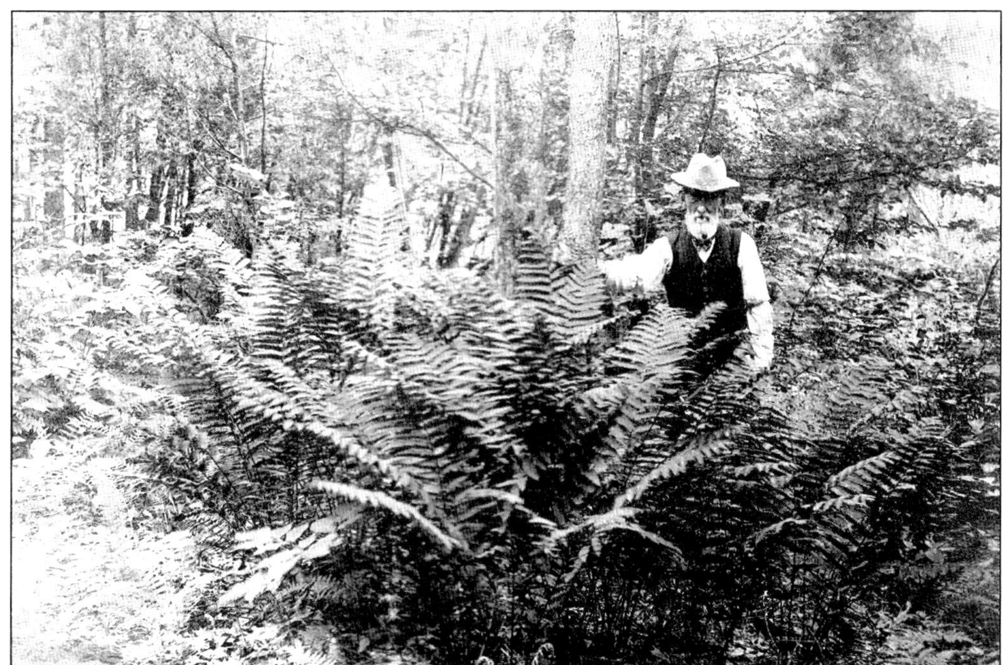

The late 19th and early 20th centuries were the time of John Muir, Gifford Pinchot, Theodore Roosevelt, and the establishment of the national park system. An appreciation for nature and the outdoor life was emerging as a part of the American character. Mount Tabor and the camp meeting movement were solidly aligned with the escape from industrialization and urbanization to a more natural environment. Part of the Mount Tabor experience was the opportunity to return to nature. In nearby woods, an early naturalist shows the size of ostrich ferns, a favorite in Victorian times. Clusters of these ferns are still abundant in the area. In the photograph below, Franklin N. Barrett's family enjoys a picnic in lovely wooded surroundings. Pictured are Mary Edith Barrett and two of her sons, Noyes (left) and Will. (Jeanne Apgar.)

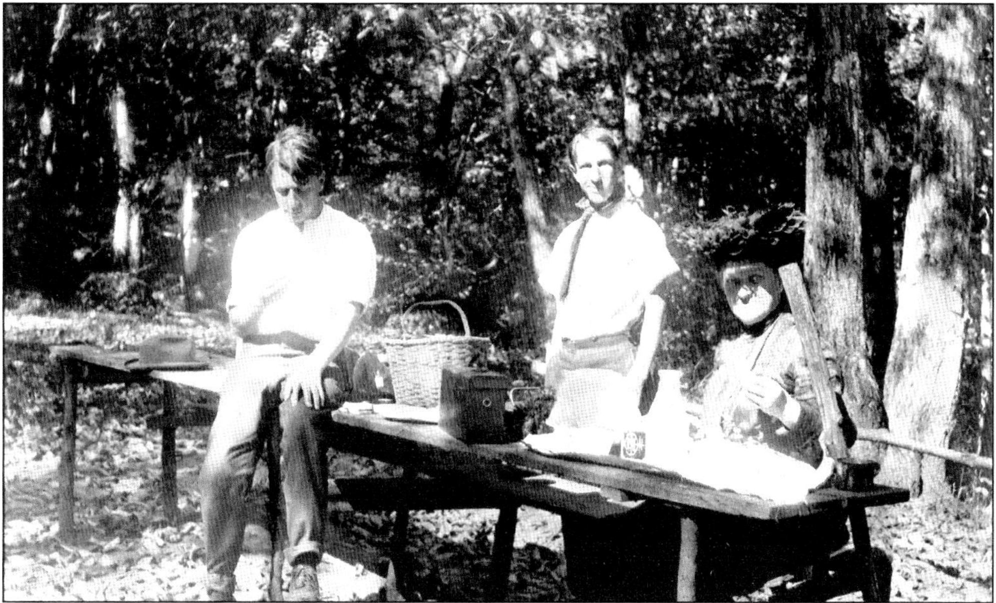

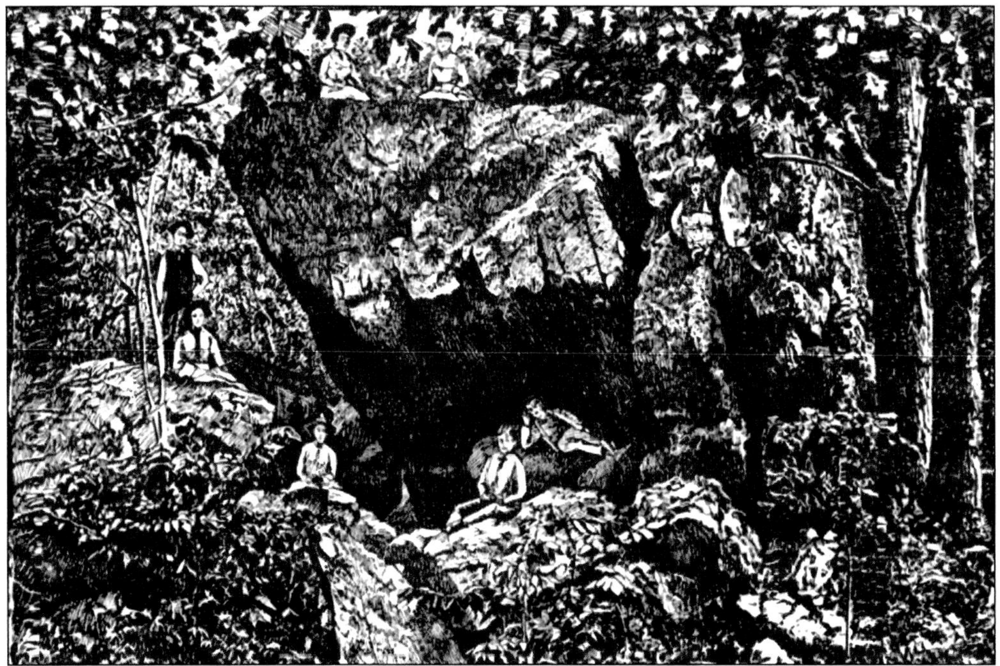

In describing the local scenery, the *Mount Tabor Record* stated, "the rocks and mountains are thrown about 'promiscuous like,' and sometimes loom up where least expected." Above is one of these huge rock formations, known as the Parsippany Rock House and termed a "house" because it is capable of sheltering a dozen people. A second nearby formation, known as the Dover Rock House, was a favorite destination for young people. Louis Menagh Sr. wrote in 1940, "At both the Dover Rock House and at the top of Point Lookout there were wooden observatories about twenty feet in height, affording a splendid view of the surrounding country." The Dover Rock House is not close to Dover but is accessed from Old Dover Road, hence the name. (Above, Mount Tabor Record, 1880s; below, Ann Britten Wilson.)

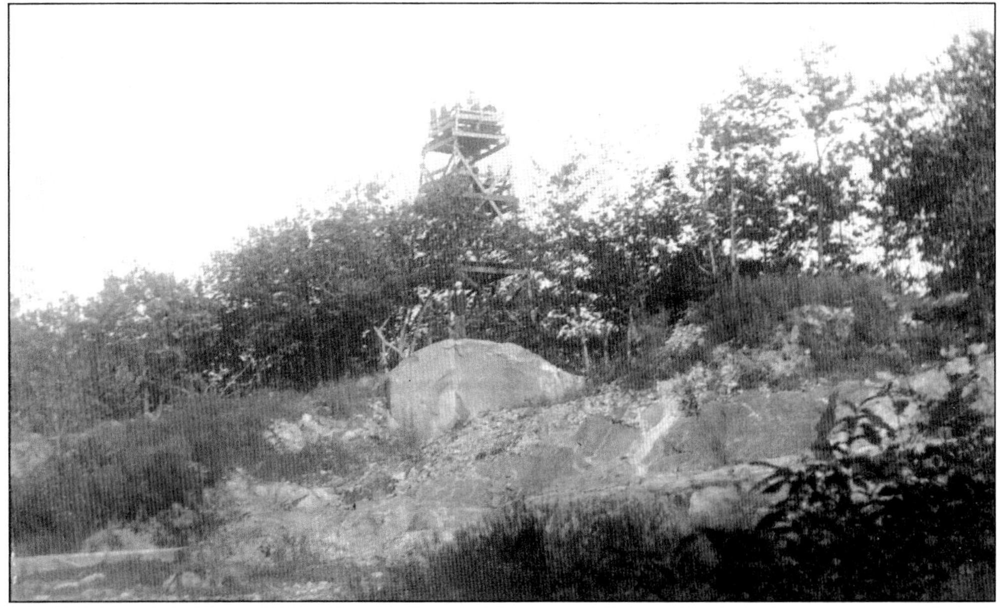

Seven

SERVING MOUNT TABOR

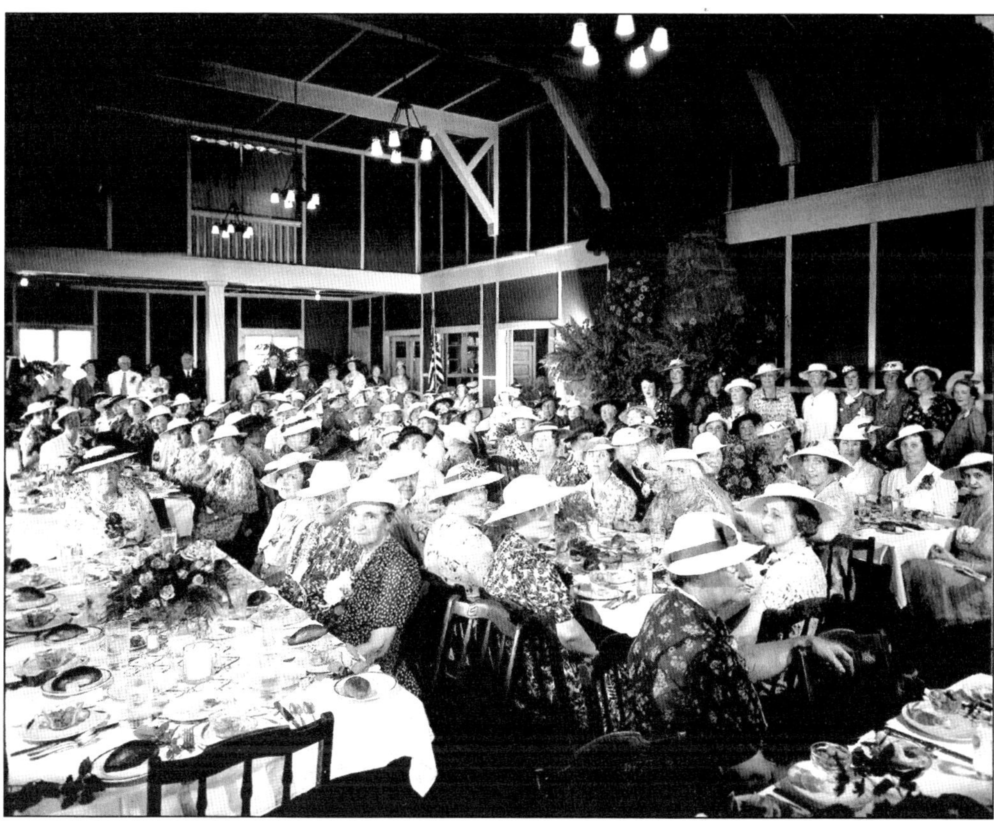

The members of the Women's Club of Mount Tabor gather for a gala luncheon to celebrate the club's golden anniversary at the Mount Tabor Country Club on July 27, 1938. Although the group had been instrumental in raising money for the construction of the clubhouse, it was several years and a general change in the social climate before women were accorded full membership privileges at the club. (Ann Britten Wilson.)

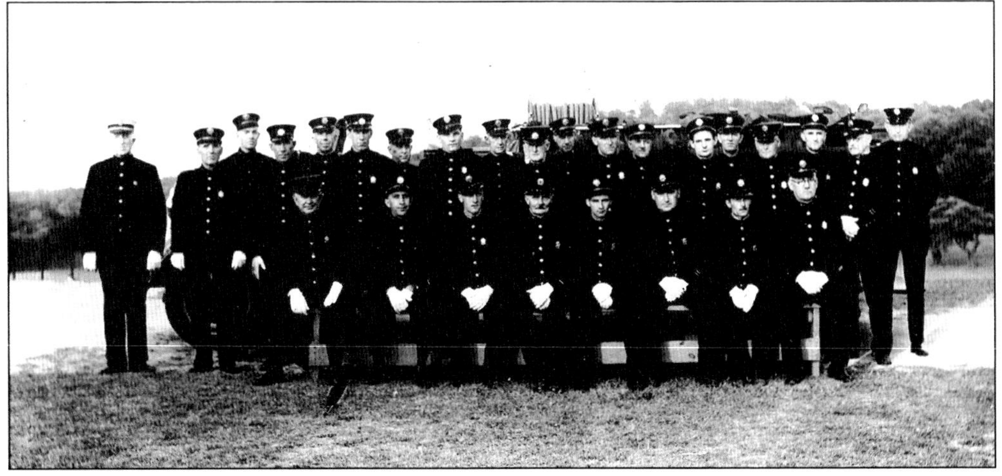

The founding members of the Mount Tabor Fire Department pose for an official photograph in front of a hose cart on the baseball field. The Mount Tabor Fire Department was organized on June 11, 1910, and incorporated in 1915. Prior to 1910, fire protection was provided by the Protection Hook and Ladder Company from Dover. (Mount Tabor Fire Department.)

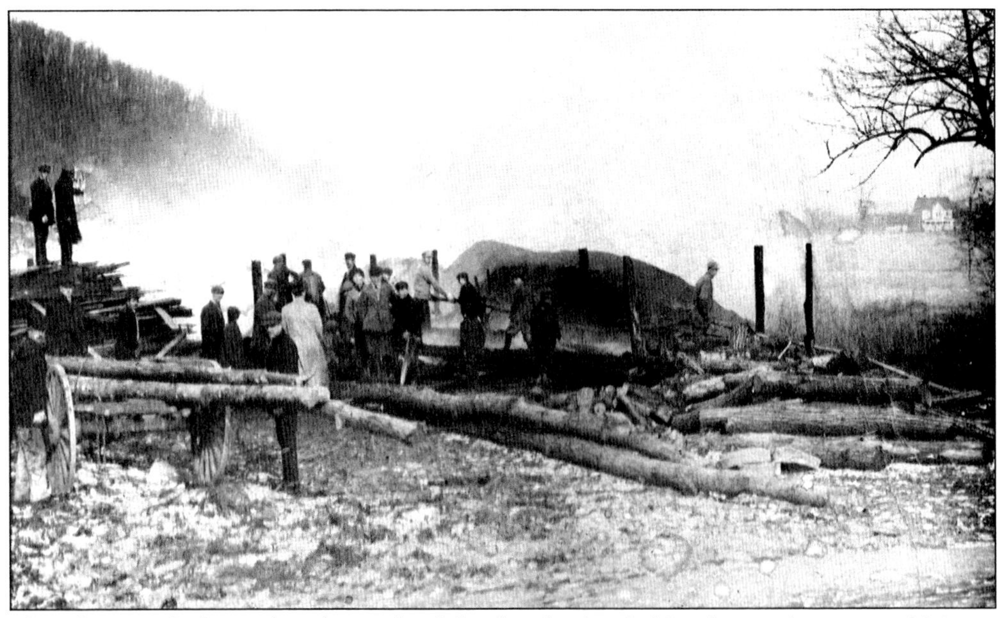

This photograph shows the aftermath of the first fire battled by the newly organized Mount Tabor Fire Department. The blaze destroyed the old sawmill that stood at the corner of what is now Dickerson Road and Route 53. (Mount Tabor Fire Department.)

The initial equipment of the fire department was comprised of hose carts; because of the steep streets, one cart was kept in the old firehouse and one was kept on top of the hill, in the vicinity of North Place. Eventually in 1923, a Buffalo water pumper was purchased. It had a 30-gallon steel tank and was the first pumper in the area between Morristown and Dover. The ladies' auxiliary was organized on March 21, 1934. In 1936, in compliance with state statutes, the Township of Parsippany–Troy Hills established the six fire districts that exist today. (Mount Tabor Fire Department.)

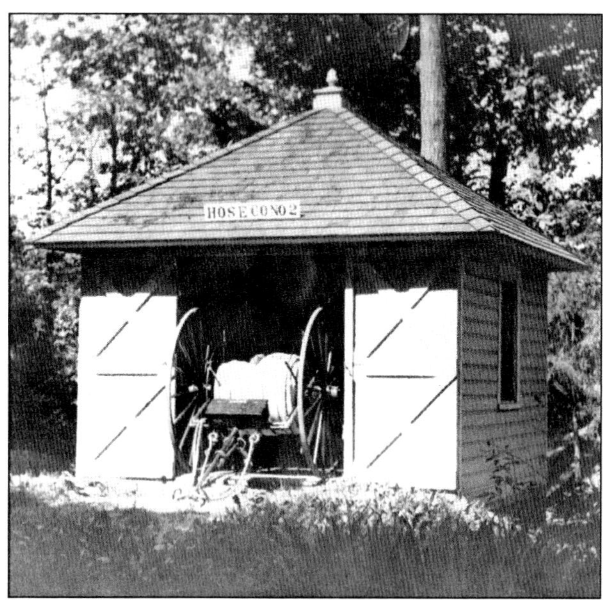

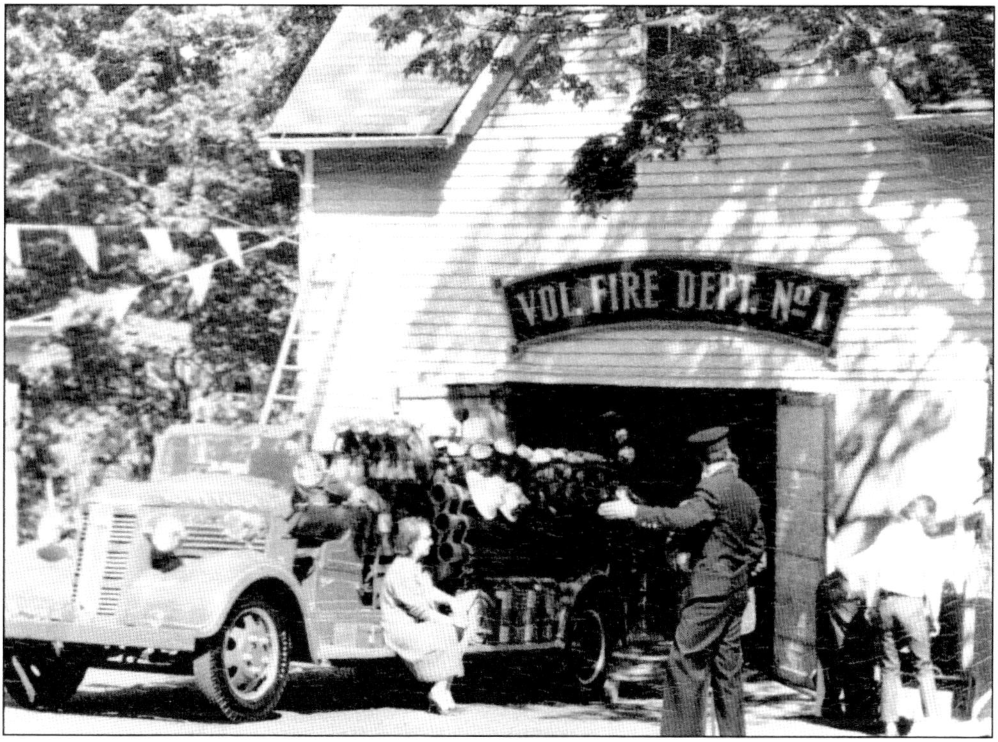

The building seen here is the old firehouse. Originally it was used to house the horse and coach that carried passengers and luggage up the hill from the train station. It became the first firehouse for the Mount Tabor Volunteer Fire Department in 1911 and was also used for hose drying, socializing, and meetings. In 1913, the cupola and 500-pound bell were added. The bell was used as a fire alarm for Mount Tabor until 1923, when it was replaced by a siren. The building was used as the location for a 1960 Coca-Cola commercial. The fire department moved across the street to the lower level of the tabernacle in 1953. (Mount Tabor Fire Department.)

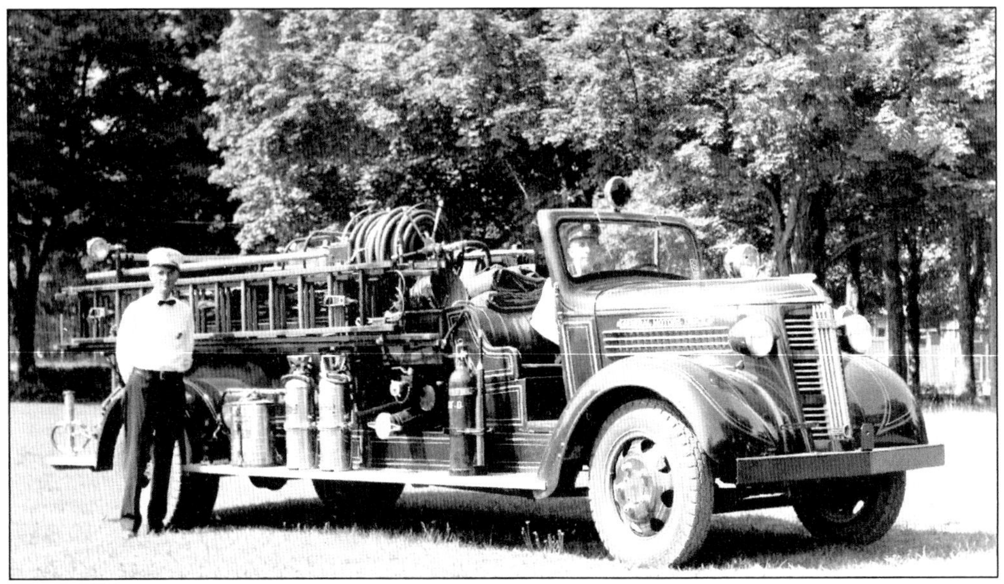

On Children's Day, 1944, Claude Dickerson, standing on the side of the truck, and Ken Smith, behind the steering wheel, proudly pose with the Mount Tabor Fire Department's 1937 GMC pumper truck. Dickerson joined the department in 1918 and held every office, serving as chief from 1949 to 1950. The fire department was and continues to be an important part of the Children's Day parade. Today the fire trucks both enhance the early afternoon parade and, joined by trucks from the surrounding communities, follow the parade route once again. Several members of the fire department valiantly battle a blaze in the photograph below. The close proximity of the cottages raises the risk of fire spreading quickly. In the early days, all residents were required to keep a bucket of water outside their dwelling in the event of a fire. (Mount Tabor Fire Department.)

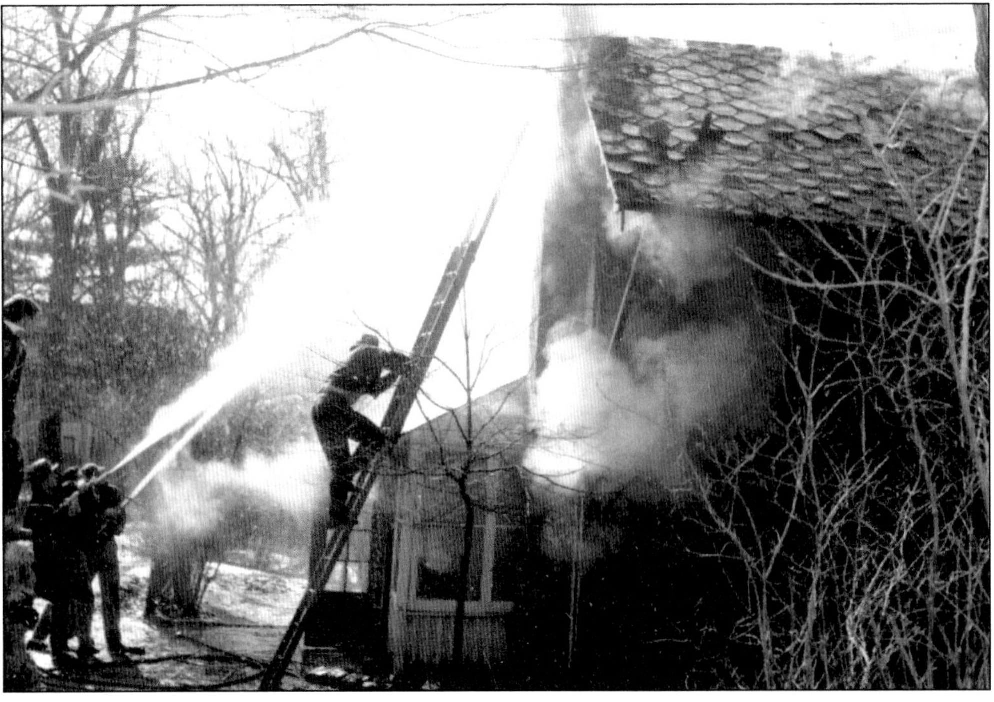

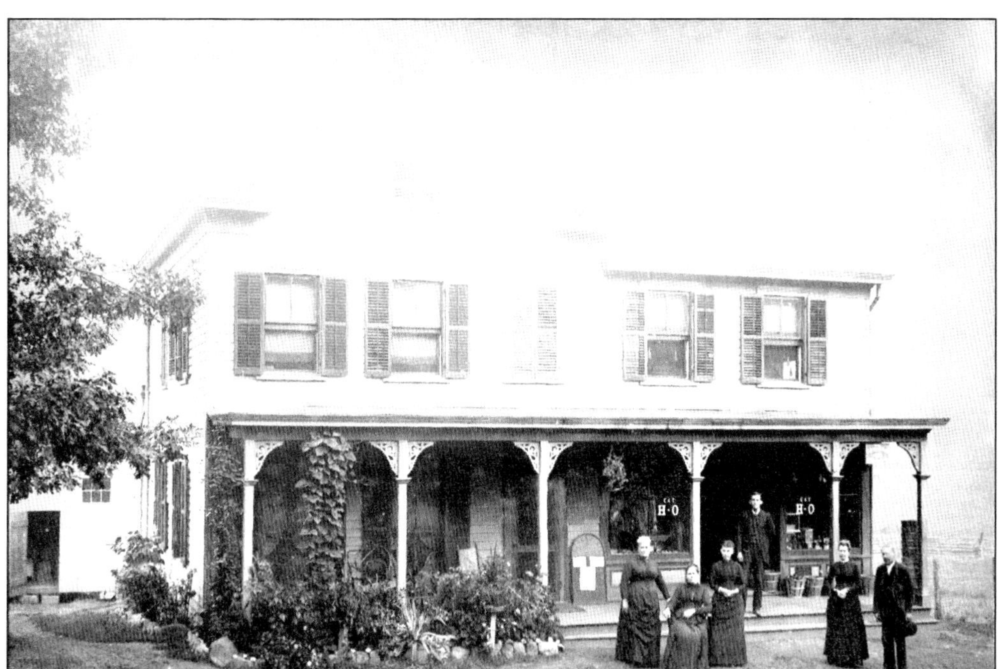

The building in this photograph was located across from the campgrounds. It was built for Albert Davis and his wife. For 20 years after the campground was established, over a dozen grocers served the community. Most owned full-time stores the rest of the year in surrounding communities, some as far away as Morristown and Dover. Few stayed long in Mount Tabor. In 1893, Davis sold his establishment to Elmer Dickerson and his sister Susan. In the 1934 photograph at right, Claude Dickerson poses alongside the Dickerson Store delivery truck. Delivery service to outlying farms considerably expanded the circle of customers supporting the market. The shelves could also be stocked with fresh meats and vegetables obtained locally. (Ron Dickerson.)

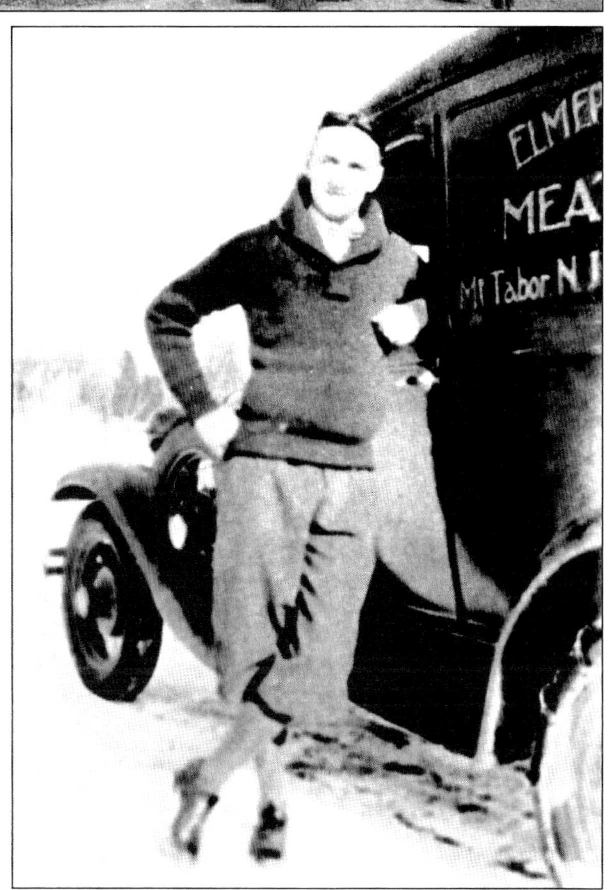

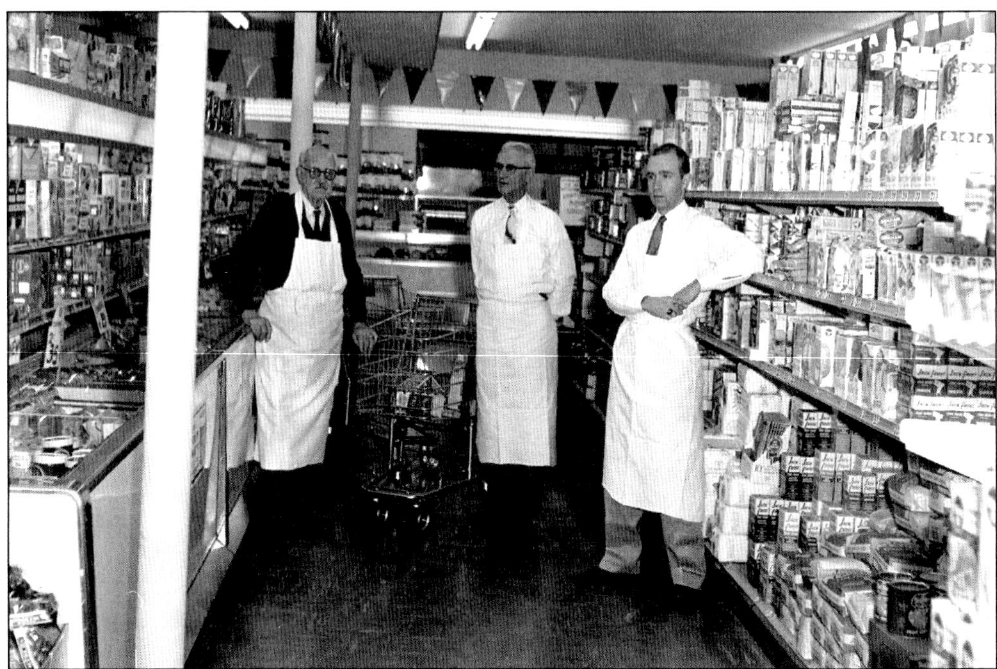

After Elmer and Susan Dickerson bought the store in 1893, they took over the summer store next to the Arlington Hotel on Simpson Avenue in 1895. In 1918, they built a new larger store a few hundred feet away. Here, from left to right, Elmer, Claude, and Ronald, three generations of Dickersons, pose inside the store around 1958. The fourth generation, Jeff Dickerson, continues the tradition as proprietor of the Foodtown market at the same location. (Ron Dickerson.)

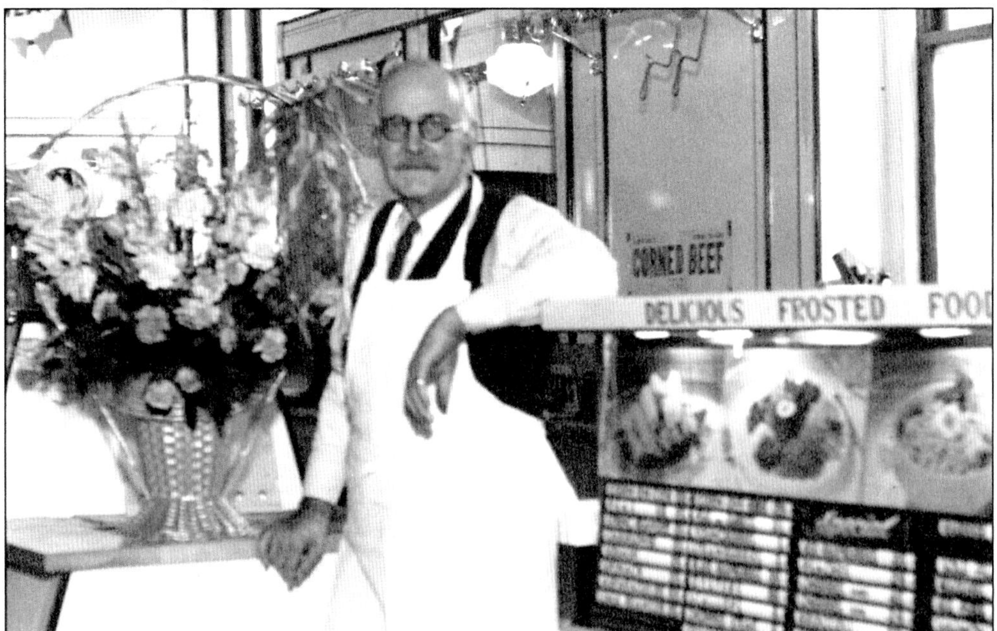

Elmer Dickerson, proprietor and head of the family, was also widely known as an avid gardener. He was particularly proud of his gladiolus, which regularly won him prizes at the county fair. A bouquet of his prize-winning blooms is displayed here in the 1940s. (Ron Dickerson.)

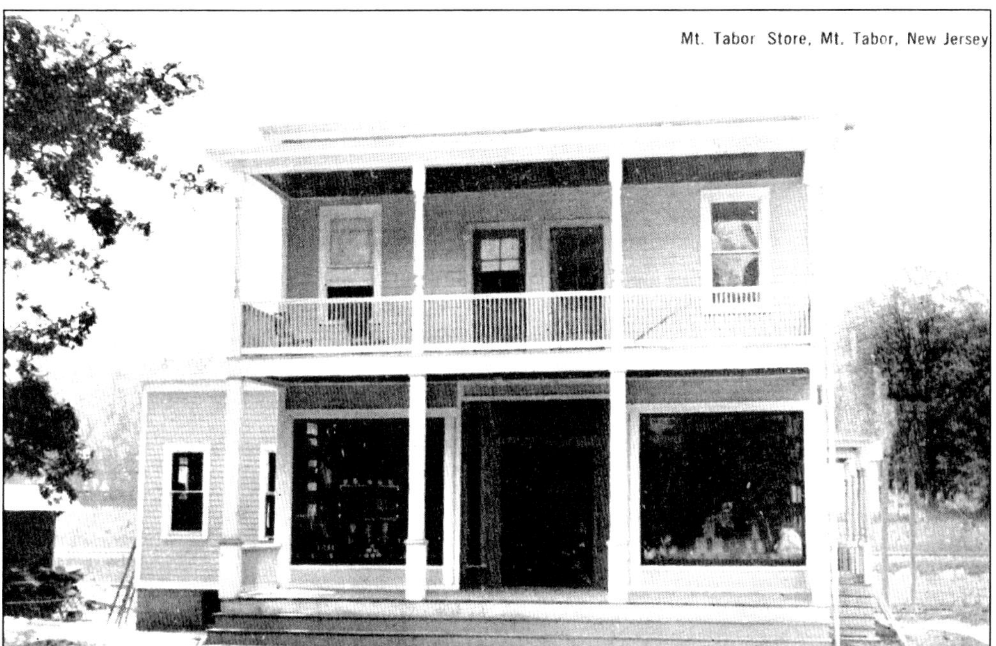

This postcard image shows the new Dickerson Market built in 1918 on the corner of Station Road opposite the camp entrance. The Dickerson family has successfully met the provisioning needs of Mount Tabor and the surrounding community for over 100 years. The store was expanded and modernized in 1956, as shown below. The family lived over the original store. The building was demolished in 1969. The present market can be seen directly behind the old building, in what is now a small shopping center. The new building was built on the location of the former ice hockey rink. (Ron Dickerson.)

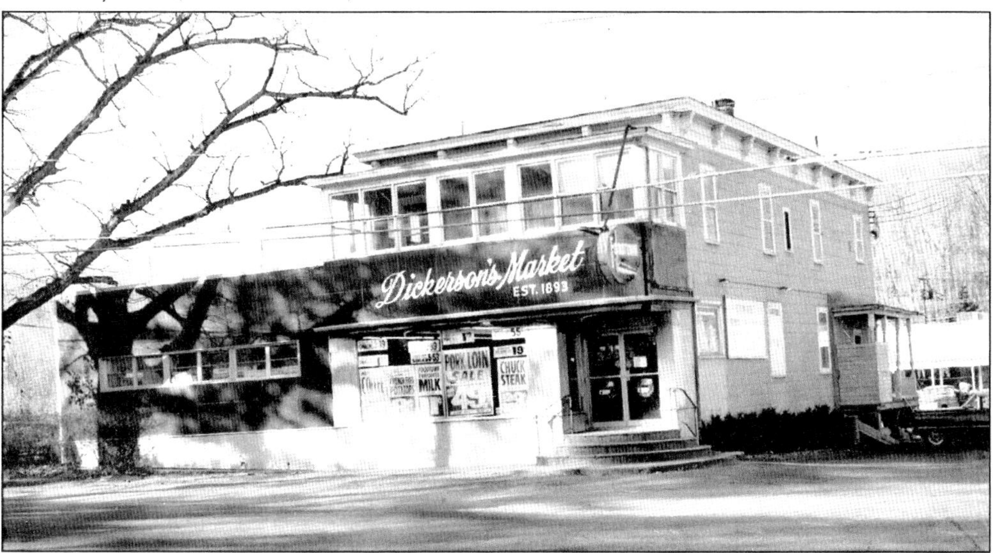

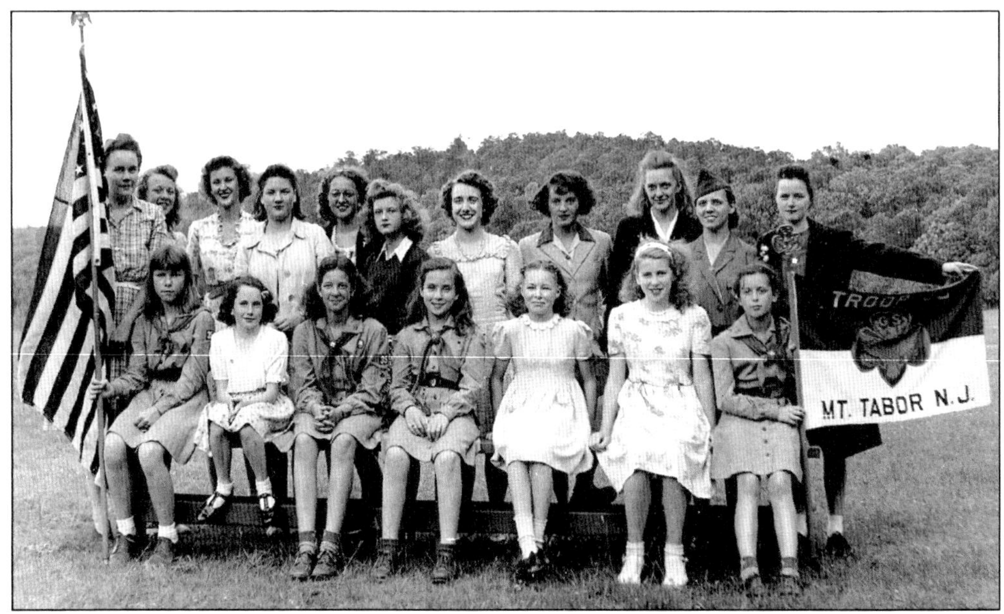

Seated on the golf course is Girl Scout Troop 35 of Mount Tabor in 1945. From left to right they are (first row) Martha McDougall, Pat Slee, Jane Wertz, Carolyn Dell, Jean Davis, Ruth Keener, and Janet Wythe Noll; (second row) Betty Sherman Kay, (leader), Joan Parks Patrick, Vivianne Carter Shorr, Katherine Stager, Ruth Lynch Blazure, Betty Tonking Perrelli, Anne Stephenson Lane, Edna Rawlings Bessemer, Audrey Lynch Gilligan, Mildred Blazure (leader), and Barbara Surphen. (Ruth Lynch Blazure.)

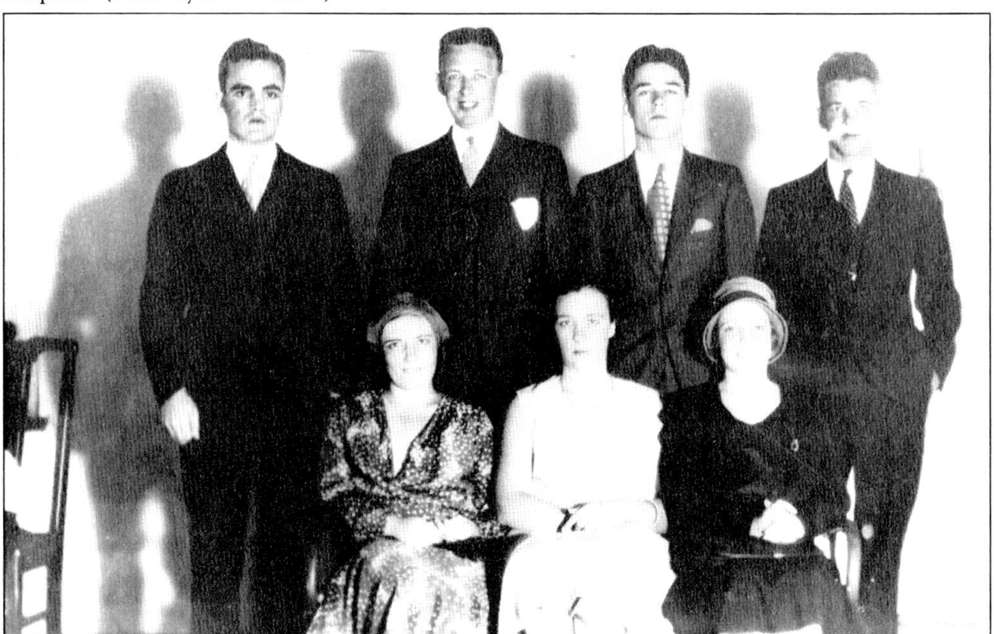

The Library Players performed plays to raise money for the library. The production *Applesauce* was presented on August 21, 1931. The players from left to right are (first row) Helen Swenerton-Swenker, Kate Louise Daniels, and Kathryn Abernathy; (second row) Henry W. Fout Jr., Henry L. Brown, Wesley A. Cale, and H. Brooks Everett. (Camp Meeting Association.)

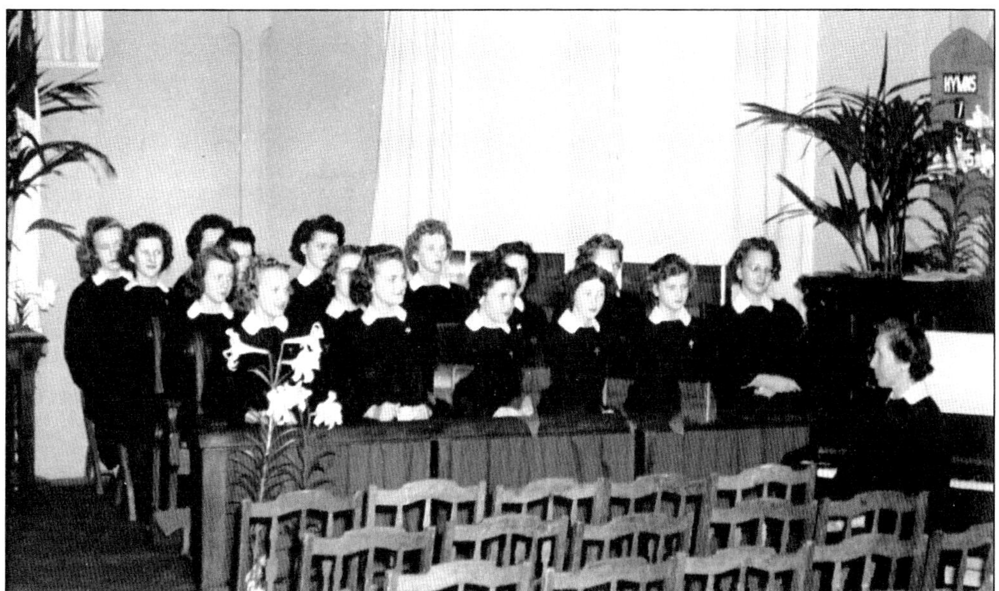

As the community grew and more families were in residence year-round, there was a need for a program of religious activities throughout the year as well. A church body was formed called the Community Church of Mount Tabor. Beginning in October 1939, services were held weekly in the Bethel. During the summer, services were moved to the tabernacle. In 1942, the Community Methodist Church was organized, and a modern church building was constructed, largely with volunteer labor, and opened in July 1950. The picture above shows the church choir in the Bethel. The wooden chairs in the foreground were each marked "N.C.C.M.A. (Newark Conference Camp Meeting Association) Mt. Tabor" under the seat with a branding iron purchased for that purpose in 1885. (Ruth Lynch Blazure.)

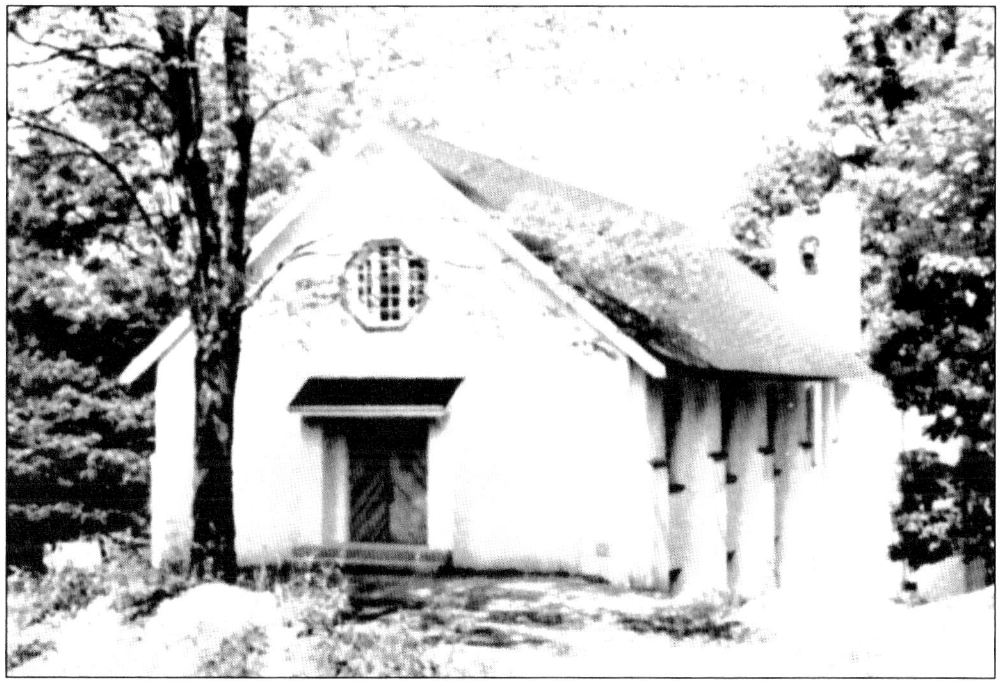

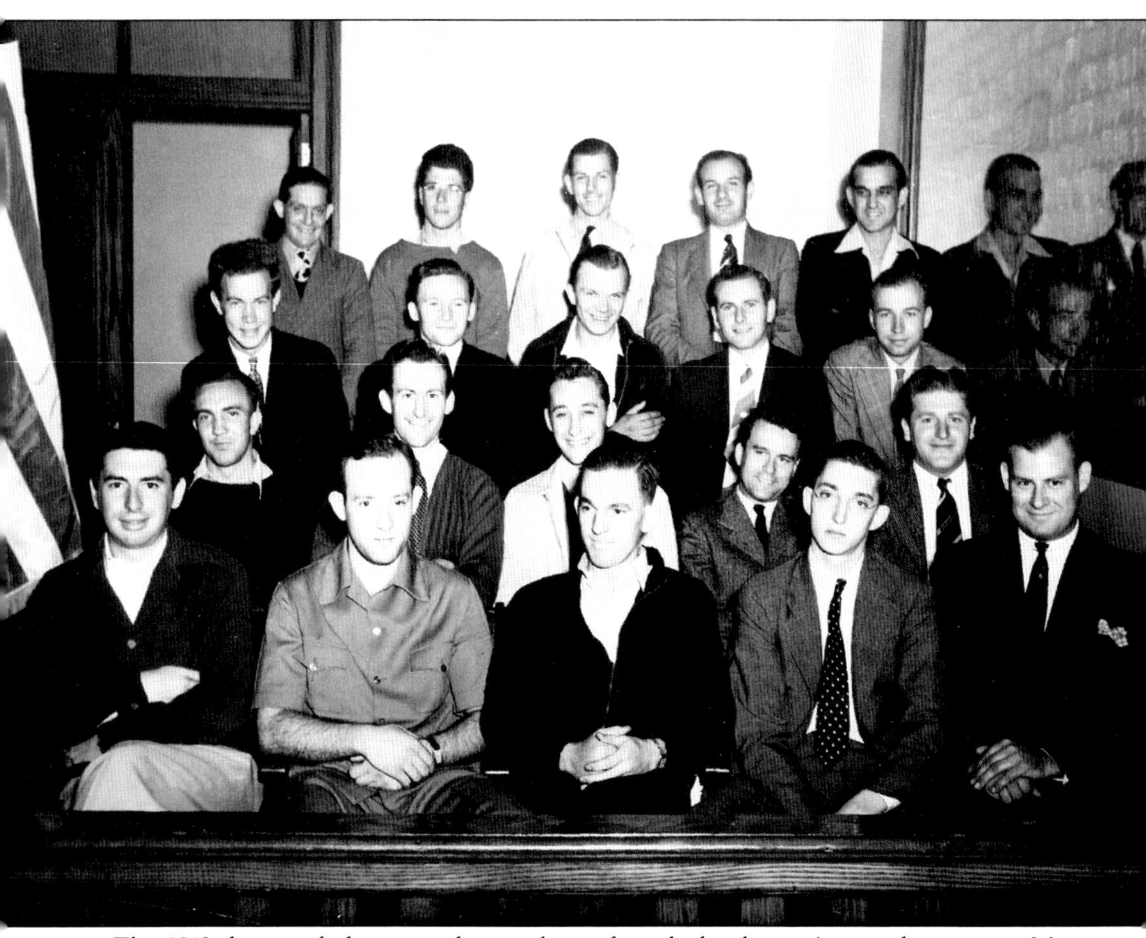

This 1942 photograph shows proud new enlistees from the local area. Among them are two Mount Tabor men: William Lloyd Apgar and Carter Childs. Apgar is seated in the center of the second row and Childs is next to him on the right. Over 100 men and women from Mount Tabor served in World War II. (Jeanne Apgar.)

Standing on the porch of the Parsippany clerk's office on April 25, 1942, William Lloyd Apgar (known as Lloyd) and his new bride, Jeanne (Barrett) Apgar, proudly display their marriage license. Recently enlisted, Lloyd left soon after their wedding, and the couple was not reunited until the end of the war. (Jeanne Apgar.)

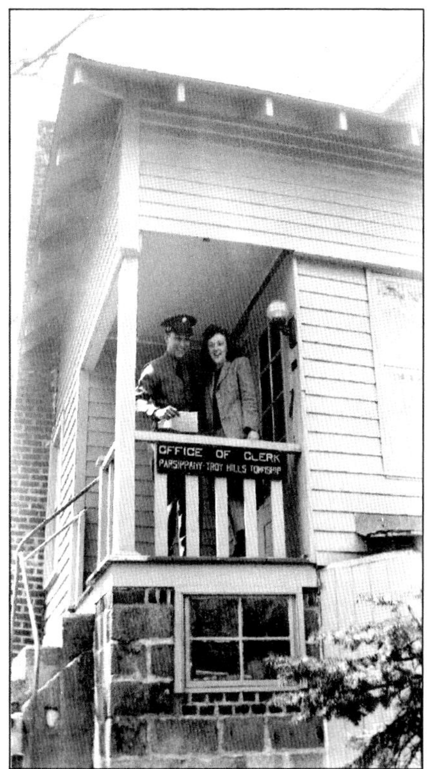

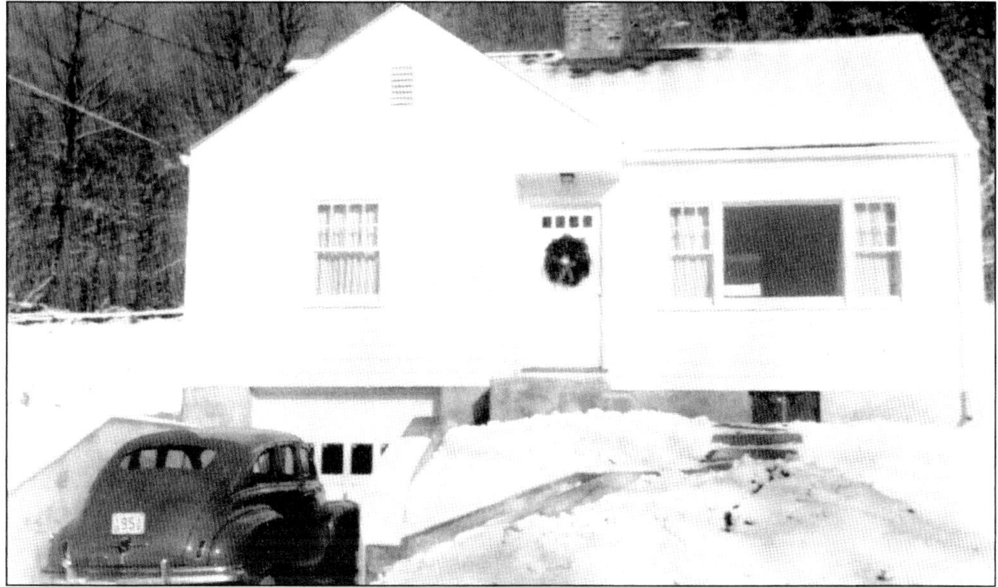

In 1939, 12 acres were purchased from the Howell estate for $3,500. This property adjoined Mount Tabor and is known today as the "new section" of town. One lot was sold and a house was built similar to the one shown in this 1950 photograph of 21 Hilsinger Road. World War II brought a halt to construction, which was resumed when the veterans returned. This land was reserved for building houses, and no other use was to be considered. Nearly 100 houses occupy this area now. (Richard Morgan.)